Garfield
OLDER & WIDER

BY JIM DAVIS

Ballantine Books • New York

A Ballantine Book
Published by The Random House Publishing Group
Copyright © 2005 by PAWS, Inc. All Rights Reserved.

All rights reserved under International and Pan-American Copyright Conventions. Published in the United States by Ballantine Books, an imprint of The Random House Publishing Group, a division of Random House, Inc., New York, and simultaneously in Canada by Random House of Canada Limited, Toronto.

Ballantine and colophon are registered trademarks of Random House, Inc.

"GARFIELD" and the GARFIELD characters are trademarks of PAWS, Inc.

www.ballantinebooks.com

Library of Congress Control Number: 2004097374

ISBN 0-345-46462-1

Manufactured in the United States of America

9 8 7 6 5 4 3 2 1

First Edition: February 2005

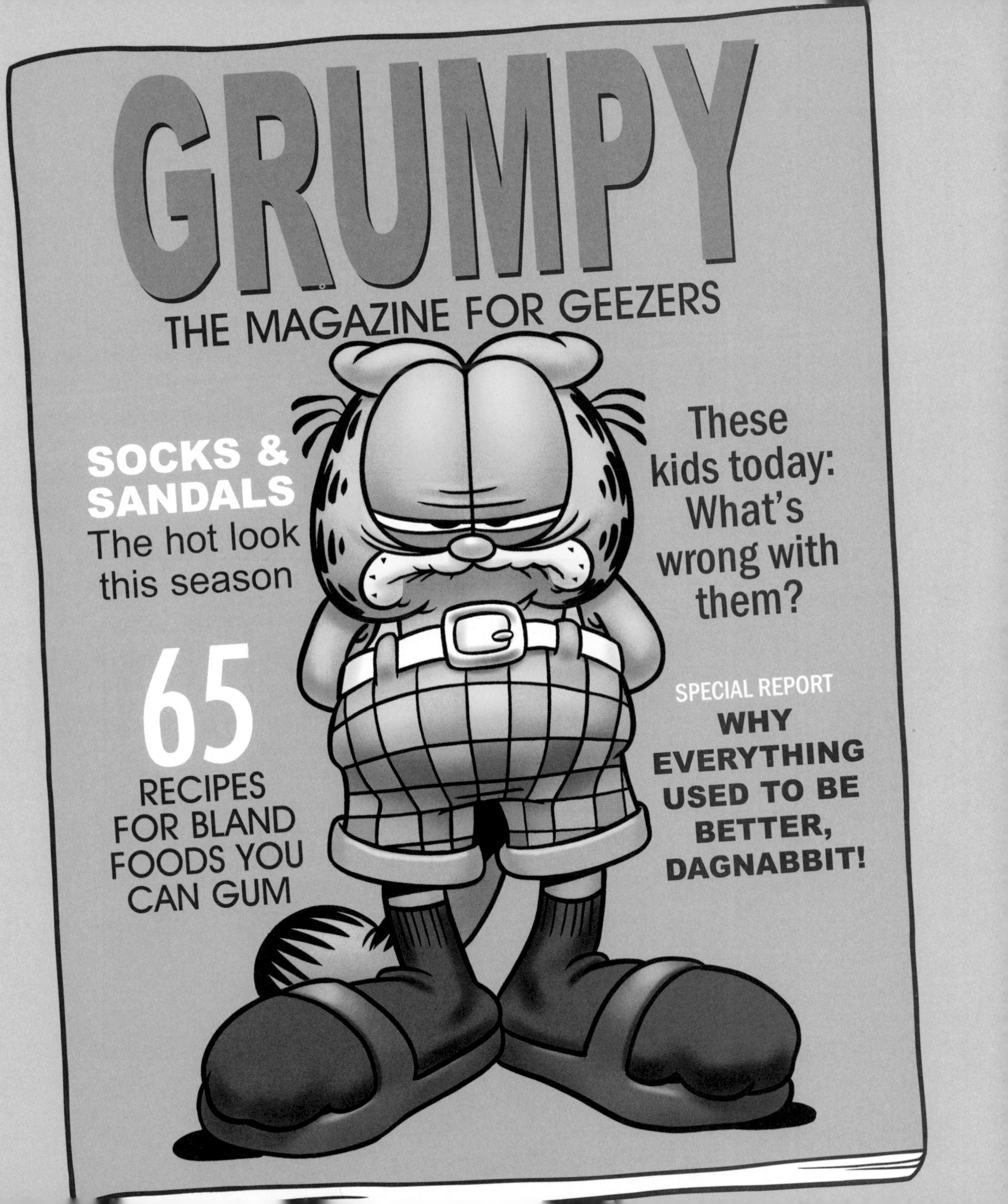
GRUMPY
THE MAGAZINE FOR GEEZERS
SOCKS & SANDALS
The hot look this season
These kids today: What's wrong with them?
65 RECIPES FOR BLAND FOODS YOU CAN GUM
SPECIAL REPORT
WHY EVERYTHING USED TO BE BETTER, DAGNABBIT!

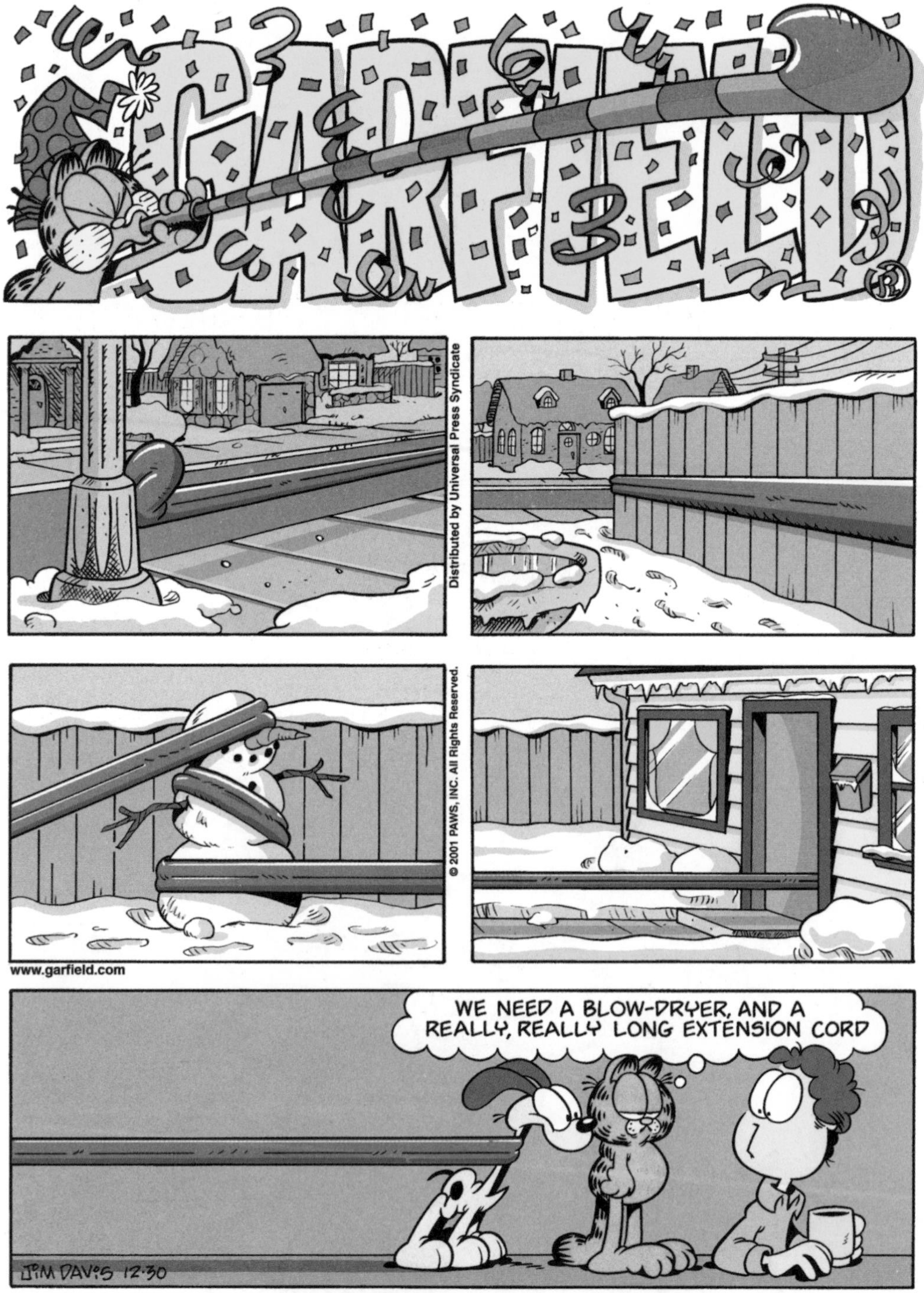
GARFIELD
Distributed by Universal Press Syndicate
© 2001 PAWS, INC. All Rights Reserved.
www.garfield.com
WE NEED A BLOW-DRYER, AND A REALLY, REALLY LONG EXTENSION CORD
JIM DAVIS 12·30

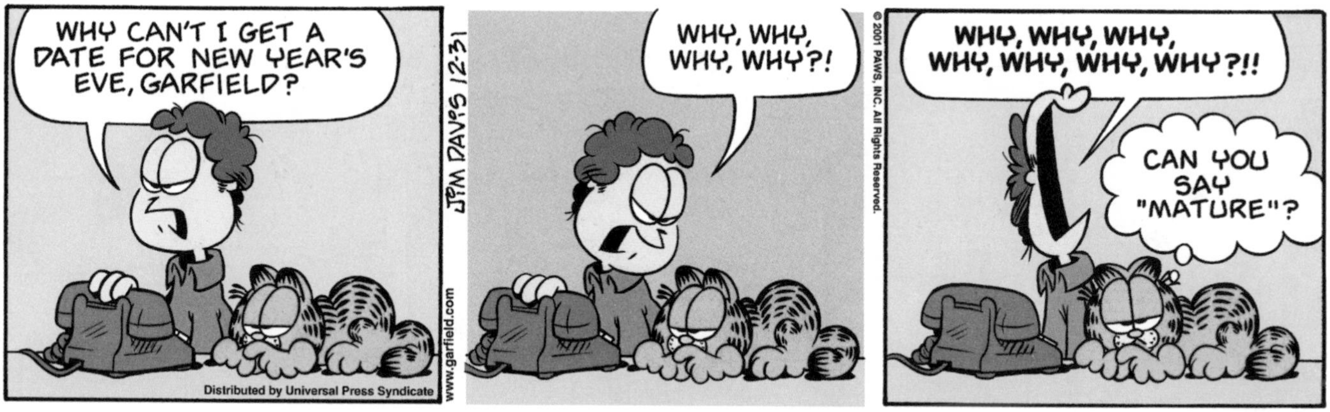
WHY CAN'T I GET A DATE FOR NEW YEAR'S EVE, GARFIELD?
WHY, WHY, WHY, WHY?!
WHY, WHY, WHY, WHY, WHY, WHY, WHY?!!
CAN YOU SAY "MATURE"?
Distributed by Universal Press Syndicate
www.garfield.com
JIM DAVIS 12-31
© 2001 PAWS, INC. All Rights Reserved.

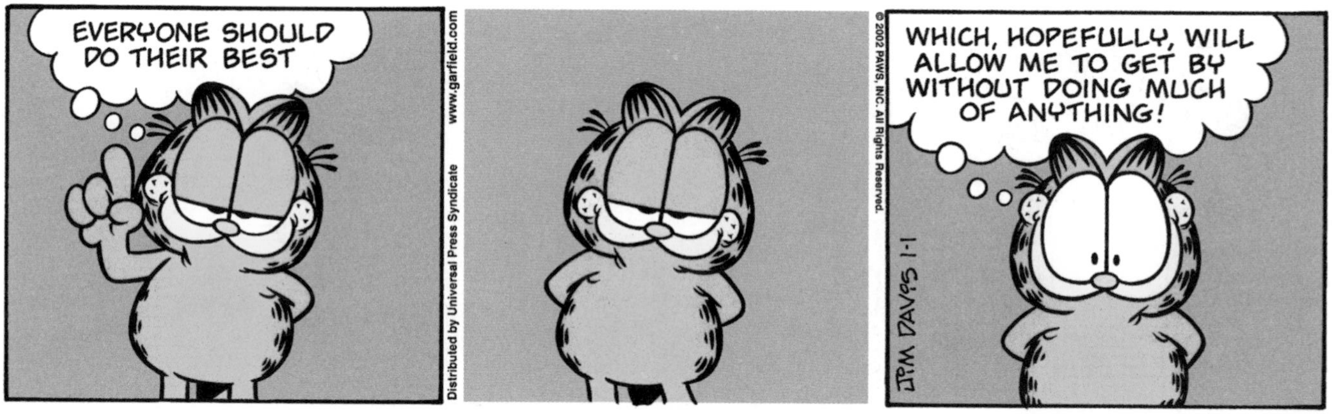
EVERYONE SHOULD DO THEIR BEST
WHICH, HOPEFULLY, WILL ALLOW ME TO GET BY WITHOUT DOING MUCH OF ANYTHING!
Distributed by Universal Press Syndicate
www.garfield.com
JIM DAVIS 1-1
© 2002 PAWS, INC. All Rights Reserved.

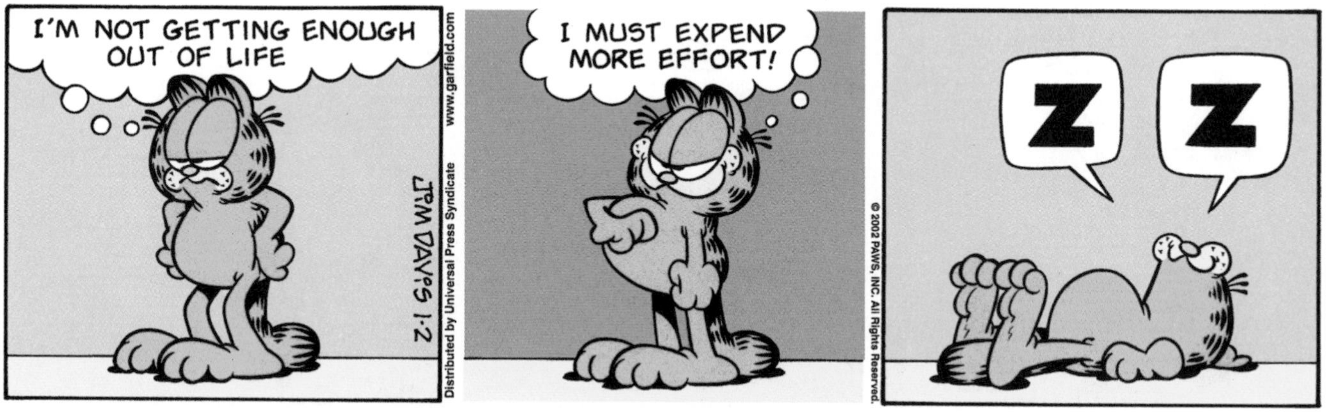
I'M NOT GETTING ENOUGH OUT OF LIFE
I MUST EXPEND MORE EFFORT!
Z
Z
Distributed by Universal Press Syndicate
www.garfield.com
JIM DAVIS 1-2
© 2002 PAWS, INC. All Rights Reserved.

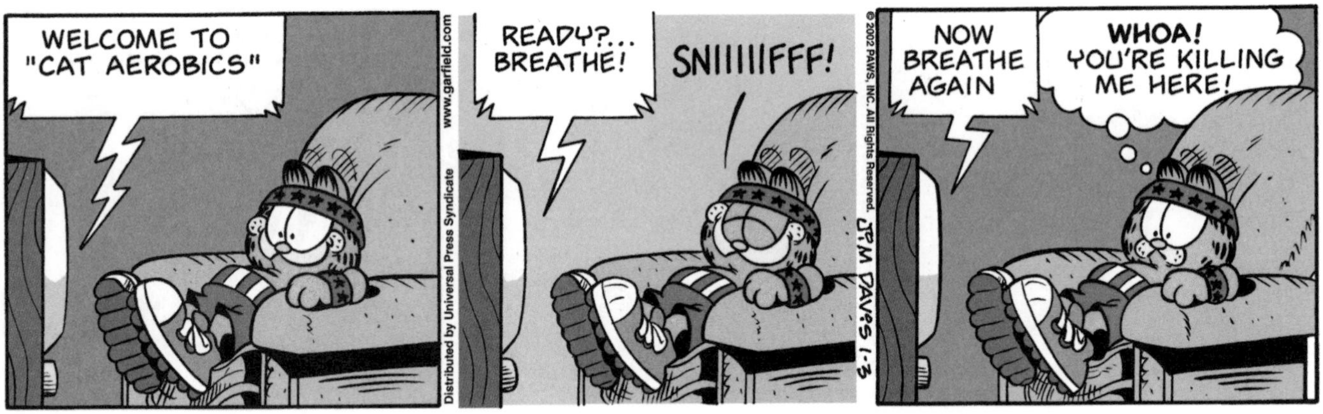
WELCOME TO "CAT AEROBICS"
READY?... BREATHE!
SNIIIIIFFF!
NOW BREATHE AGAIN
WHOA! YOU'RE KILLING ME HERE!
JIM DAVIS 1-3
www.garfield.com
Distributed by Universal Press Syndicate
© 2002 PAWS, INC. All Rights Reserved.

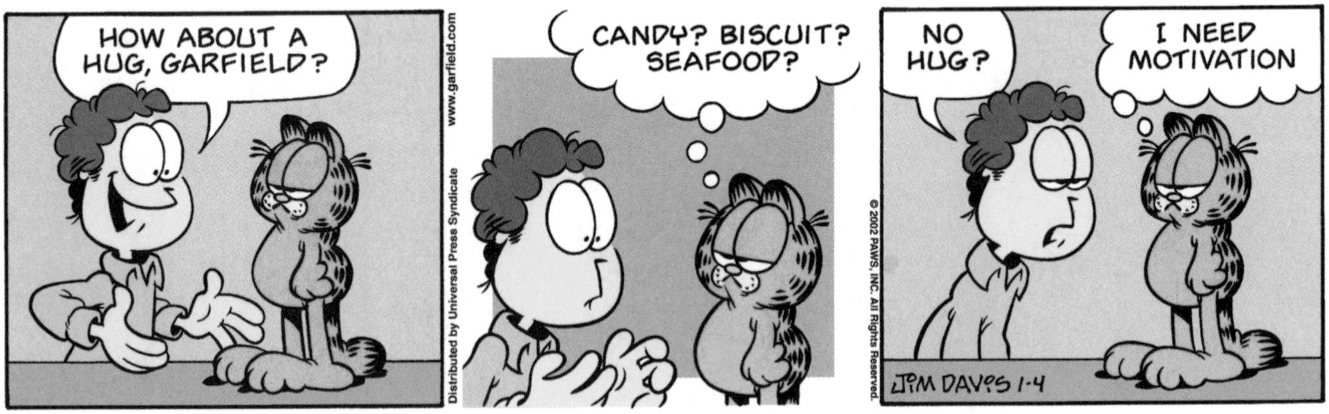
HOW ABOUT A HUG, GARFIELD?
CANDY? BISCUIT? SEAFOOD?
NO HUG?
I NEED MOTIVATION
JIM DAVIS 1-4
www.garfield.com
Distributed by Universal Press Syndicate
© 2002 PAWS, INC. All Rights Reserved.

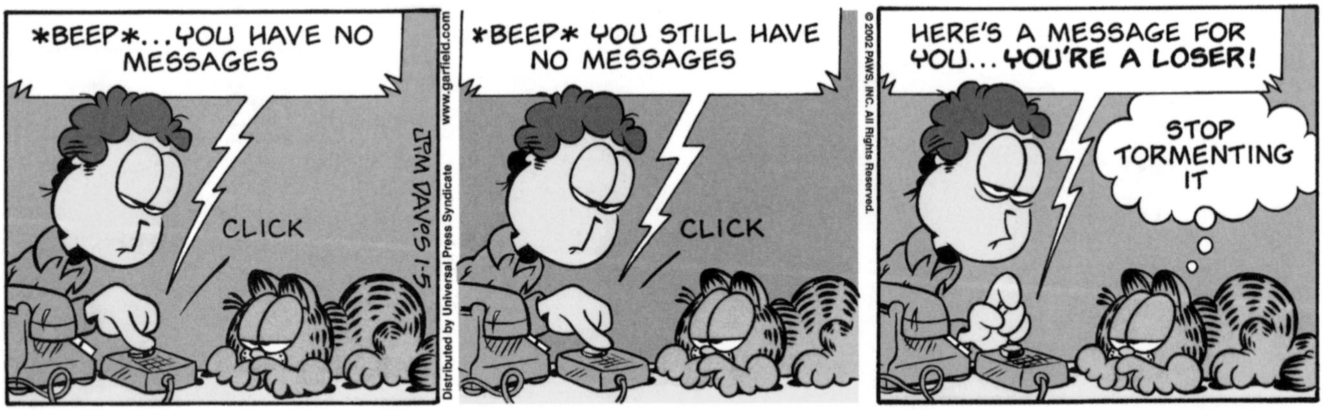
BEEP...YOU HAVE NO MESSAGES
CLICK
BEEP YOU STILL HAVE NO MESSAGES
CLICK
HERE'S A MESSAGE FOR YOU... YOU'RE A LOSER!
STOP TORMENTING IT
JIM DAVIS 1-5
www.garfield.com
Distributed by Universal Press Syndicate
© 2002 PAWS, INC. All Rights Reserved.

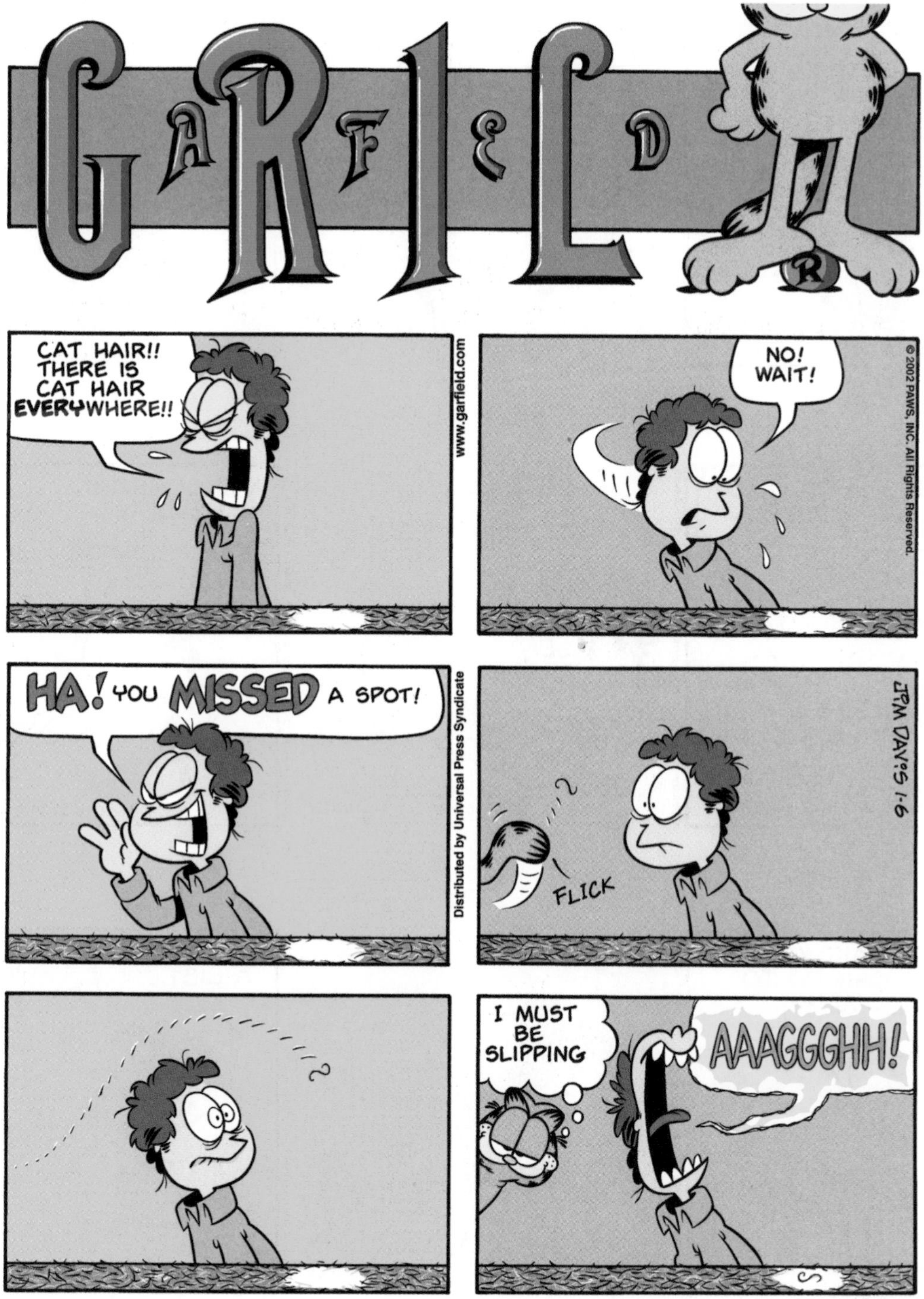
GARFIELD
CAT HAIR!! THERE IS CAT HAIR EVERYWHERE!!
www.garfield.com
NO! WAIT!
© 2002 PAWS, INC. All Rights Reserved.
HA! YOU MISSED A SPOT!
Distributed by Universal Press Syndicate
JIM DAVIS 1-6
FLICK
I MUST BE SLIPPING
AAAGGGHH!

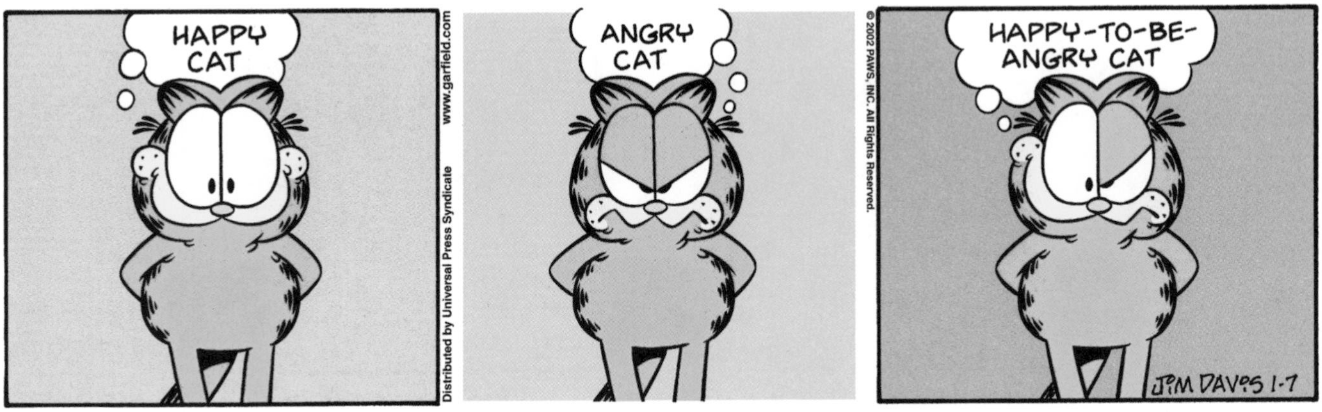
HAPPY CAT
ANGRY CAT
HAPPY-TO-BE-ANGRY CAT
JIM DAVIS 1-7
Distributed by Universal Press Syndicate www.garfield.com
© 2002 PAWS, INC. All Rights Reserved.

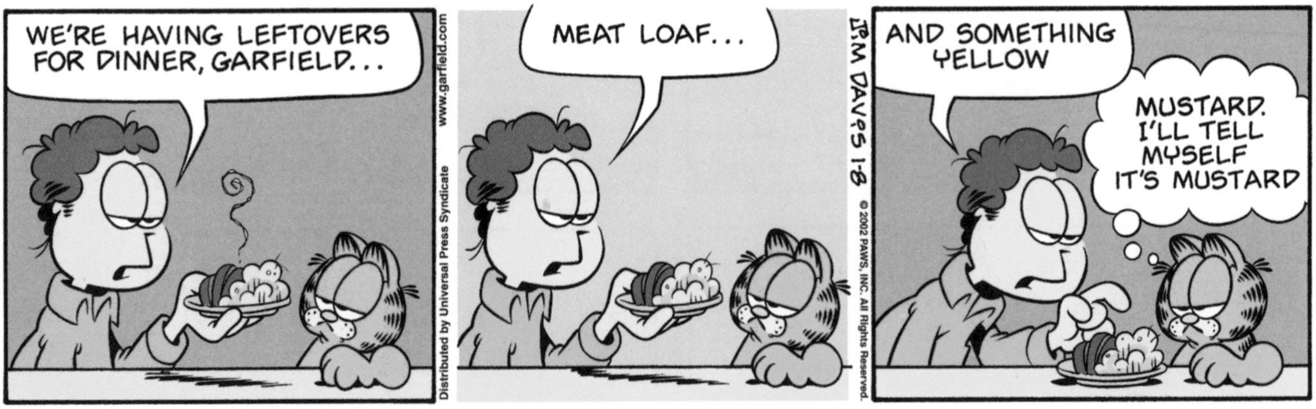
WE'RE HAVING LEFTOVERS FOR DINNER, GARFIELD...
MEAT LOAF...
AND SOMETHING YELLOW
MUSTARD. I'LL TELL MYSELF IT'S MUSTARD
JIM DAVIS 1-8
Distributed by Universal Press Syndicate www.garfield.com
© 2002 PAWS, INC. All Rights Reserved.

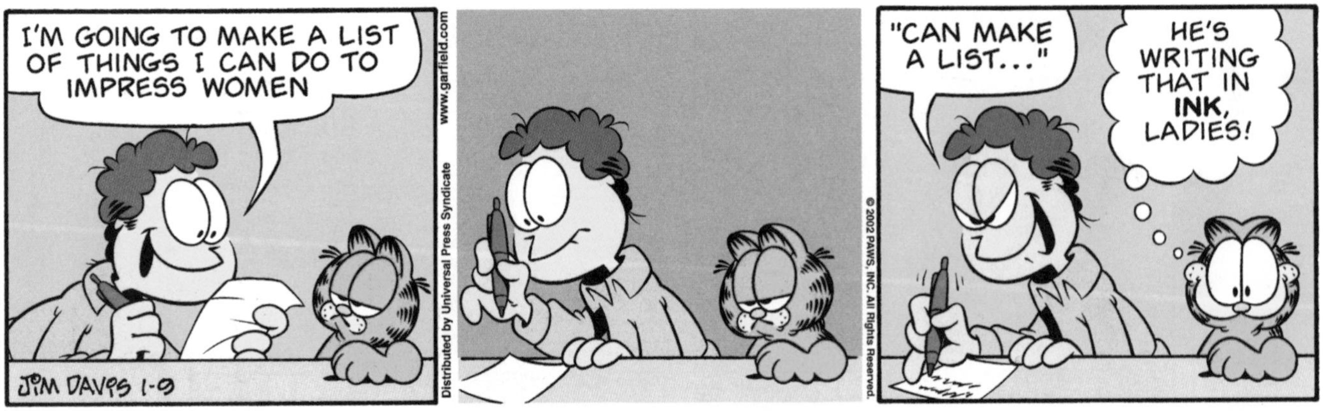
I'M GOING TO MAKE A LIST OF THINGS I CAN DO TO IMPRESS WOMEN
JIM DAVIS 1-9
"CAN MAKE A LIST..."
HE'S WRITING THAT IN **INK**, LADIES!
Distributed by Universal Press Syndicate www.garfield.com
© 2002 PAWS, INC. All Rights Reserved.

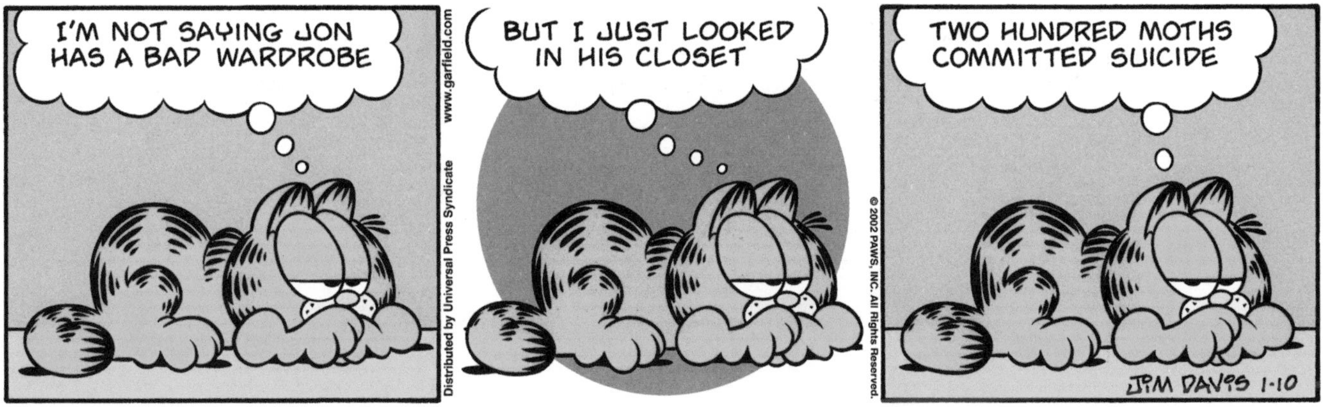
I'M NOT SAYING JON HAS A BAD WARDROBE
www.garfield.com
Distributed by Universal Press Syndicate
BUT I JUST LOOKED IN HIS CLOSET
© 2002 PAWS, INC. All Rights Reserved.
TWO HUNDRED MOTHS COMMITTED SUICIDE
JIM DAVIS 1-10

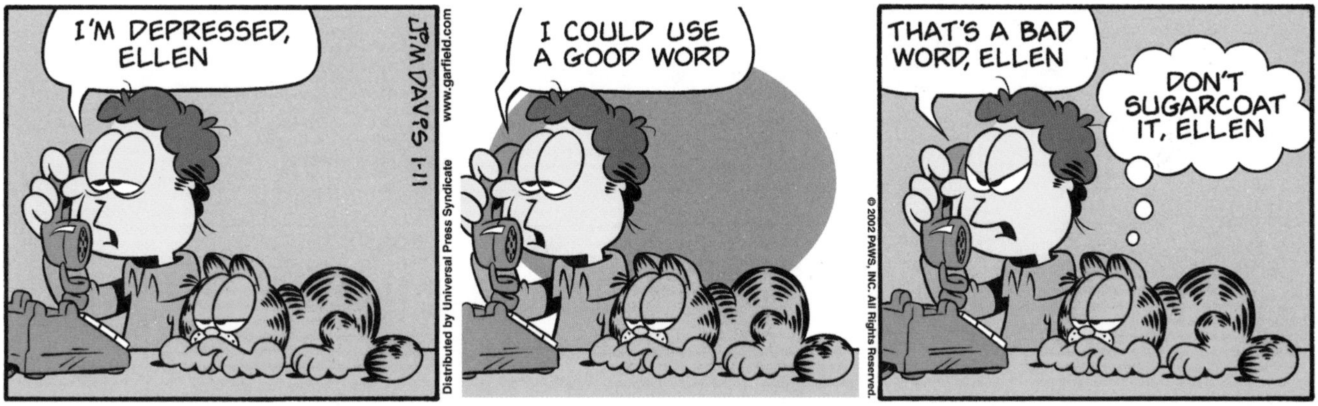
I'M DEPRESSED, ELLEN
JIM DAVIS 1-11
www.garfield.com
Distributed by Universal Press Syndicate
I COULD USE A GOOD WORD
© 2002 PAWS, INC. All Rights Reserved.
THAT'S A BAD WORD, ELLEN
DON'T SUGARCOAT IT, ELLEN

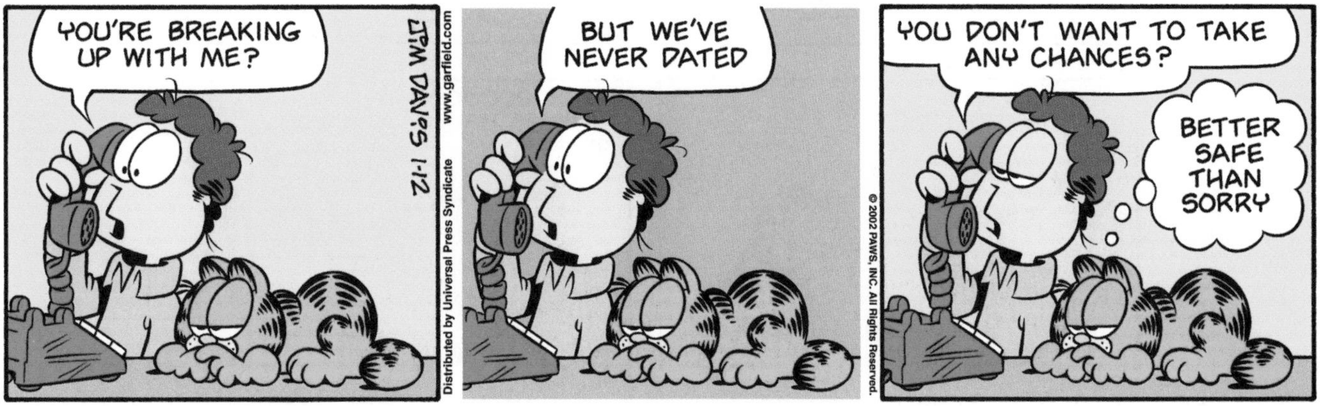
YOU'RE BREAKING UP WITH ME?
JIM DAVIS 1-12
www.garfield.com
Distributed by Universal Press Syndicate
BUT WE'VE NEVER DATED
© 2002 PAWS, INC. All Rights Reserved.
YOU DON'T WANT TO TAKE ANY CHANCES?
BETTER SAFE THAN SORRY

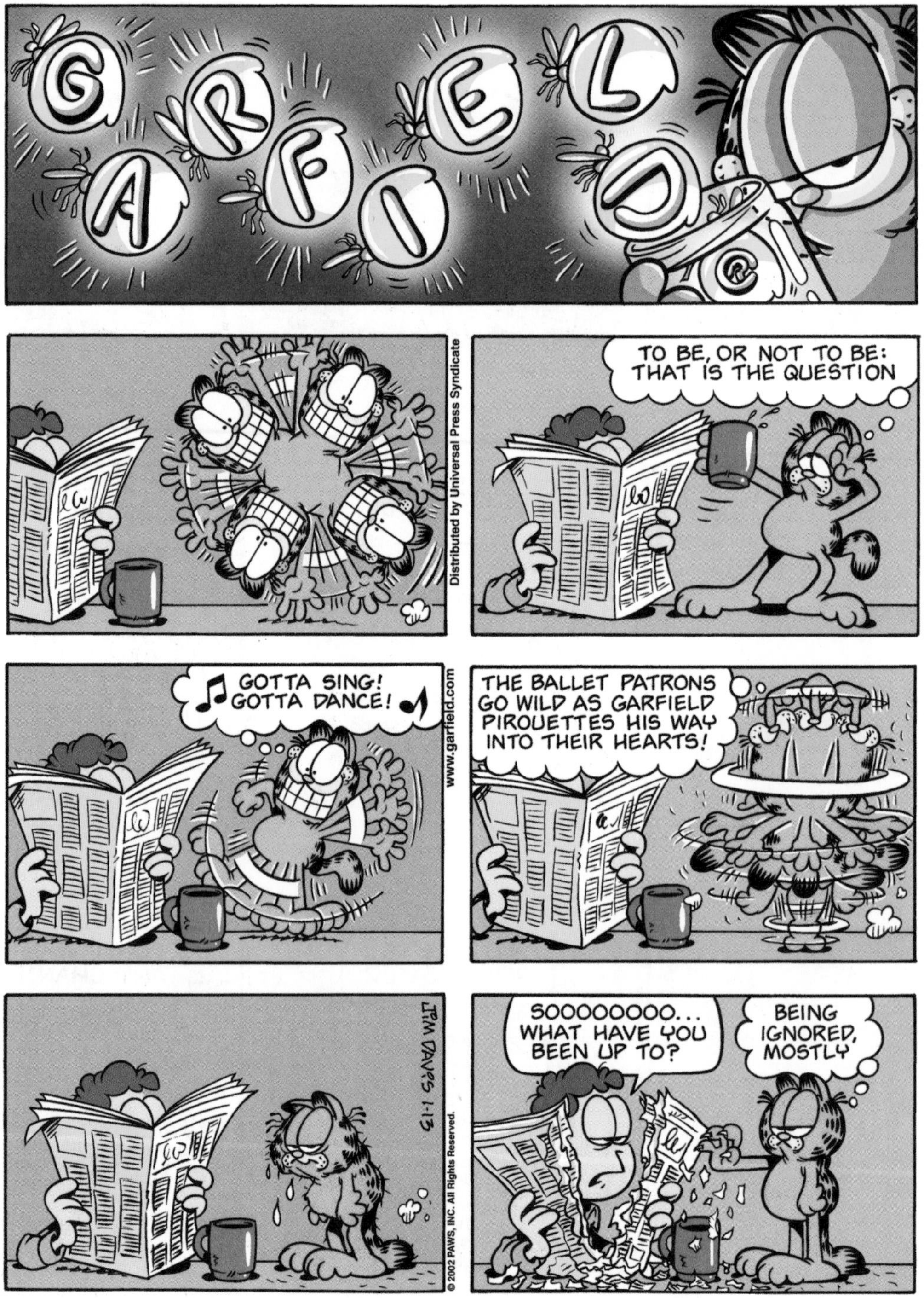
GARFIELD
Distributed by Universal Press Syndicate
TO BE, OR NOT TO BE: THAT IS THE QUESTION
GOTTA SING! GOTTA DANCE!
www.garfield.com
THE BALLET PATRONS GO WILD AS GARFIELD PIROUETTES HIS WAY INTO THEIR HEARTS!
JPM DAVIS 1-13
© 2002 PAWS, INC. All Rights Reserved.
SOOOOOOOO... WHAT HAVE YOU BEEN UP TO?
BEING IGNORED, MOSTLY

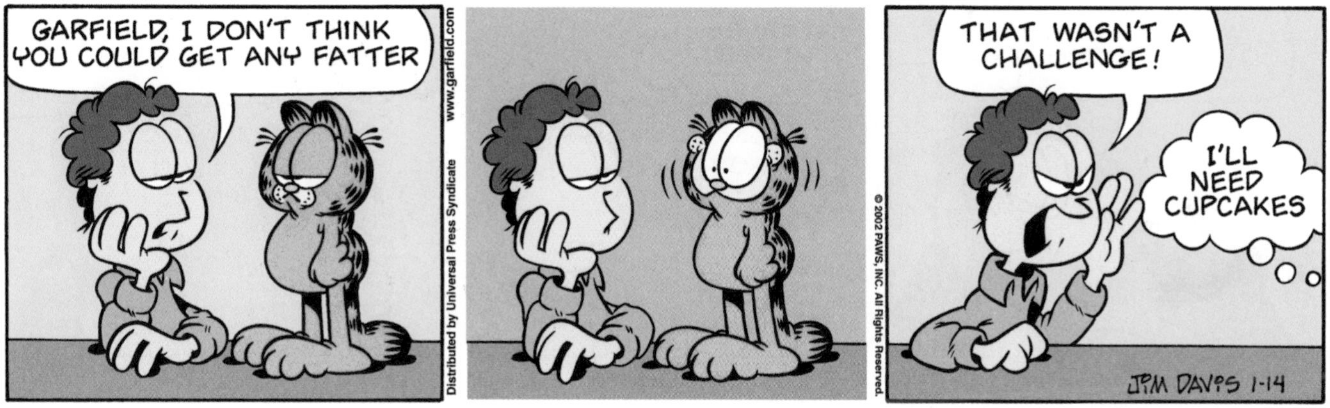
GARFIELD, I DON'T THINK YOU COULD GET ANY FATTER
www.garfield.com
Distributed by Universal Press Syndicate
THAT WASN'T A CHALLENGE!
I'LL NEED CUPCAKES
© 2002 PAWS, INC. All Rights Reserved.
JIM DAVIS 1-14

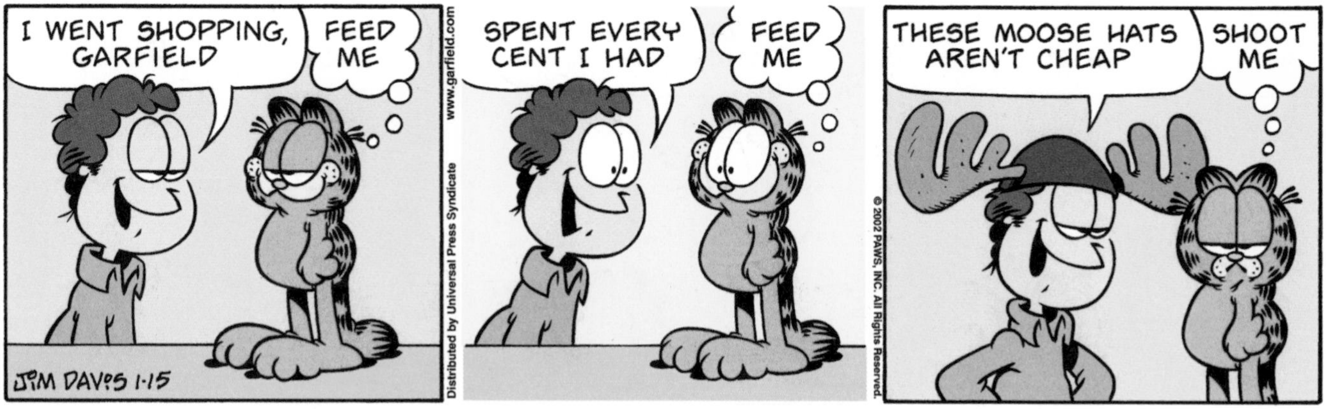
I WENT SHOPPING, GARFIELD
FEED ME
JIM DAVIS 1-15
www.garfield.com
Distributed by Universal Press Syndicate
SPENT EVERY CENT I HAD
FEED ME
© 2002 PAWS, INC. All Rights Reserved.
THESE MOOSE HATS AREN'T CHEAP
SHOOT ME

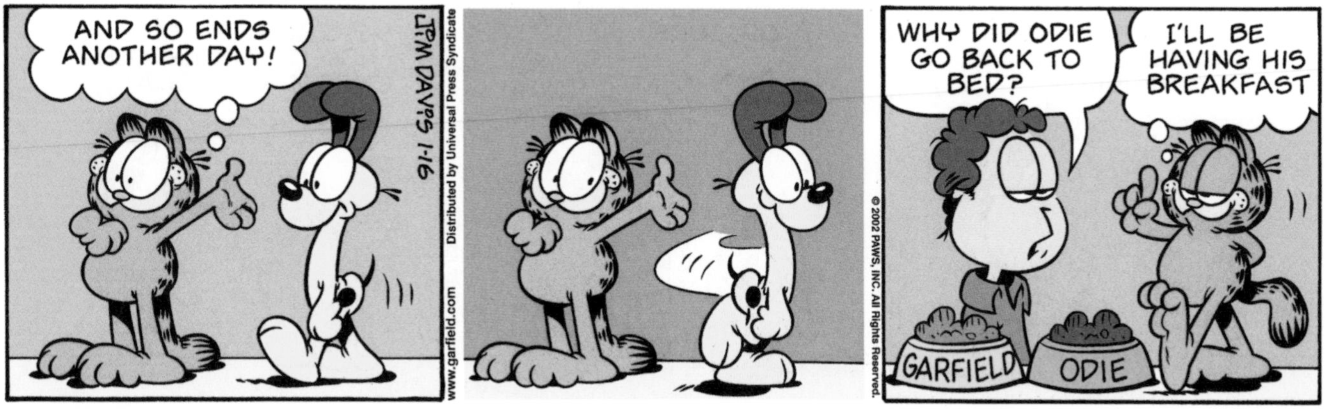
AND SO ENDS ANOTHER DAY!
JIM DAVIS 1-16
Distributed by Universal Press Syndicate
www.garfield.com
© 2002 PAWS, INC. All Rights Reserved.
WHY DID ODIE GO BACK TO BED?
I'LL BE HAVING HIS BREAKFAST
GARFIELD
ODIE

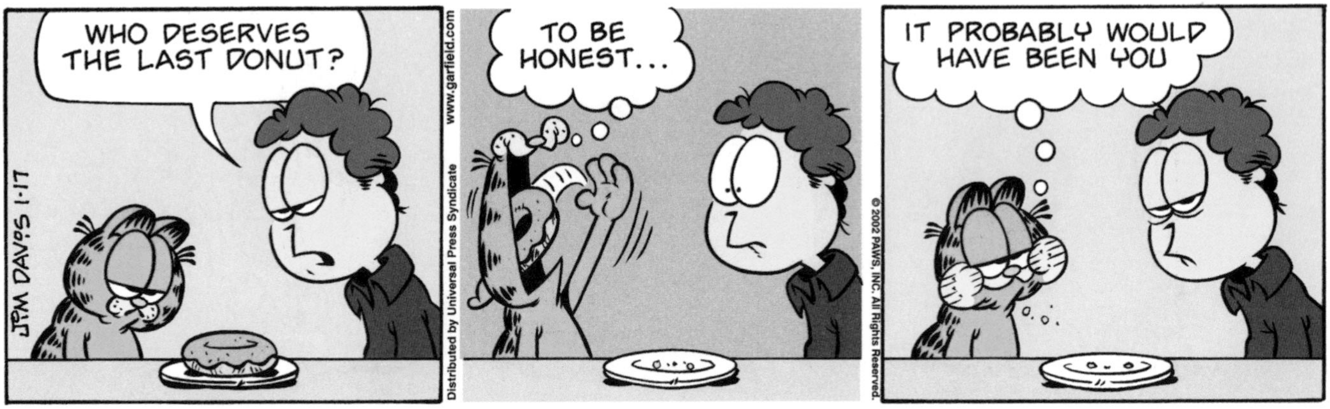
WHO DESERVES THE LAST DONUT?
TO BE HONEST...
IT PROBABLY WOULD HAVE BEEN YOU
JIM DAVIS 1·17
www.garfield.com
Distributed by Universal Press Syndicate
© 2002 PAWS, INC. All Rights Reserved.

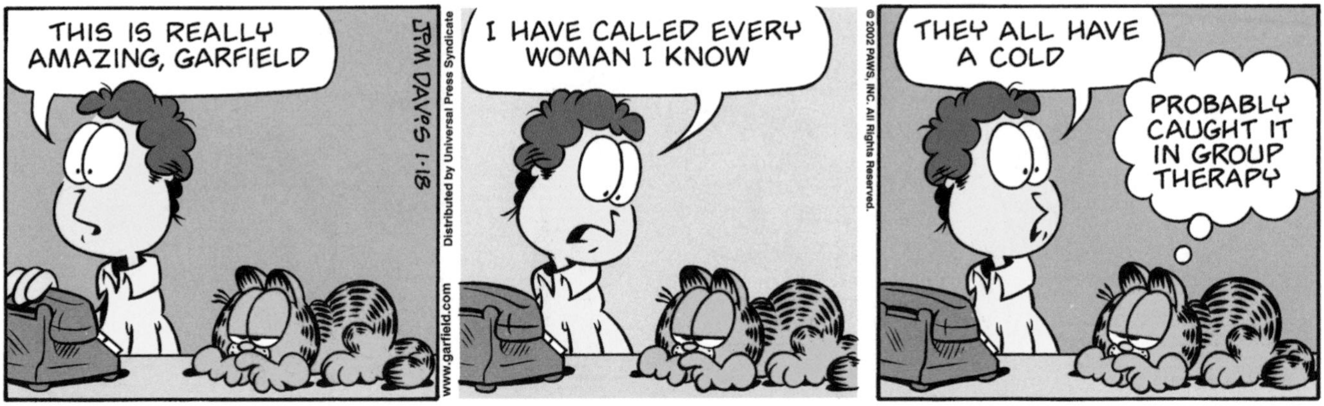
THIS IS REALLY AMAZING, GARFIELD
I HAVE CALLED EVERY WOMAN I KNOW
THEY ALL HAVE A COLD
PROBABLY CAUGHT IT IN GROUP THERAPY
JIM DAVIS 1·18
Distributed by Universal Press Syndicate
www.garfield.com
© 2002 PAWS, INC. All Rights Reserved.

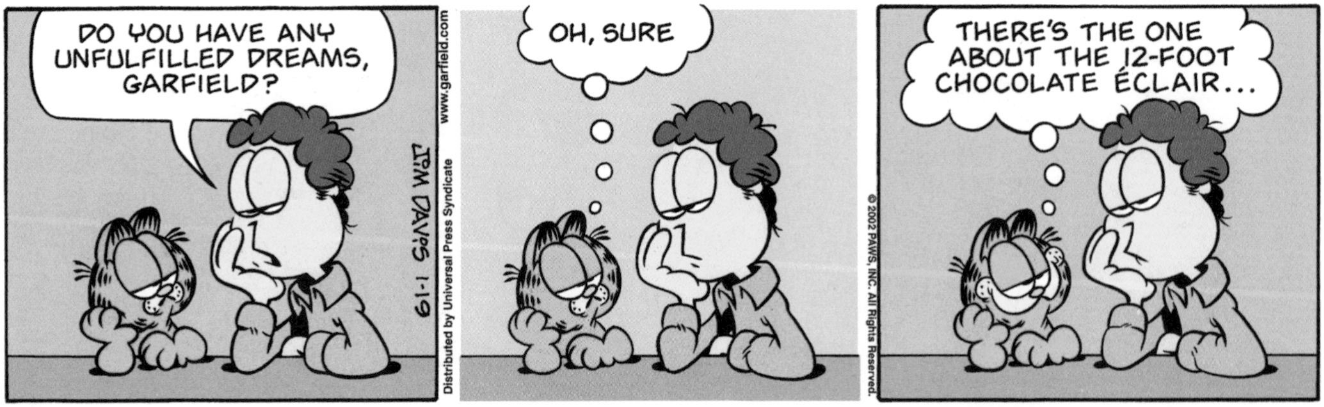
DO YOU HAVE ANY UNFULFILLED DREAMS, GARFIELD?
OH, SURE
THERE'S THE ONE ABOUT THE 12-FOOT CHOCOLATE ÉCLAIR...
JIM DAVIS 1·19
www.garfield.com
Distributed by Universal Press Syndicate
© 2002 PAWS, INC. All Rights Reserved.

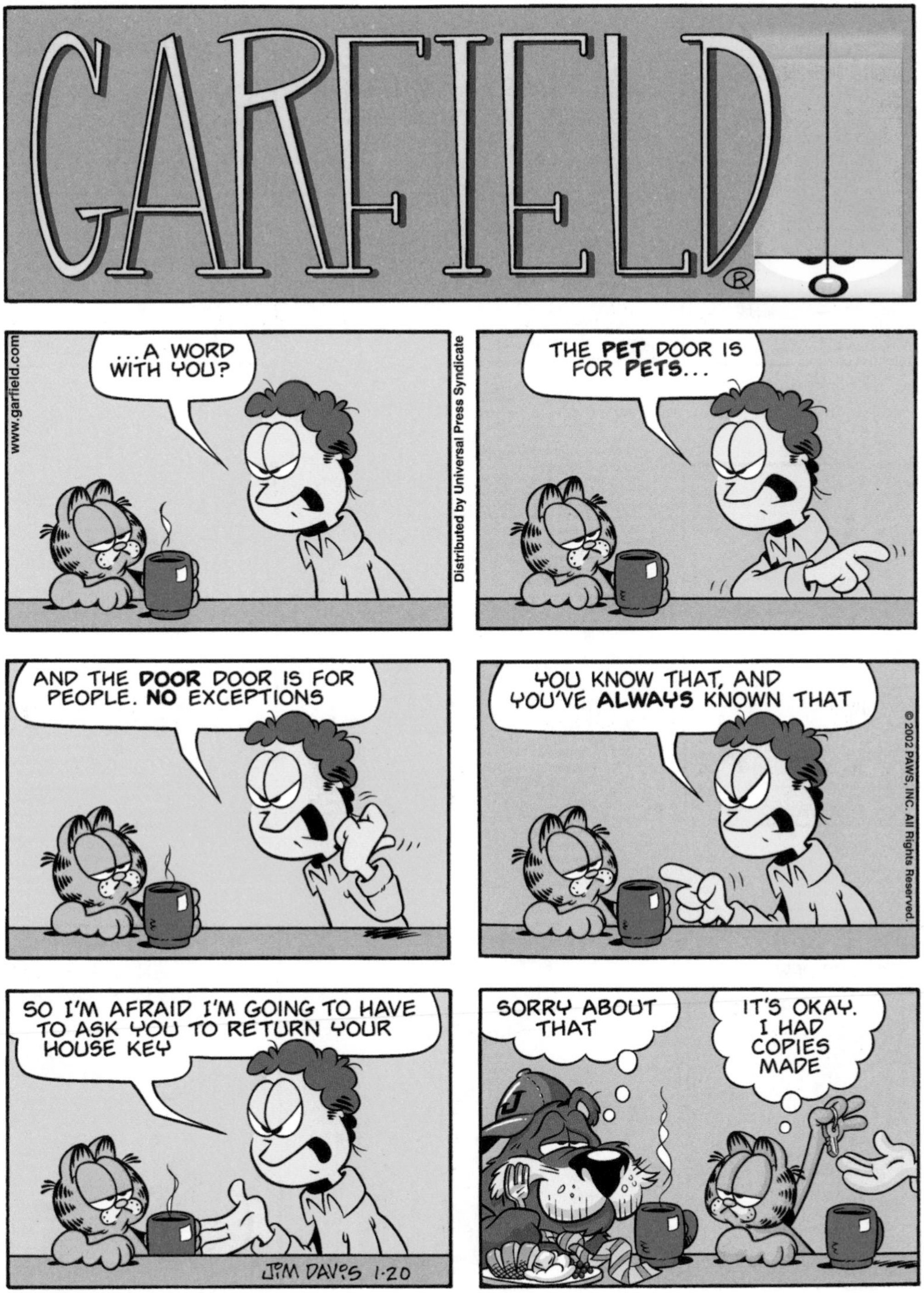
GARFIELD
www.garfield.com
Distributed by Universal Press Syndicate
...A WORD WITH YOU?
THE PET DOOR IS FOR PETS...
AND THE DOOR DOOR IS FOR PEOPLE. NO EXCEPTIONS
YOU KNOW THAT, AND YOU'VE ALWAYS KNOWN THAT
© 2002 PAWS, INC. All Rights Reserved.
SO I'M AFRAID I'M GOING TO HAVE TO ASK YOU TO RETURN YOUR HOUSE KEY
JIM DAVIS 1·20
SORRY ABOUT THAT
IT'S OKAY. I HAD COPIES MADE

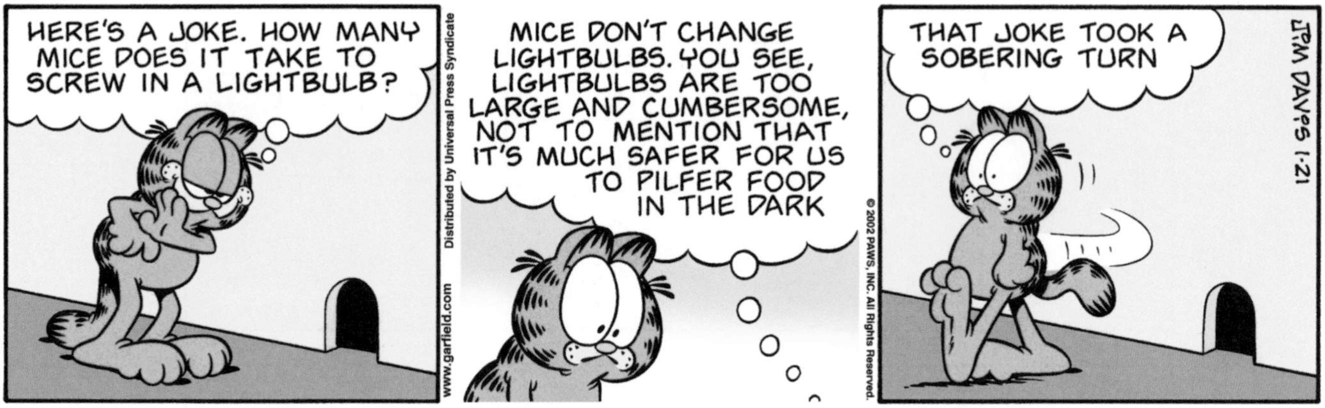
HERE'S A JOKE. HOW MANY MICE DOES IT TAKE TO SCREW IN A LIGHTBULB?
MICE DON'T CHANGE LIGHTBULBS. YOU SEE, LIGHTBULBS ARE TOO LARGE AND CUMBERSOME, NOT TO MENTION THAT IT'S MUCH SAFER FOR US TO PILFER FOOD IN THE DARK
THAT JOKE TOOK A SOBERING TURN
JIM DAVIS 1-21
www.garfield.com Distributed by Universal Press Syndicate
© 2002 PAWS, INC. All Rights Reserved.

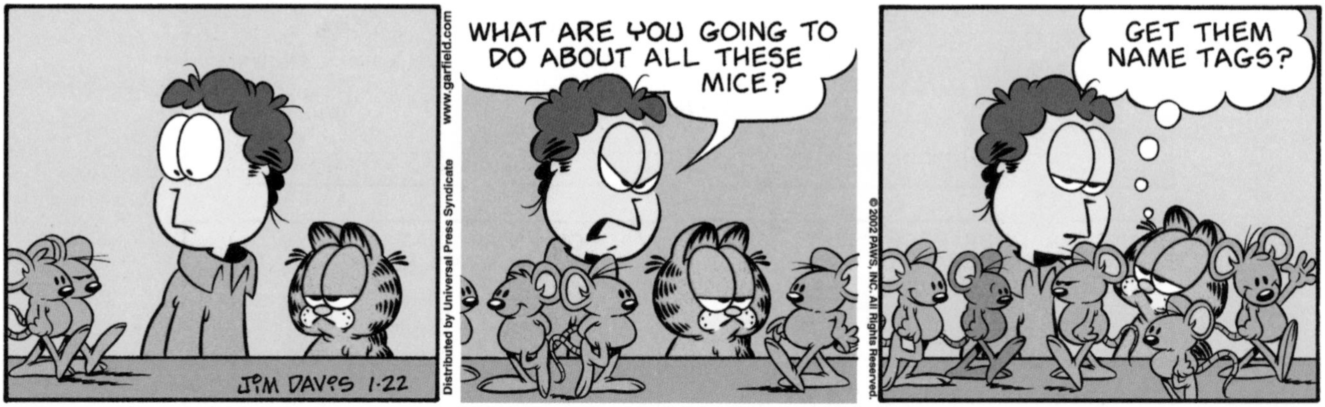
JIM DAVIS 1-22
WHAT ARE YOU GOING TO DO ABOUT ALL THESE MICE?
GET THEM NAME TAGS?
www.garfield.com Distributed by Universal Press Syndicate
© 2002 PAWS, INC. All Rights Reserved.

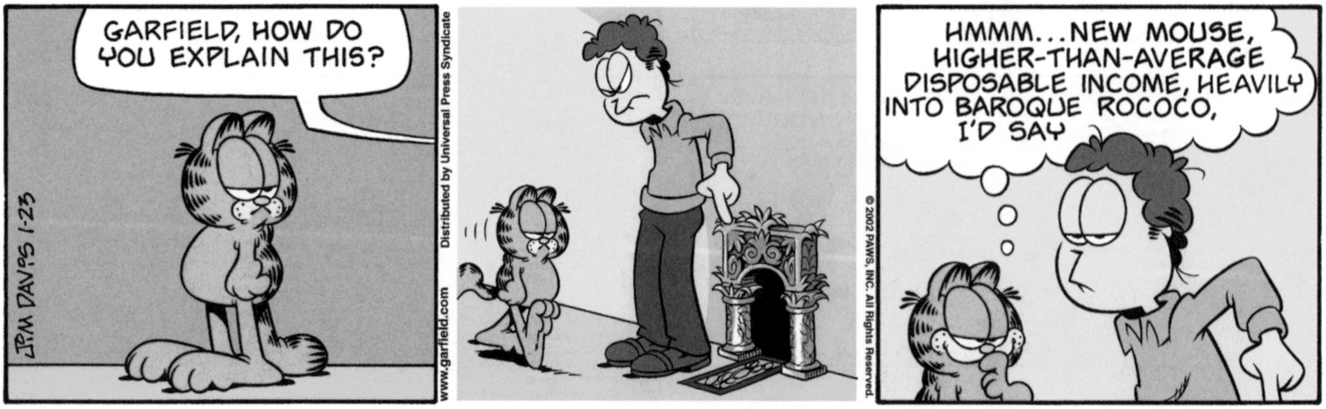
GARFIELD, HOW DO YOU EXPLAIN THIS?
JIM DAVIS 1-23
HMMM...NEW MOUSE, HIGHER-THAN-AVERAGE DISPOSABLE INCOME, HEAVILY INTO BAROQUE ROCOCO, I'D SAY
www.garfield.com Distributed by Universal Press Syndicate
© 2002 PAWS, INC. All Rights Reserved.

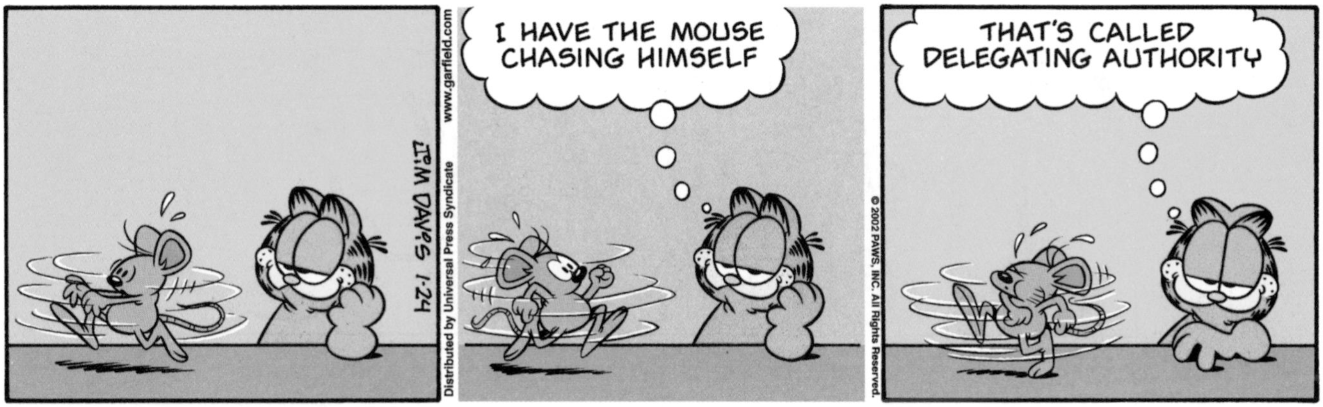
JIM DAVIS 1·24
www.garfield.com
Distributed by Universal Press Syndicate
I HAVE THE MOUSE CHASING HIMSELF
© 2002 PAWS, INC. All Rights Reserved.
THAT'S CALLED DELEGATING AUTHORITY

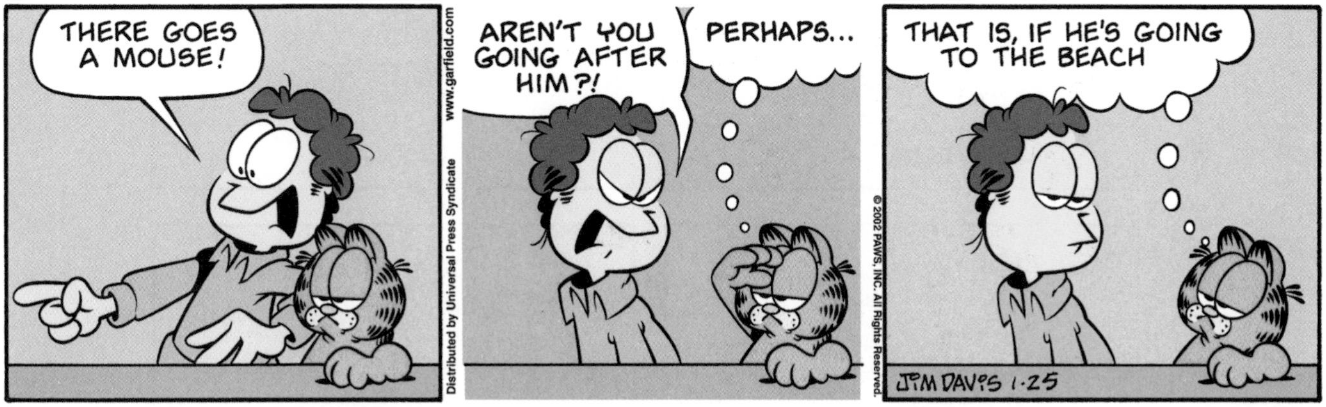
THERE GOES A MOUSE!
www.garfield.com
Distributed by Universal Press Syndicate
AREN'T YOU GOING AFTER HIM?!
PERHAPS...
© 2002 PAWS, INC. All Rights Reserved.
THAT IS, IF HE'S GOING TO THE BEACH
JIM DAVIS 1·25

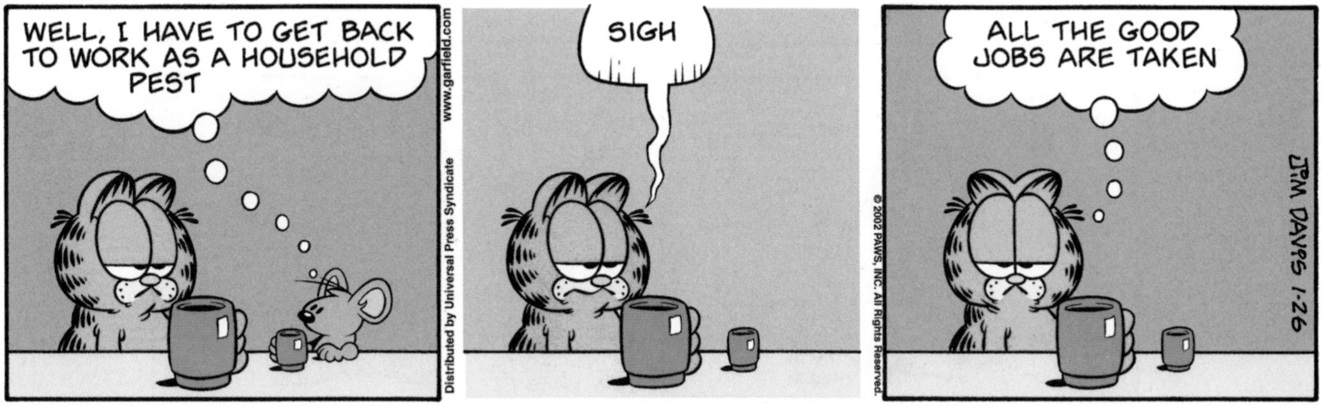
WELL, I HAVE TO GET BACK TO WORK AS A HOUSEHOLD PEST
www.garfield.com
Distributed by Universal Press Syndicate
SIGH
© 2002 PAWS, INC. All Rights Reserved.
ALL THE GOOD JOBS ARE TAKEN
JIM DAVIS 1·26

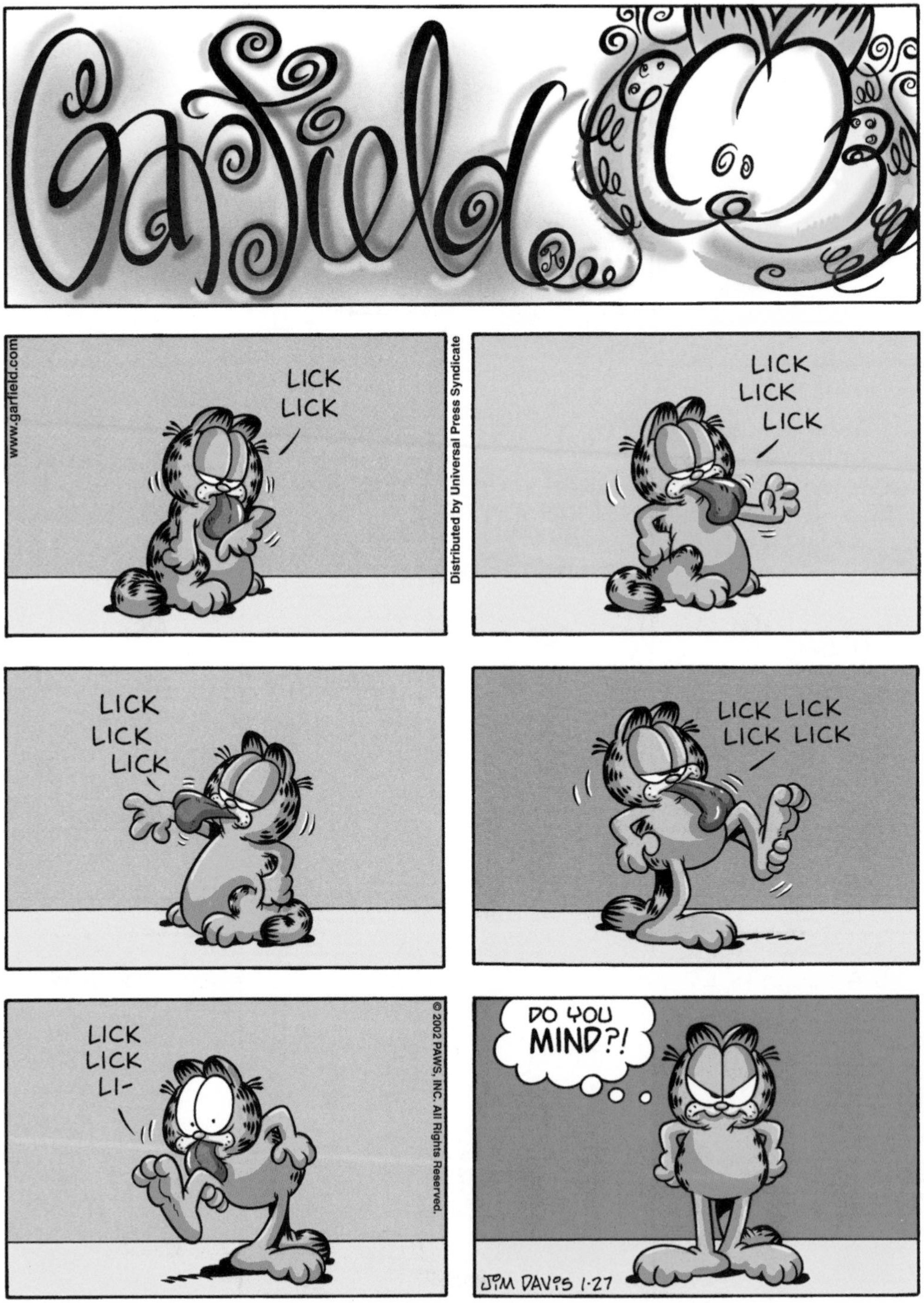
Garfield
www.garfield.com
LICK
LICK
Distributed by Universal Press Syndicate
LICK
LICK
LICK
LICK
LICK
LICK
LICK LICK
LICK LICK
LICK
LICK
LI-
© 2002 PAWS, INC. All Rights Reserved.
DO YOU
MIND?!
JIM DAVIS 1-27

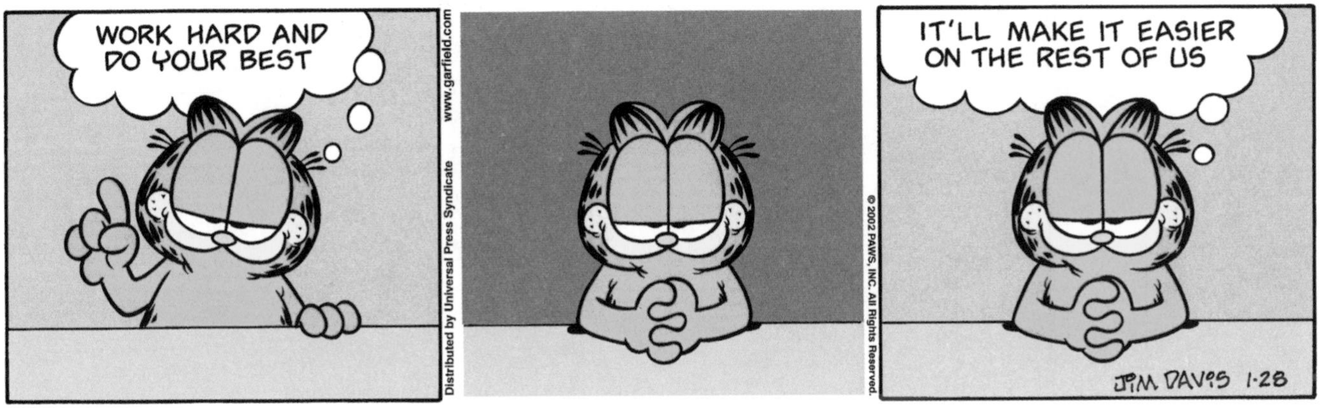
WORK HARD AND DO YOUR BEST
www.garfield.com
Distributed by Universal Press Syndicate
© 2002 PAWS, INC. All Rights Reserved.
IT'LL MAKE IT EASIER ON THE REST OF US
JIM DAVIS 1·28

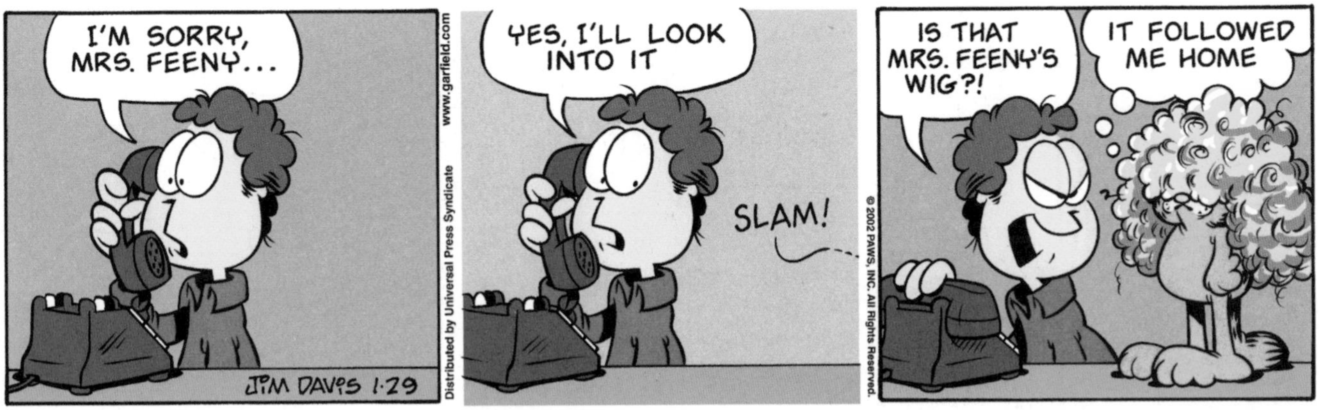
I'M SORRY, MRS. FEENY...
JIM DAVIS 1·29
www.garfield.com
Distributed by Universal Press Syndicate
YES, I'LL LOOK INTO IT
SLAM!
© 2002 PAWS, INC. All Rights Reserved.
IS THAT MRS. FEENY'S WIG?!
IT FOLLOWED ME HOME

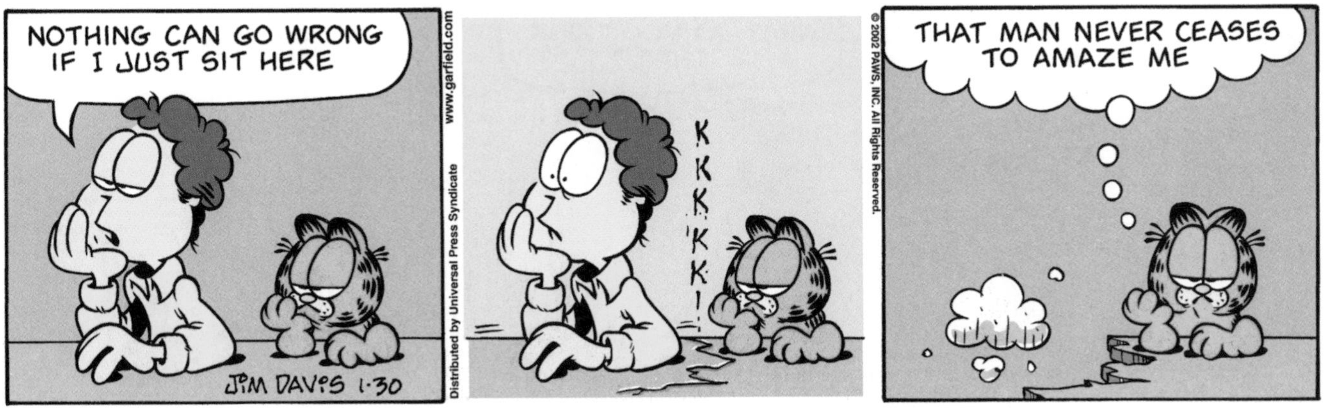
NOTHING CAN GO WRONG IF I JUST SIT HERE
JIM DAVIS 1·30
www.garfield.com
Distributed by Universal Press Syndicate
KKKK!
© 2002 PAWS, INC. All Rights Reserved.
THAT MAN NEVER CEASES TO AMAZE ME

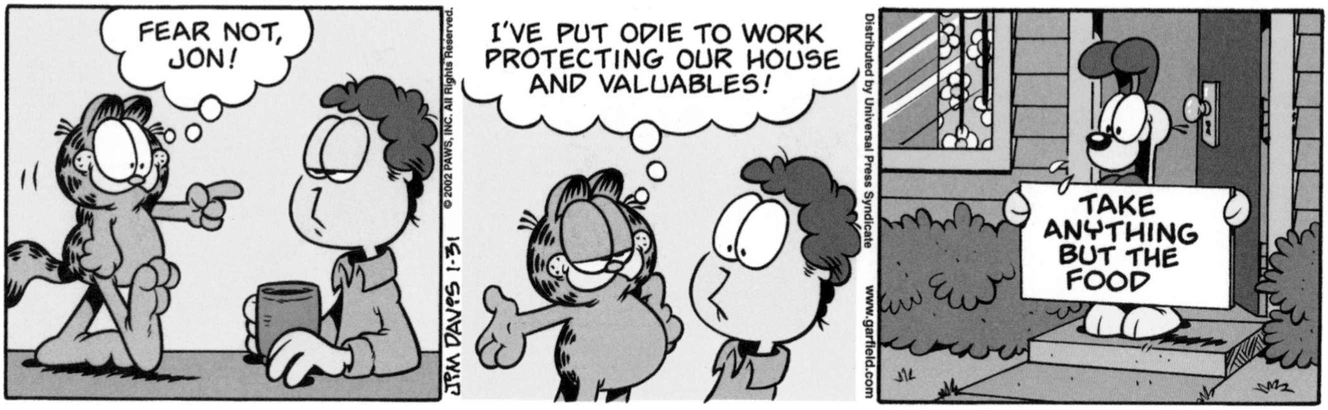
FEAR NOT, JON!
JIM DAVIS 1·31
© 2002 PAWS, INC. All Rights Reserved.
I'VE PUT ODIE TO WORK PROTECTING OUR HOUSE AND VALUABLES!
Distributed by Universal Press Syndicate
www.garfield.com
TAKE ANYTHING BUT THE FOOD

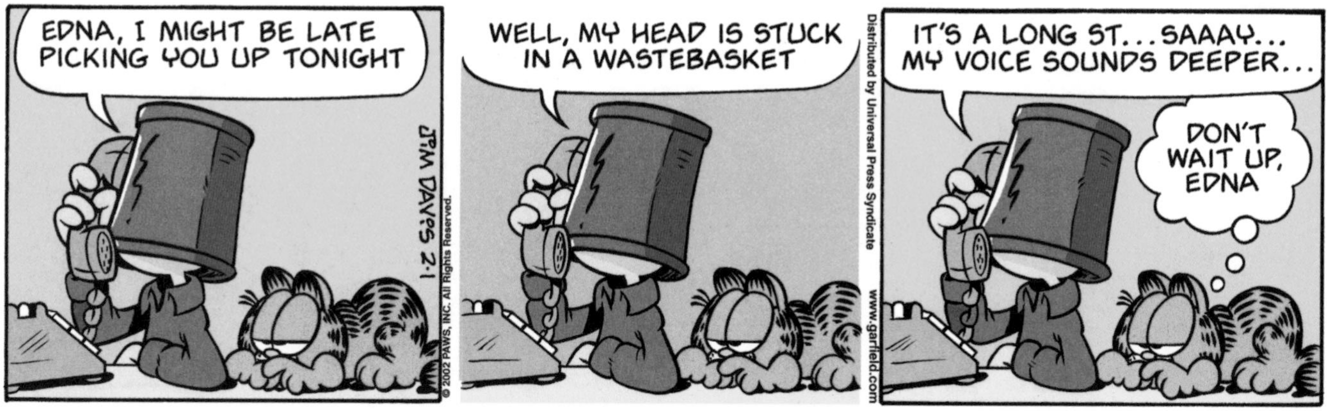
EDNA, I MIGHT BE LATE PICKING YOU UP TONIGHT
JIM DAVIS 2·1
© 2002 PAWS, INC. All Rights Reserved.
WELL, MY HEAD IS STUCK IN A WASTEBASKET
Distributed by Universal Press Syndicate
www.garfield.com
IT'S A LONG ST... SAAAY... MY VOICE SOUNDS DEEPER...
DON'T WAIT UP, EDNA

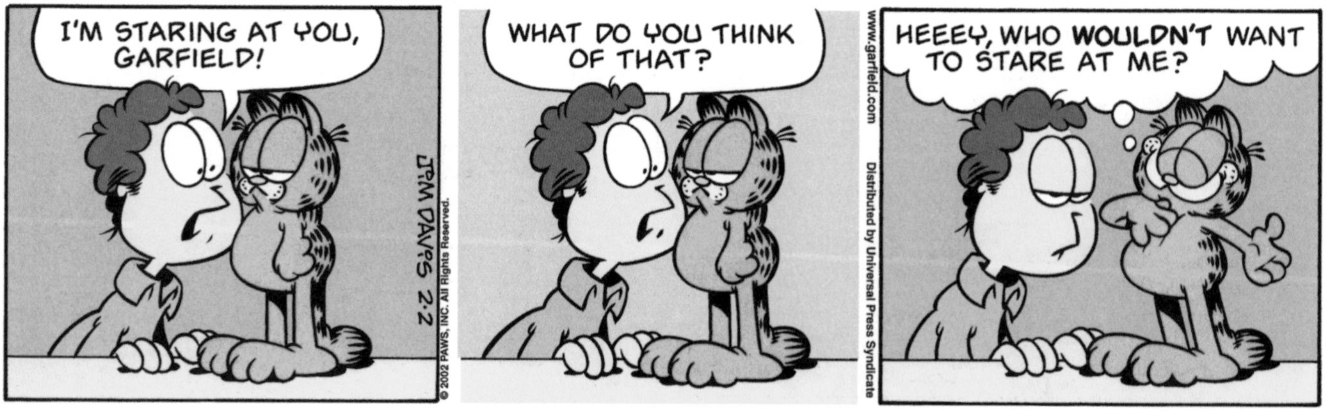
I'M STARING AT YOU, GARFIELD!
JIM DAVIS 2·2
© 2002 PAWS, INC. All Rights Reserved.
WHAT DO YOU THINK OF THAT?
www.garfield.com
Distributed by Universal Press Syndicate
HEEEY, WHO **WOULDN'T** WANT TO STARE AT ME?

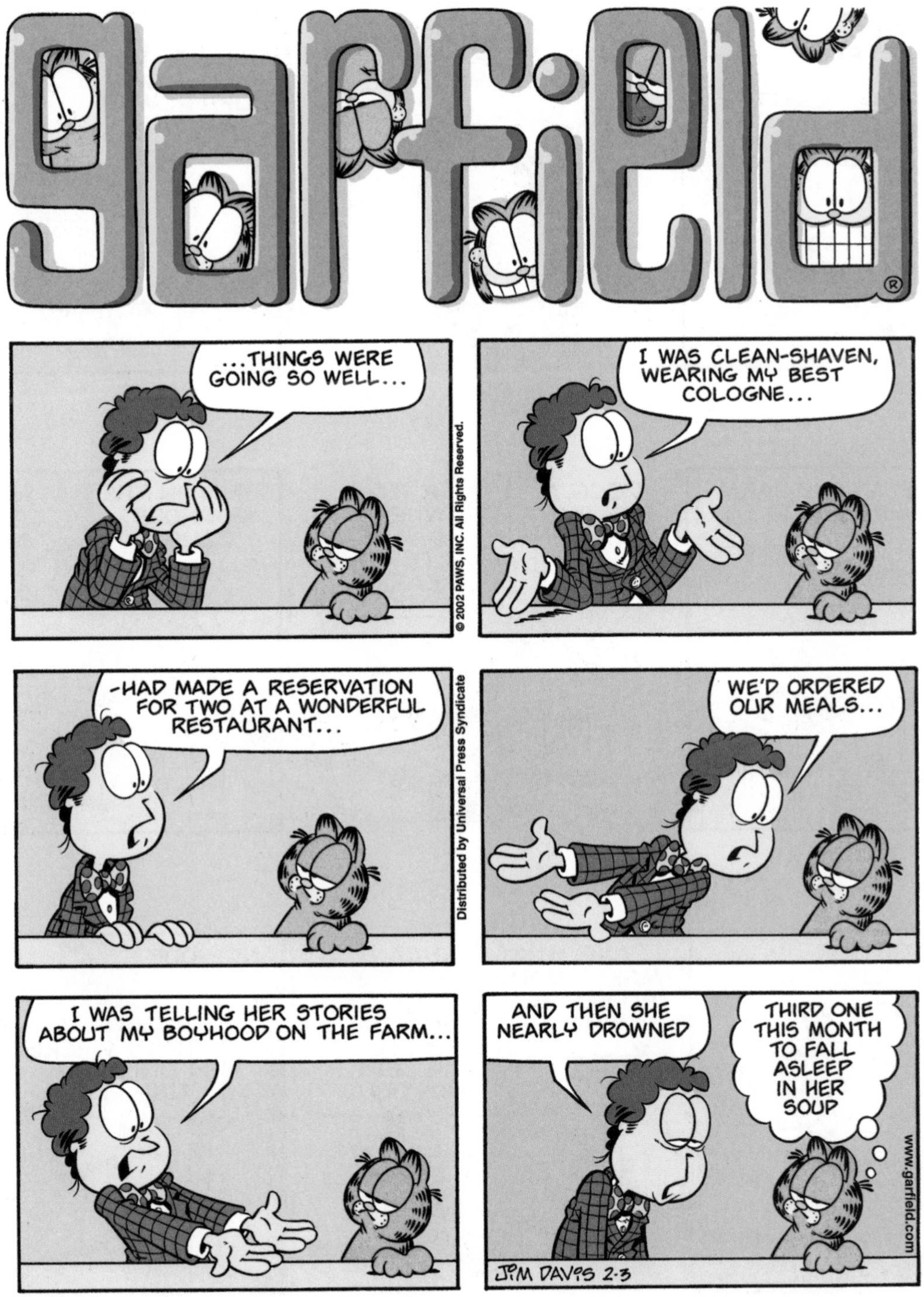
garfield
...THINGS WERE GOING SO WELL...
© 2002 PAWS, INC. All Rights Reserved.
I WAS CLEAN-SHAVEN, WEARING MY BEST COLOGNE...
-HAD MADE A RESERVATION FOR TWO AT A WONDERFUL RESTAURANT...
Distributed by Universal Press Syndicate
WE'D ORDERED OUR MEALS...
I WAS TELLING HER STORIES ABOUT MY BOYHOOD ON THE FARM...
AND THEN SHE NEARLY DROWNED
THIRD ONE THIS MONTH TO FALL ASLEEP IN HER SOUP
www.garfield.com
JIM DAVIS 2-3

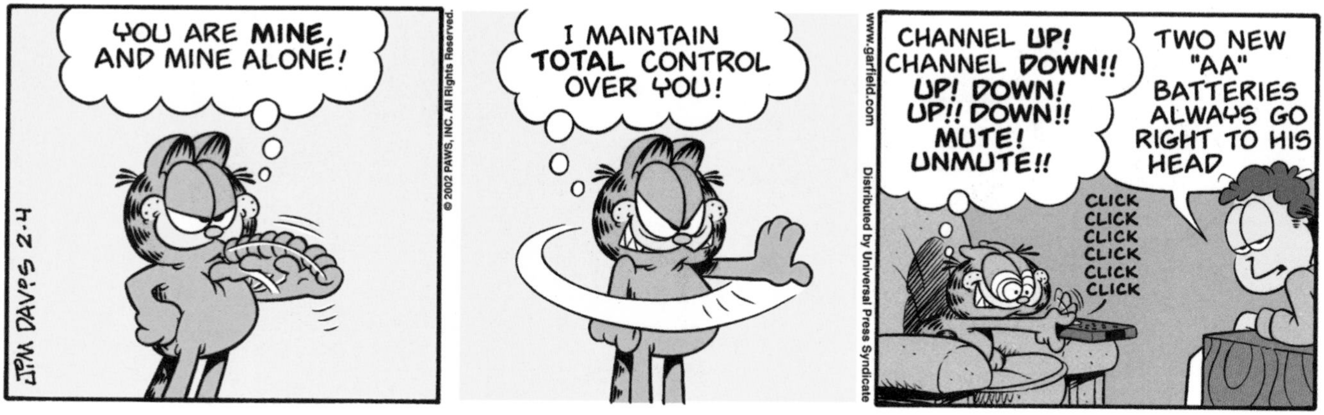
YOU ARE MINE, AND MINE ALONE!
JPM DAVPS 2-4
© 2002 PAWS, INC. All Rights Reserved.
I MAINTAIN TOTAL CONTROL OVER YOU!
www.garfield.com
Distributed by Universal Press Syndicate
CHANNEL UP! CHANNEL DOWN!! UP! DOWN! UP!! DOWN!! MUTE! UNMUTE!!
CLICK CLICK CLICK CLICK CLICK CLICK
TWO NEW "AA" BATTERIES ALWAYS GO RIGHT TO HIS HEAD

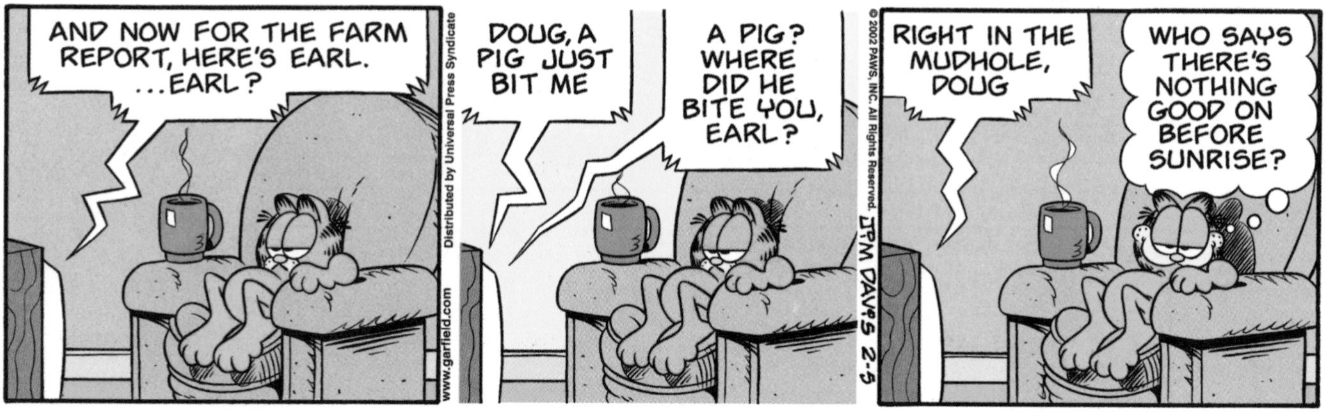
AND NOW FOR THE FARM REPORT, HERE'S EARL. ...EARL?
Distributed by Universal Press Syndicate
www.garfield.com
DOUG, A PIG JUST BIT ME
A PIG? WHERE DID HE BITE YOU, EARL?
© 2002 PAWS, INC. All Rights Reserved.
JPM DAVPS 2-5
RIGHT IN THE MUDHOLE, DOUG
WHO SAYS THERE'S NOTHING GOOD ON BEFORE SUNRISE?

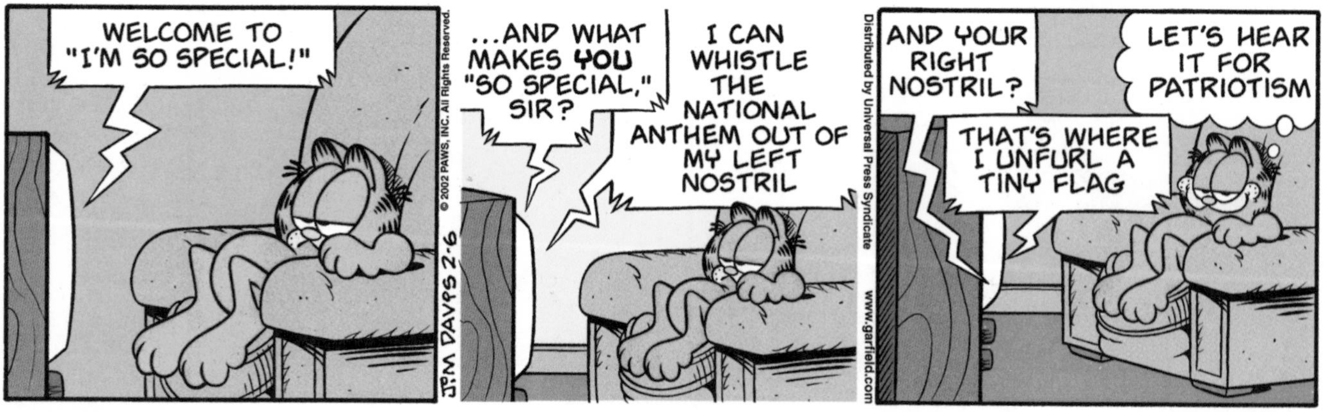
WELCOME TO "I'M SO SPECIAL!"
© 2002 PAWS, INC. All Rights Reserved.
JPM DAVPS 2-6
...AND WHAT MAKES YOU "SO SPECIAL," SIR?
I CAN WHISTLE THE NATIONAL ANTHEM OUT OF MY LEFT NOSTRIL
Distributed by Universal Press Syndicate
www.garfield.com
AND YOUR RIGHT NOSTRIL?
THAT'S WHERE I UNFURL A TINY FLAG
LET'S HEAR IT FOR PATRIOTISM

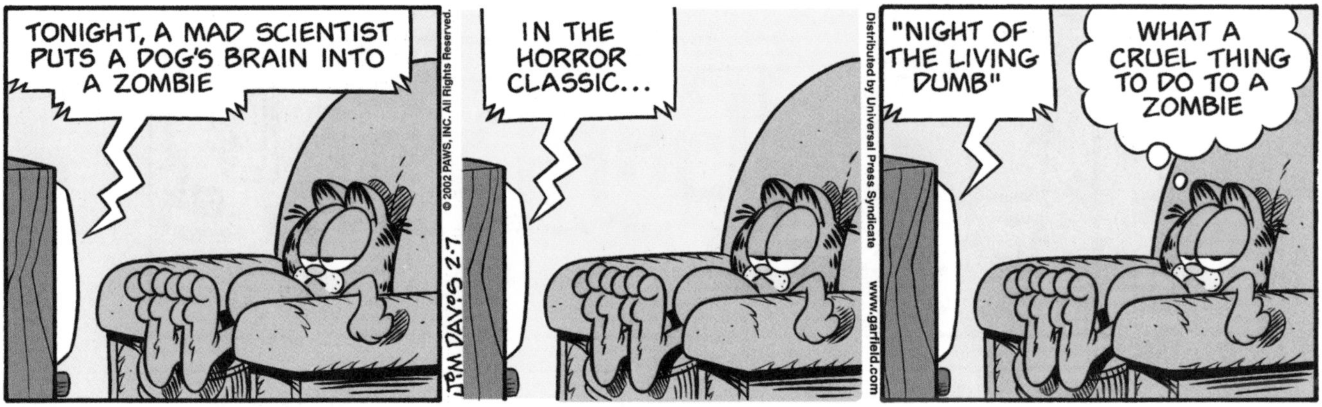
TONIGHT, A MAD SCIENTIST PUTS A DOG'S BRAIN INTO A ZOMBIE
IN THE HORROR CLASSIC...
"NIGHT OF THE LIVING DUMB"
WHAT A CRUEL THING TO DO TO A ZOMBIE
JPM DAVPS 2-7
© 2002 PAWS, INC. All Rights Reserved.
Distributed by Universal Press Syndicate
www.garfield.com

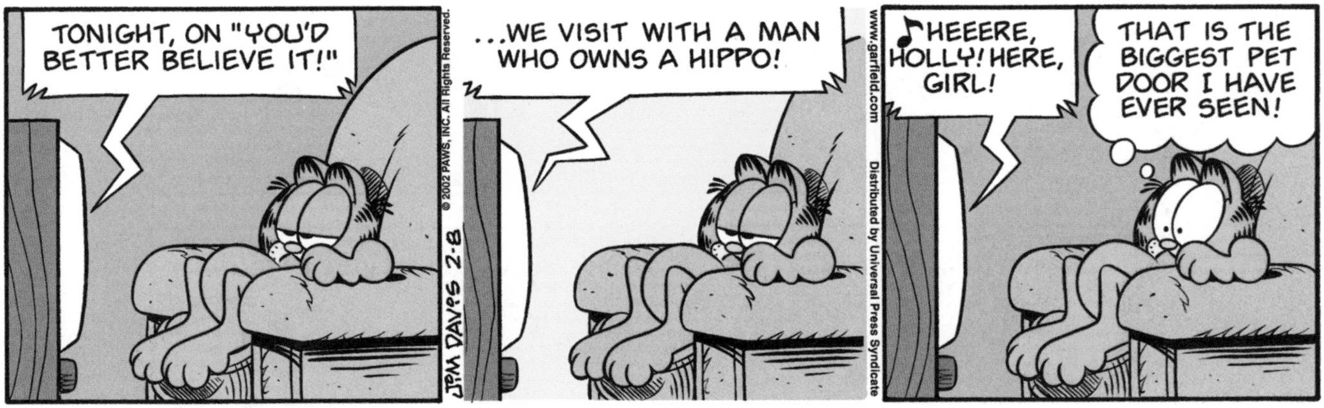
TONIGHT, ON "YOU'D BETTER BELIEVE IT!"
...WE VISIT WITH A MAN WHO OWNS A HIPPO!
♪HEEERE, HOLLY! HERE, GIRL!
THAT IS THE BIGGEST PET DOOR I HAVE EVER SEEN!
JPM DAVPS 2-8
© 2002 PAWS, INC. All Rights Reserved.
www.garfield.com
Distributed by Universal Press Syndicate

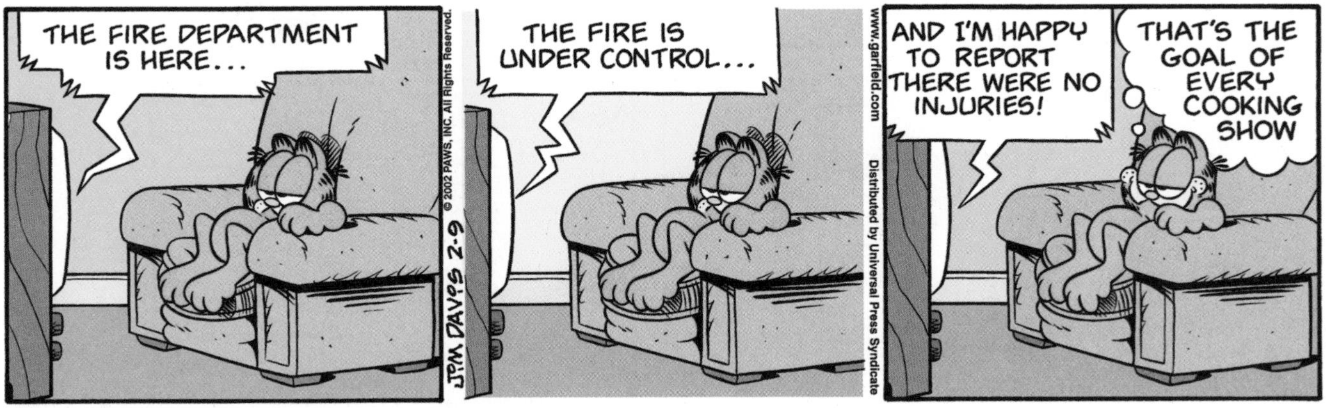
THE FIRE DEPARTMENT IS HERE...
THE FIRE IS UNDER CONTROL...
AND I'M HAPPY TO REPORT THERE WERE NO INJURIES!
THAT'S THE GOAL OF EVERY COOKING SHOW
JPM DAVPS 2-9
© 2002 PAWS, INC. All Rights Reserved.
www.garfield.com
Distributed by Universal Press Syndicate

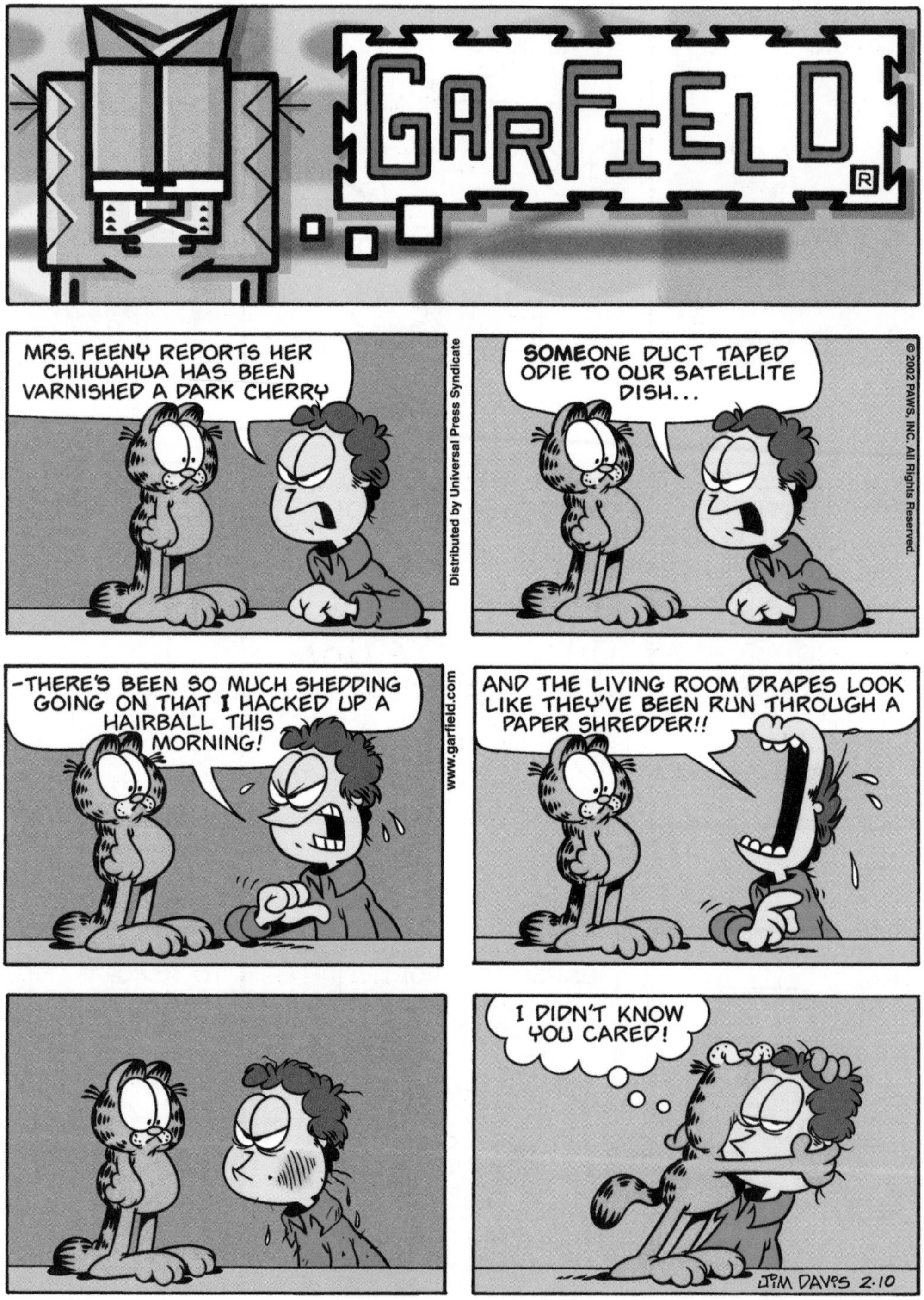
GARFIELD
MRS. FEENY REPORTS HER CHIHUAHUA HAS BEEN VARNISHED A DARK CHERRY
Distributed by Universal Press Syndicate
SOMEONE DUCT TAPED ODIE TO OUR SATELLITE DISH...
© 2002 PAWS, INC. All Rights Reserved.
-THERE'S BEEN SO MUCH SHEDDING GOING ON THAT I HACKED UP A HAIRBALL THIS MORNING!
www.garfield.com
AND THE LIVING ROOM DRAPES LOOK LIKE THEY'VE BEEN RUN THROUGH A PAPER SHREDDER!!
I DIDN'T KNOW YOU CARED!
JIM DAVIS 2-10

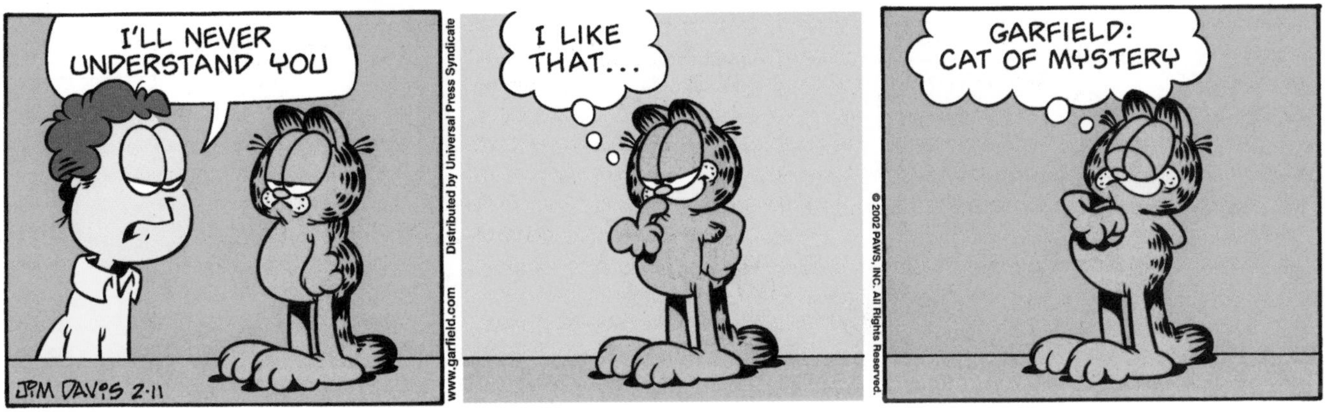
I'LL NEVER UNDERSTAND YOU
I LIKE THAT...
GARFIELD: CAT OF MYSTERY
JIM DAVIS 2-11
www.garfield.com
Distributed by Universal Press Syndicate
© 2002 PAWS, INC. All Rights Reserved.

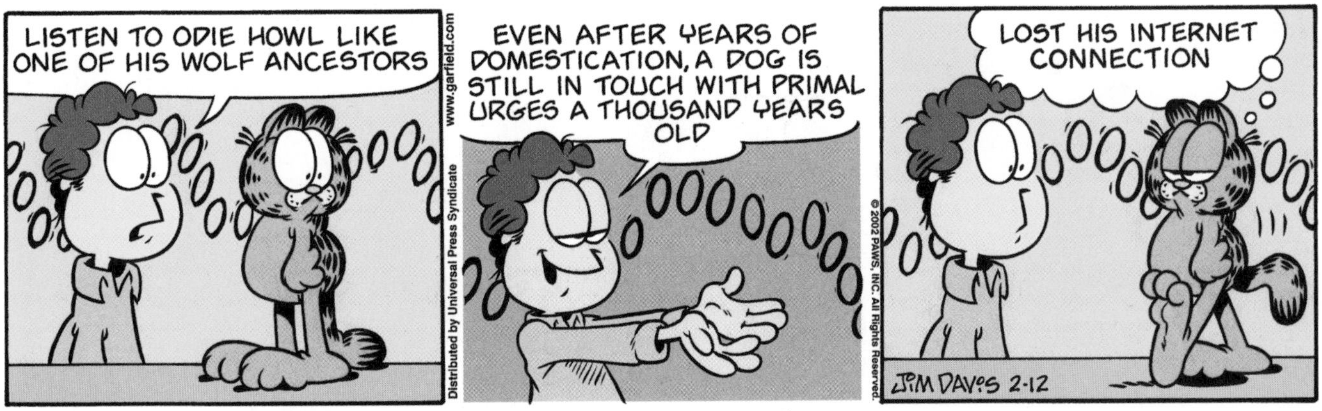
LISTEN TO ODIE HOWL LIKE ONE OF HIS WOLF ANCESTORS
EVEN AFTER YEARS OF DOMESTICATION, A DOG IS STILL IN TOUCH WITH PRIMAL URGES A THOUSAND YEARS OLD
LOST HIS INTERNET CONNECTION
JIM DAVIS 2-12
www.garfield.com
Distributed by Universal Press Syndicate
© 2002 PAWS, INC. All Rights Reserved.

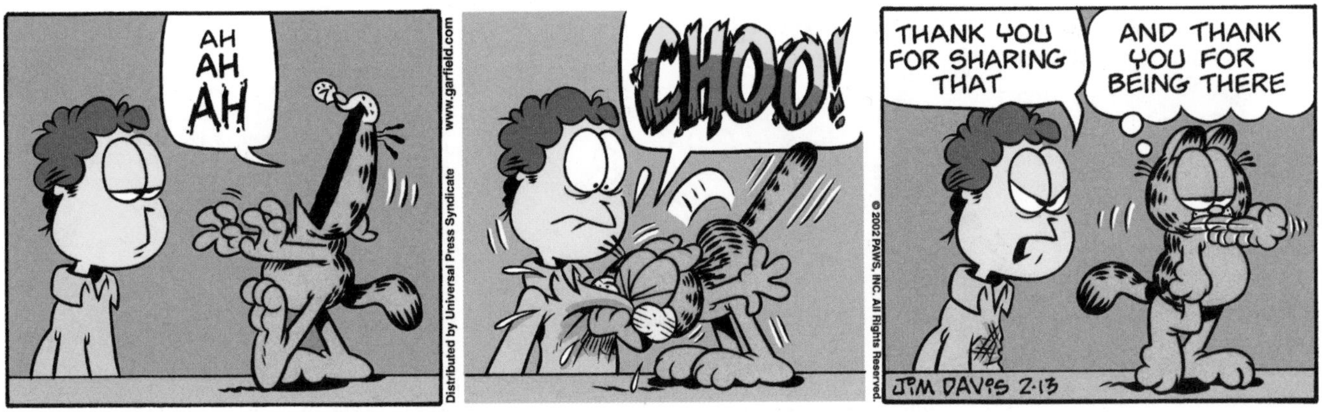
AH AH AH
CHOO!
THANK YOU FOR SHARING THAT
AND THANK YOU FOR BEING THERE
JIM DAVIS 2-13
www.garfield.com
Distributed by Universal Press Syndicate
© 2002 PAWS, INC. All Rights Reserved.

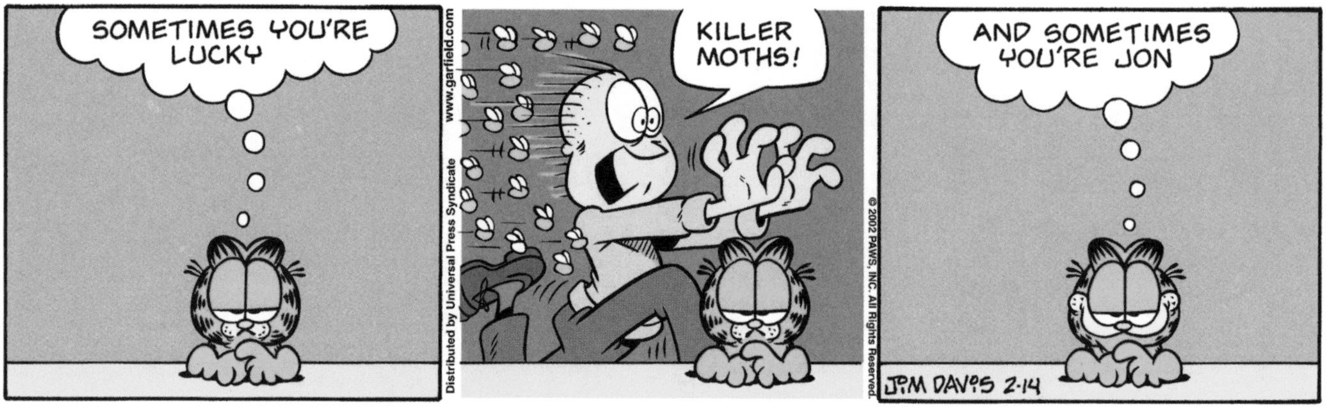
SOMETIMES YOU'RE LUCKY
KILLER MOTHS!
AND SOMETIMES YOU'RE JON
JIM DAVIS 2-14
Distributed by Universal Press Syndicate www.garfield.com
© 2002 PAWS, INC. All Rights Reserved.

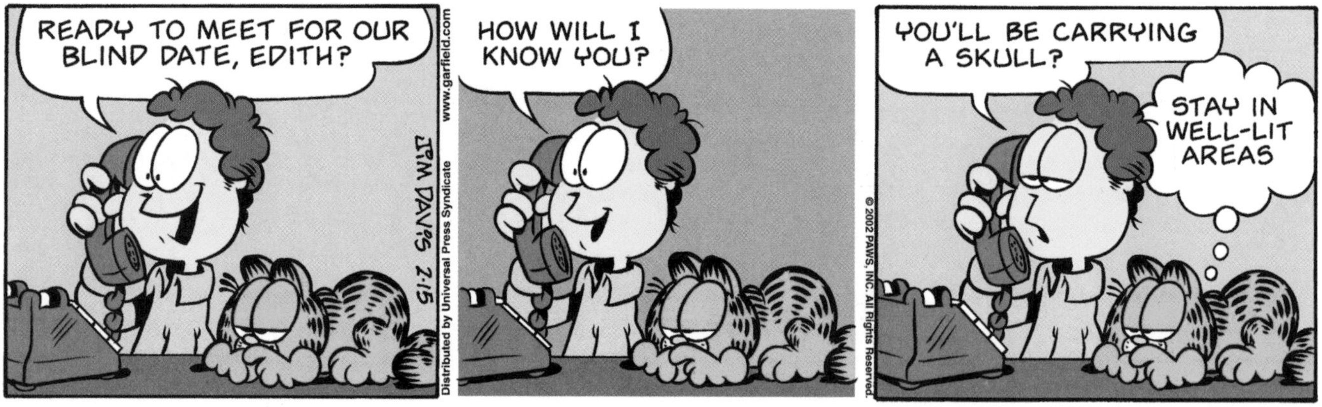
READY TO MEET FOR OUR BLIND DATE, EDITH?
HOW WILL I KNOW YOU?
YOU'LL BE CARRYING A SKULL?
STAY IN WELL-LIT AREAS
JIM DAVIS 2-15
Distributed by Universal Press Syndicate www.garfield.com
© 2002 PAWS, INC. All Rights Reserved.

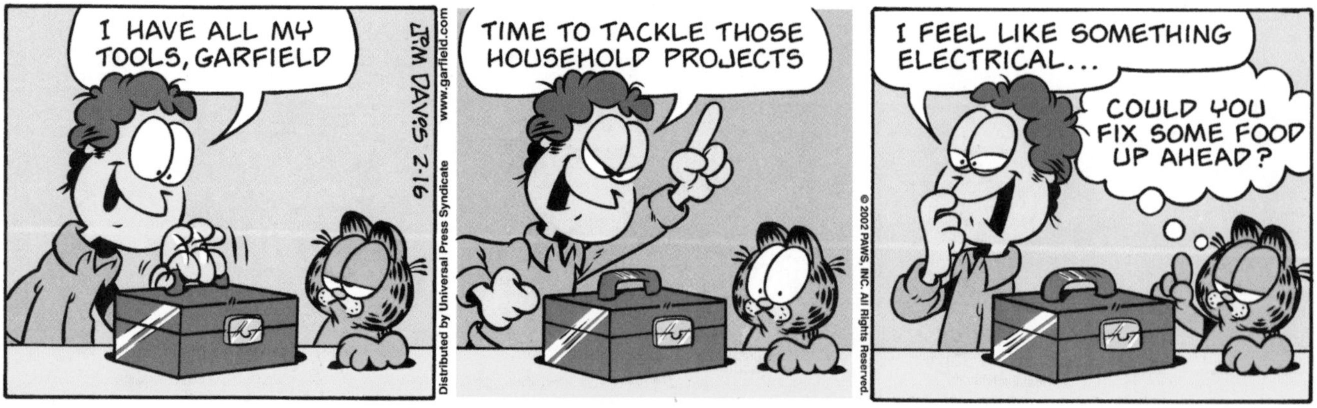
I HAVE ALL MY TOOLS, GARFIELD
TIME TO TACKLE THOSE HOUSEHOLD PROJECTS
I FEEL LIKE SOMETHING ELECTRICAL...
COULD YOU FIX SOME FOOD UP AHEAD?
JIM DAVIS 2-16
Distributed by Universal Press Syndicate www.garfield.com
© 2002 PAWS, INC. All Rights Reserved.

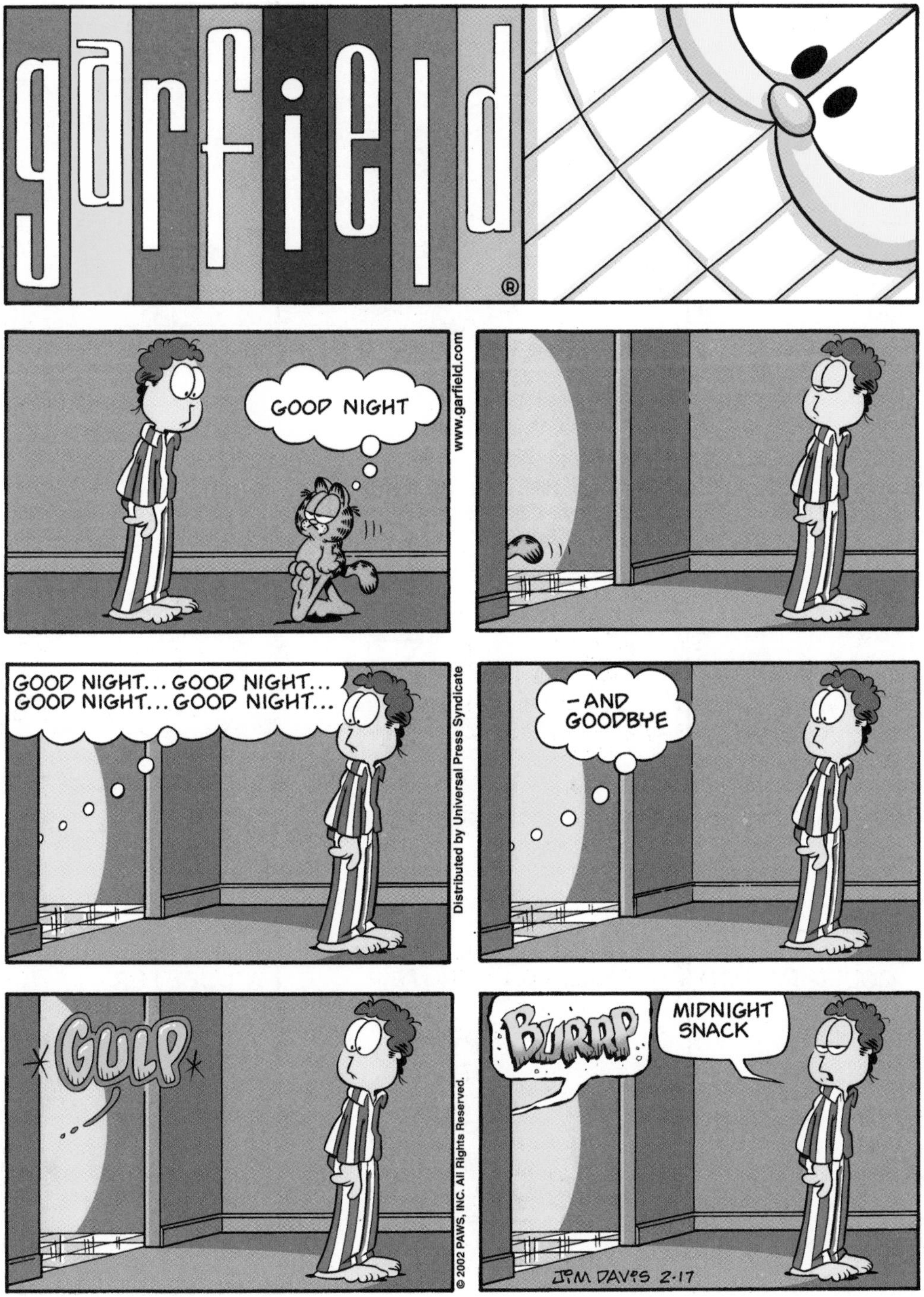
garfield®
www.garfield.com
GOOD NIGHT
GOOD NIGHT... GOOD NIGHT... GOOD NIGHT... GOOD NIGHT...
Distributed by Universal Press Syndicate
-AND GOODBYE
GULP
© 2002 PAWS, INC. All Rights Reserved.
BURRP
MIDNIGHT SNACK
JIM DAVIS 2-17

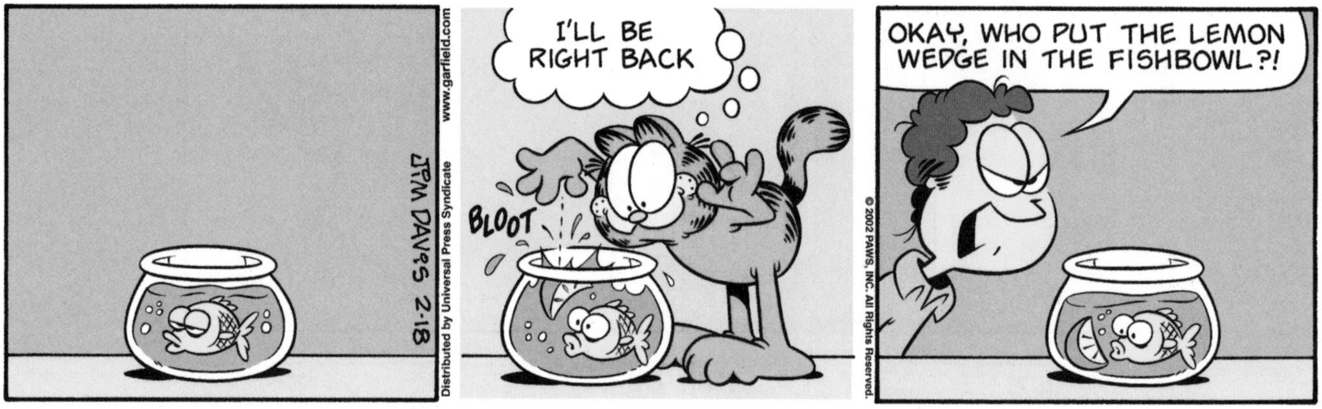
JIM DAVIS 2-18
www.garfield.com
Distributed by Universal Press Syndicate
I'LL BE RIGHT BACK
BLOOT
© 2002 PAWS, INC. All Rights Reserved.
OKAY, WHO PUT THE LEMON WEDGE IN THE FISHBOWL?!

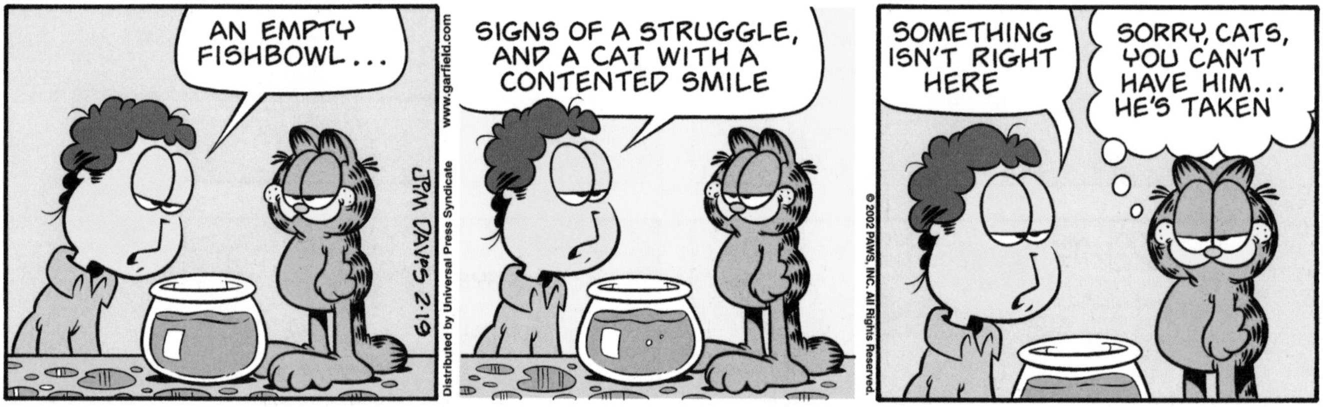
AN EMPTY FISHBOWL...
JIM DAVIS 2-19
www.garfield.com
Distributed by Universal Press Syndicate
SIGNS OF A STRUGGLE, AND A CAT WITH A CONTENTED SMILE
© 2002 PAWS, INC. All Rights Reserved.
SOMETHING ISN'T RIGHT HERE
SORRY, CATS, YOU CAN'T HAVE HIM... HE'S TAKEN

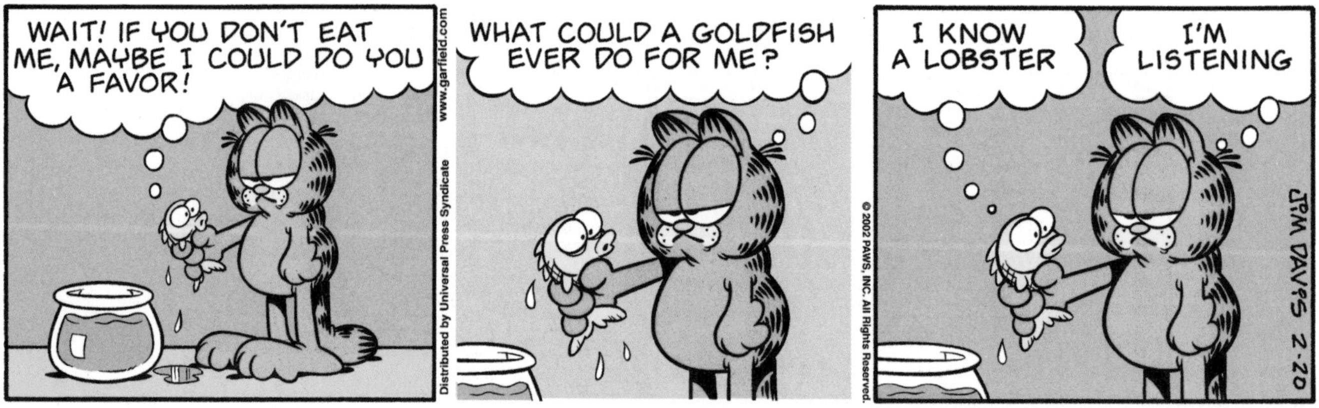
WAIT! IF YOU DON'T EAT ME, MAYBE I COULD DO YOU A FAVOR!
www.garfield.com
Distributed by Universal Press Syndicate
WHAT COULD A GOLDFISH EVER DO FOR ME?
© 2002 PAWS, INC. All Rights Reserved.
I KNOW A LOBSTER
I'M LISTENING
JIM DAVIS 2-20

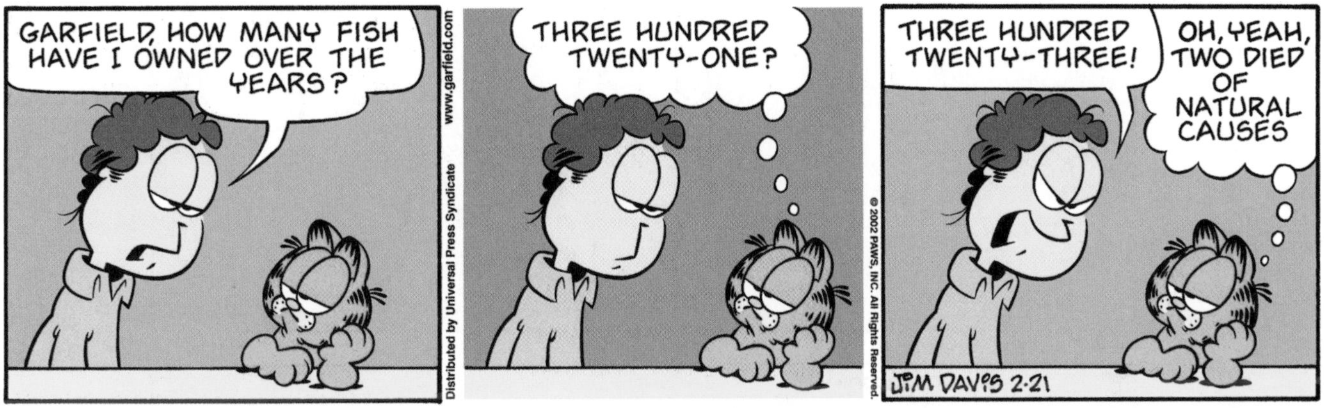
GARFIELD, HOW MANY FISH HAVE I OWNED OVER THE YEARS?
THREE HUNDRED TWENTY-ONE?
THREE HUNDRED TWENTY-THREE!
OH, YEAH, TWO DIED OF NATURAL CAUSES
JIM DAVIS 2·21
www.garfield.com
Distributed by Universal Press Syndicate
© 2002 PAWS, INC. All Rights Reserved.

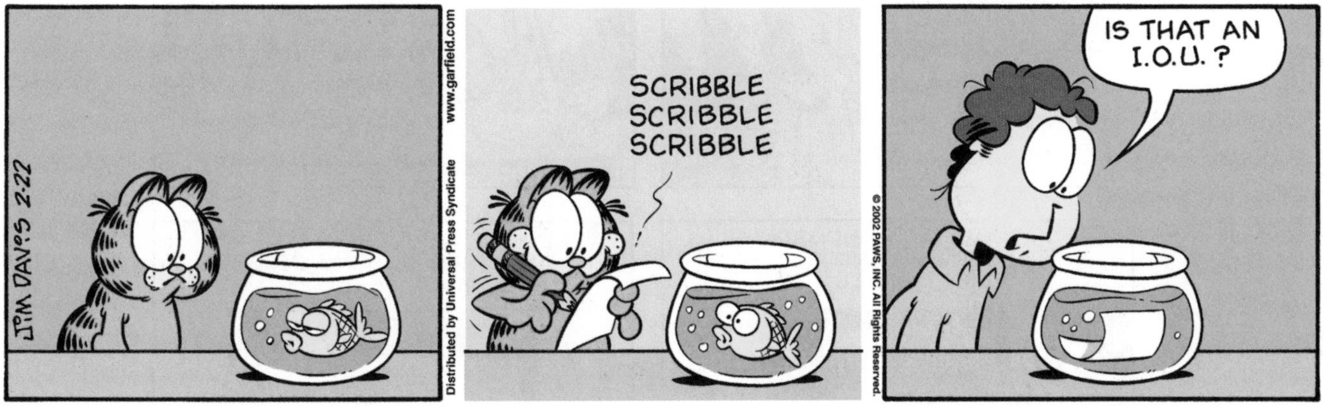
JIM DAVIS 2·22
SCRIBBLE
SCRIBBLE
SCRIBBLE
IS THAT AN I.O.U.?
www.garfield.com
Distributed by Universal Press Syndicate
© 2002 PAWS, INC. All Rights Reserved.

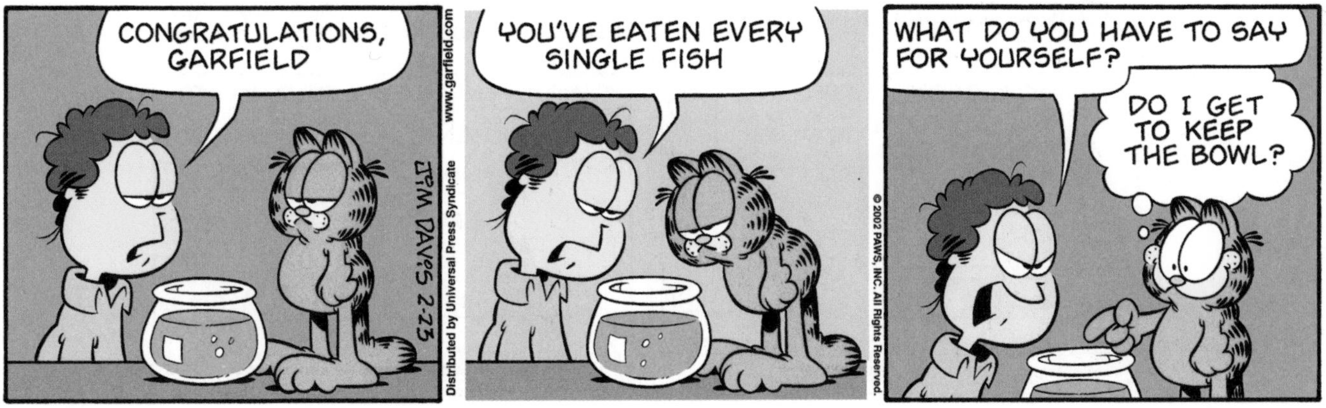
CONGRATULATIONS, GARFIELD
YOU'VE EATEN EVERY SINGLE FISH
WHAT DO YOU HAVE TO SAY FOR YOURSELF?
DO I GET TO KEEP THE BOWL?
JIM DAVIS 2·23
www.garfield.com
Distributed by Universal Press Syndicate
© 2002 PAWS, INC. All Rights Reserved.

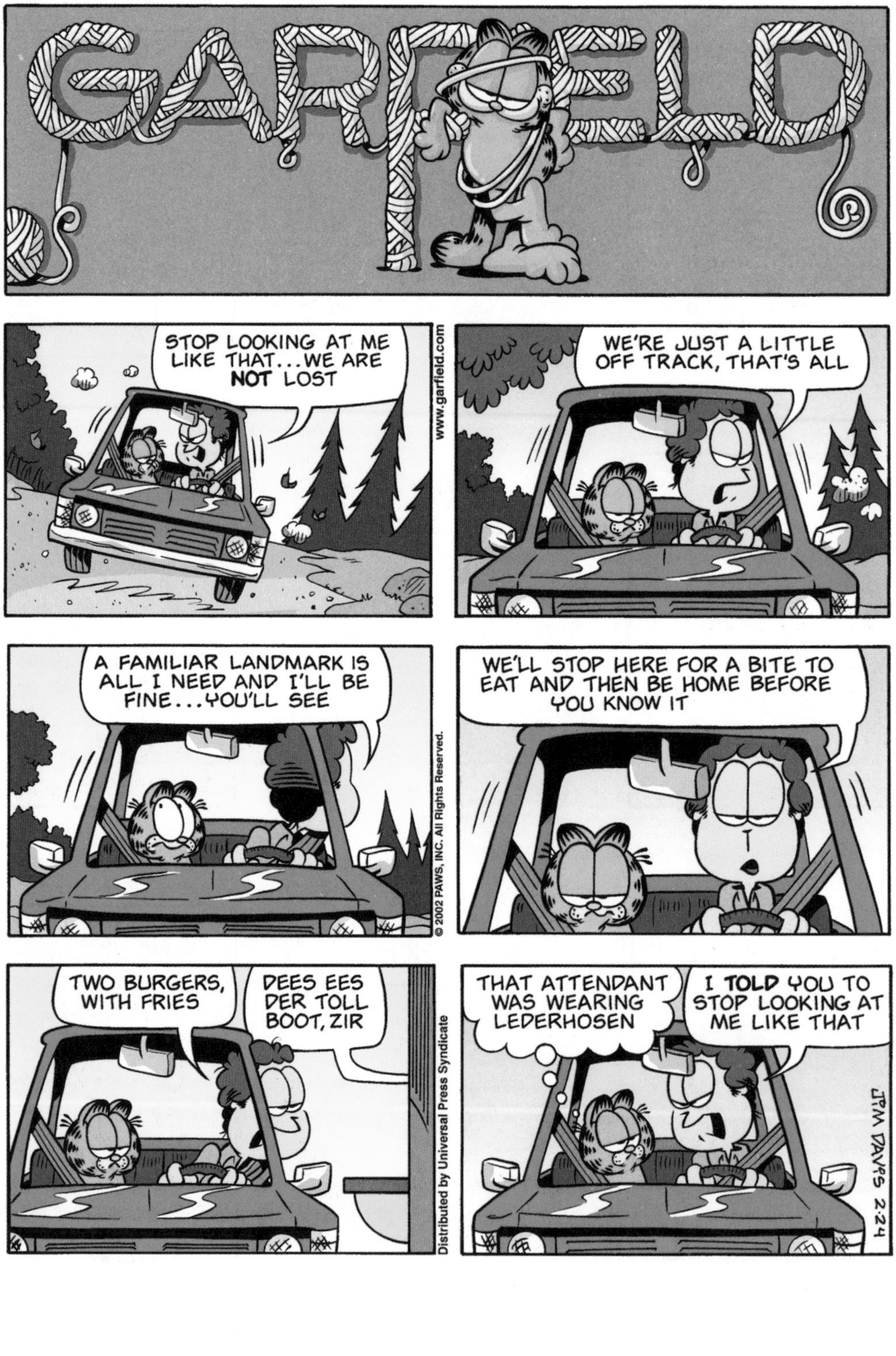
GARFIELD
STOP LOOKING AT ME LIKE THAT...WE ARE NOT LOST
www.garfield.com
WE'RE JUST A LITTLE OFF TRACK, THAT'S ALL
A FAMILIAR LANDMARK IS ALL I NEED AND I'LL BE FINE...YOU'LL SEE
© 2002 PAWS, INC. All Rights Reserved.
WE'LL STOP HERE FOR A BITE TO EAT AND THEN BE HOME BEFORE YOU KNOW IT
TWO BURGERS, WITH FRIES
DEES EES DER TOLL BOOT, ZIR
Distributed by Universal Press Syndicate
THAT ATTENDANT WAS WEARING LEDERHOSEN
I TOLD YOU TO STOP LOOKING AT ME LIKE THAT
JPM DAVPS 2-24

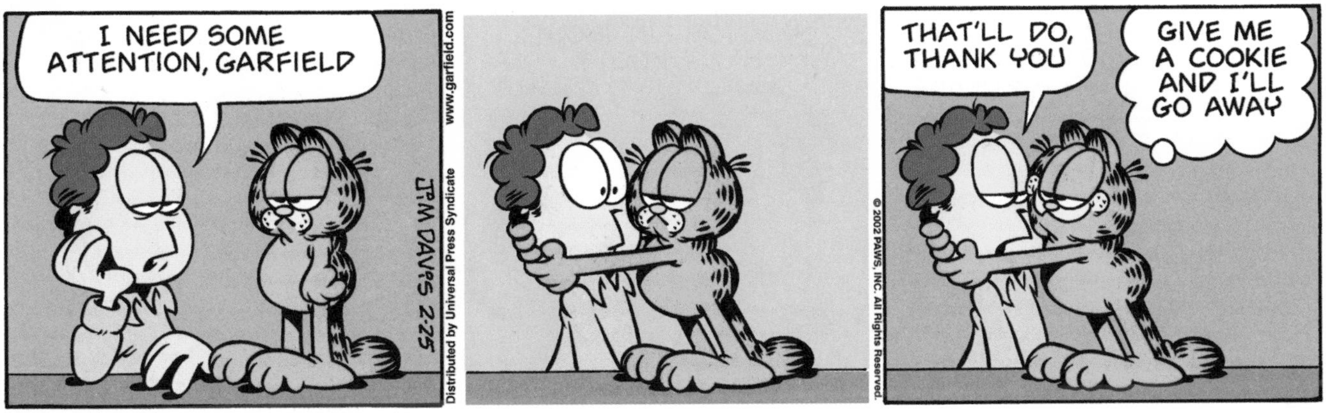
I NEED SOME ATTENTION, GARFIELD
JIM DAVIS 2·25
www.garfield.com
Distributed by Universal Press Syndicate
© 2002 PAWS, INC. All Rights Reserved.
THAT'LL DO, THANK YOU
GIVE ME A COOKIE AND I'LL GO AWAY

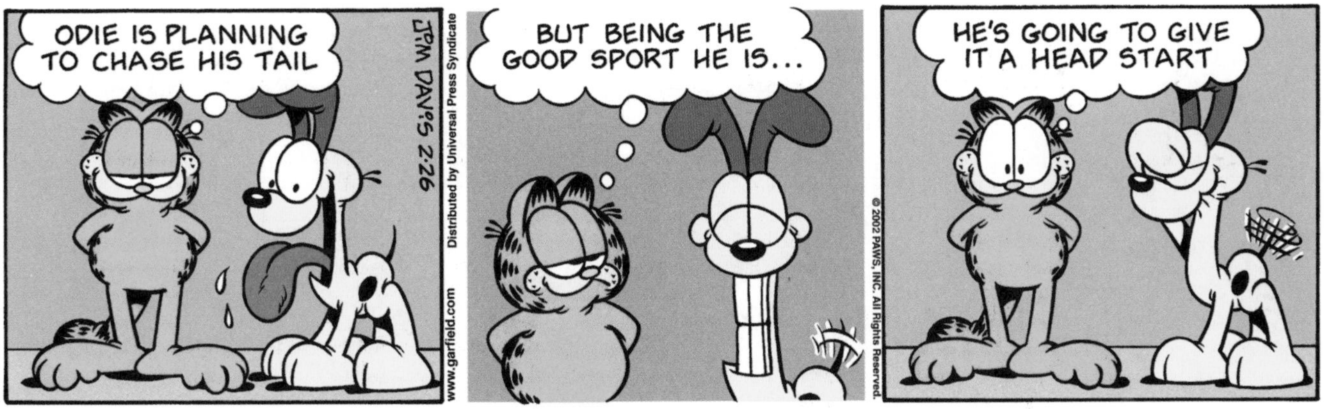
ODIE IS PLANNING TO CHASE HIS TAIL
JIM DAVIS 2·26
Distributed by Universal Press Syndicate
www.garfield.com
BUT BEING THE GOOD SPORT HE IS...
© 2002 PAWS, INC. All Rights Reserved.
HE'S GOING TO GIVE IT A HEAD START

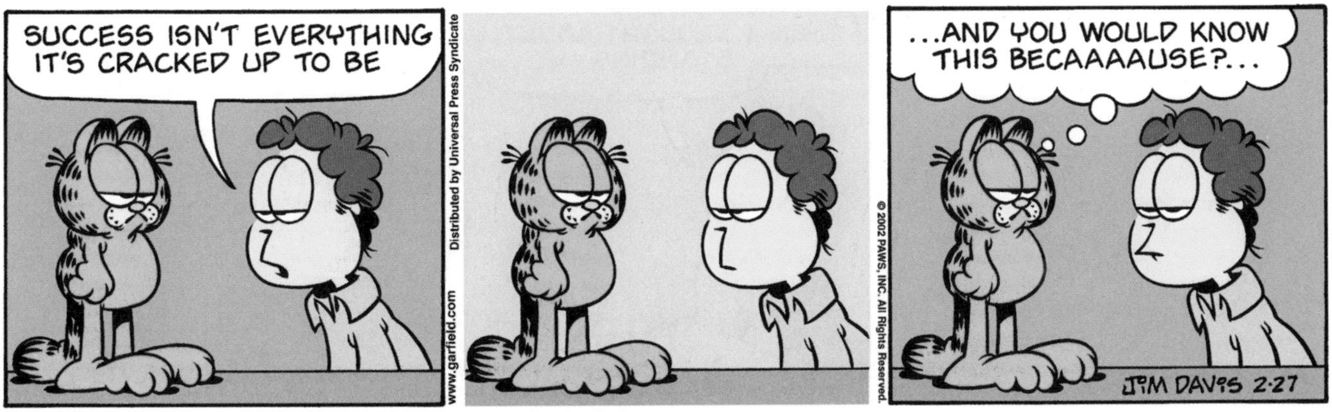
SUCCESS ISN'T EVERYTHING IT'S CRACKED UP TO BE
Distributed by Universal Press Syndicate
www.garfield.com
© 2002 PAWS, INC. All Rights Reserved.
...AND YOU WOULD KNOW THIS BECAAAAUSE?...
JIM DAVIS 2·27

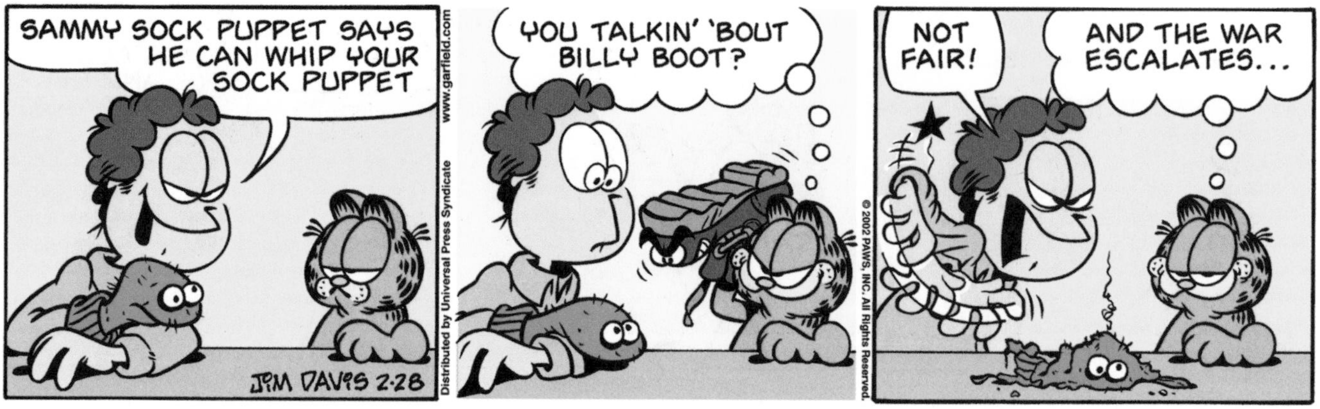
SAMMY SOCK PUPPET SAYS HE CAN WHIP YOUR SOCK PUPPET
JIM DAVIS 2-28
www.garfield.com Distributed by Universal Press Syndicate
YOU TALKIN' 'BOUT BILLY BOOT?
© 2002 PAWS, INC. All Rights Reserved.
NOT FAIR!
AND THE WAR ESCALATES...

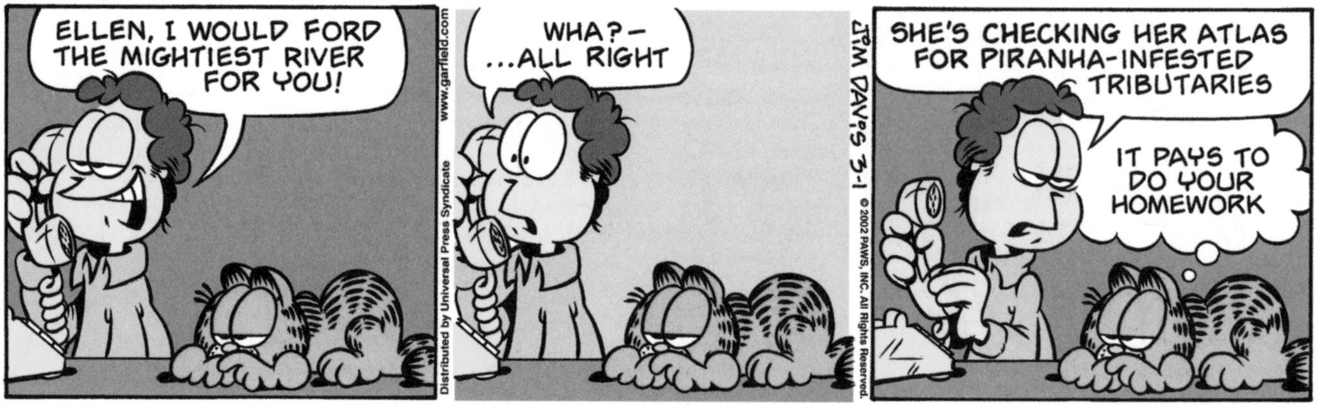
ELLEN, I WOULD FORD THE MIGHTIEST RIVER FOR YOU!
www.garfield.com Distributed by Universal Press Syndicate
WHA?– ...ALL RIGHT
JIM DAVIS 3-1
© 2002 PAWS, INC. All Rights Reserved.
SHE'S CHECKING HER ATLAS FOR PIRANHA-INFESTED TRIBUTARIES
IT PAYS TO DO YOUR HOMEWORK

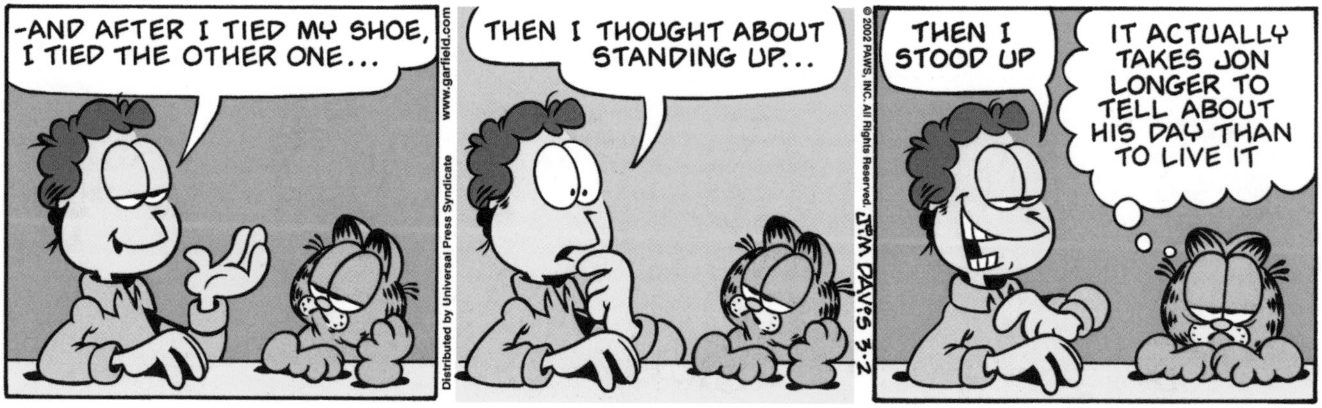
-AND AFTER I TIED MY SHOE, I TIED THE OTHER ONE...
www.garfield.com Distributed by Universal Press Syndicate
THEN I THOUGHT ABOUT STANDING UP...
© 2002 PAWS, INC. All Rights Reserved.
JIM DAVIS 3-2
THEN I STOOD UP
IT ACTUALLY TAKES JON LONGER TO TELL ABOUT HIS DAY THAN TO LIVE IT

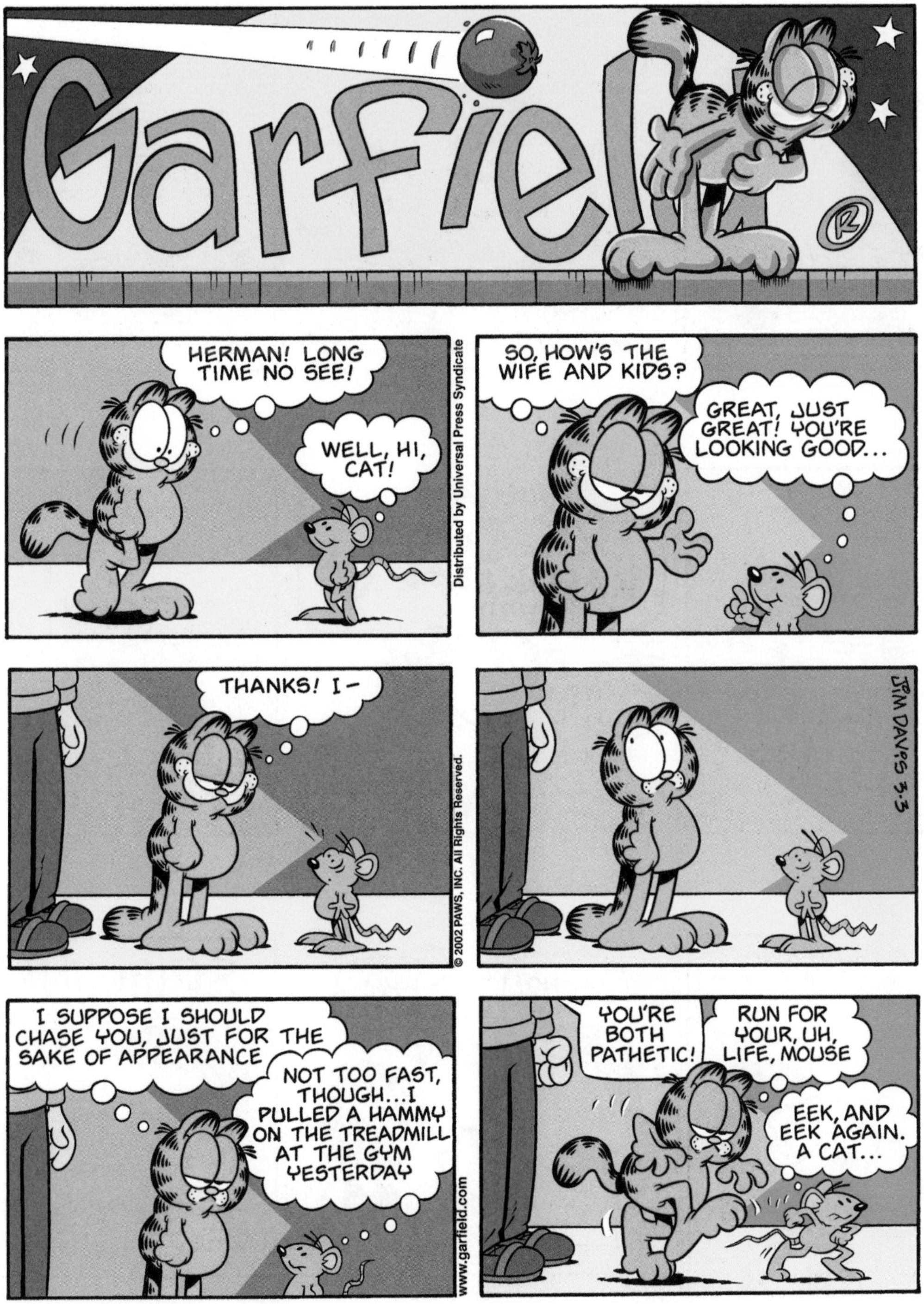
Garfield®
HERMAN! LONG TIME NO SEE!
WELL, HI, CAT!
Distributed by Universal Press Syndicate
SO, HOW'S THE WIFE AND KIDS?
GREAT, JUST GREAT! YOU'RE LOOKING GOOD...
THANKS! I-
© 2002 PAWS, INC. All Rights Reserved.
JIM DAVIS 3-3
I SUPPOSE I SHOULD CHASE YOU, JUST FOR THE SAKE OF APPEARANCE
NOT TOO FAST, THOUGH...I PULLED A HAMMY ON THE TREADMILL AT THE GYM YESTERDAY
www.garfield.com
YOU'RE BOTH PATHETIC!
RUN FOR YOUR, UH, LIFE, MOUSE
EEK, AND EEK AGAIN. A CAT...

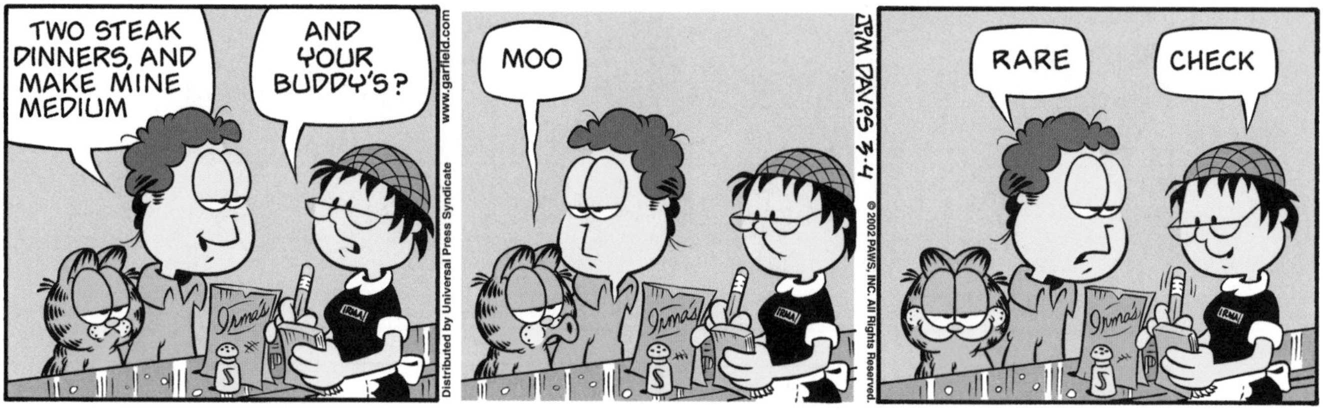
TWO STEAK DINNERS, AND MAKE MINE MEDIUM
AND YOUR BUDDY'S?
MOO
RARE
CHECK
JIM DAVIS 3-4
www.garfield.com
Distributed by Universal Press Syndicate
© 2002 PAWS, INC. All Rights Reserved.

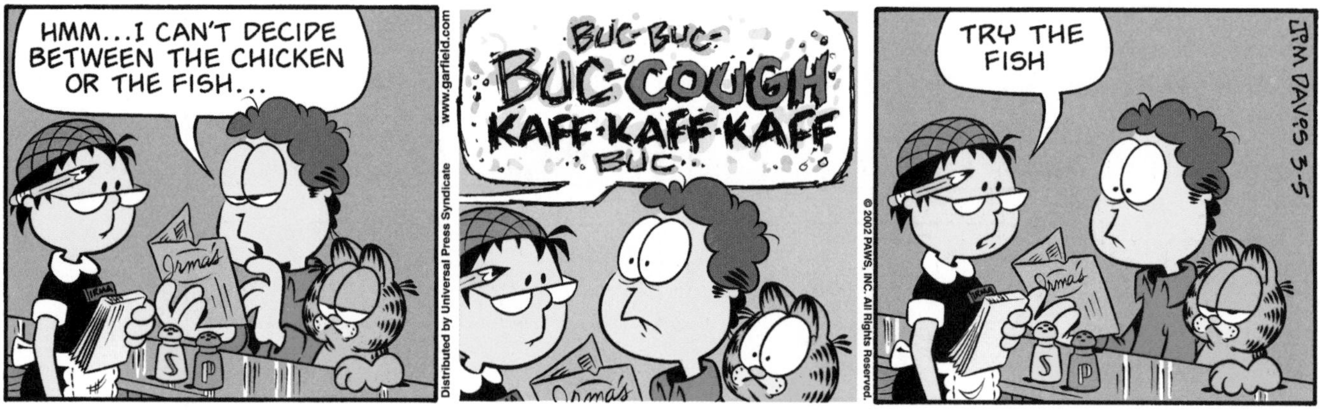
HMM...I CAN'T DECIDE BETWEEN THE CHICKEN OR THE FISH...
BUC-BUC-
BUC-COUGH
KAFF-KAFF-KAFF
BUC
TRY THE FISH
JIM DAVIS 3-5
www.garfield.com
Distributed by Universal Press Syndicate
© 2002 PAWS, INC. All Rights Reserved.

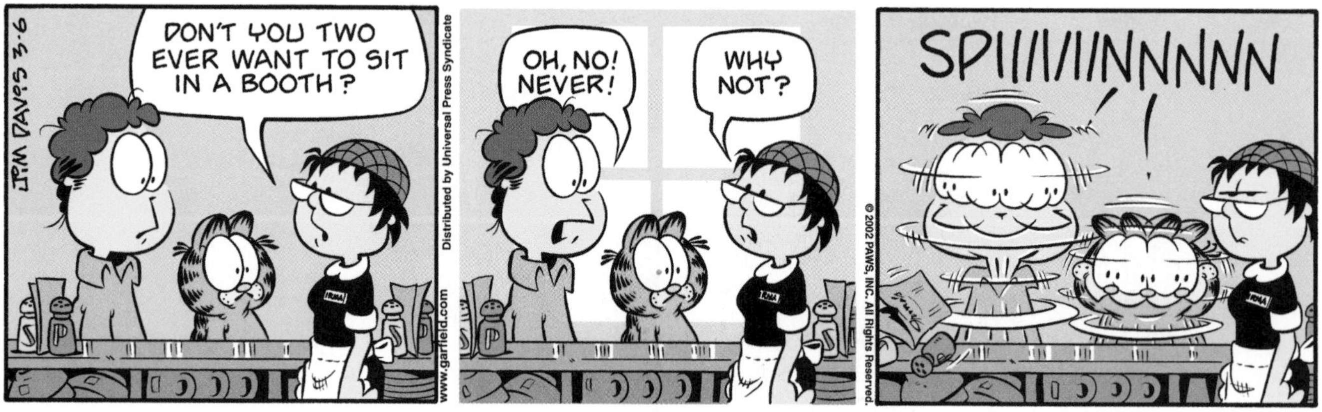
DON'T YOU TWO EVER WANT TO SIT IN A BOOTH?
OH, NO! NEVER!
WHY NOT?
SPIIIIIINNNNN
JIM DAVIS 3-6
www.garfield.com
Distributed by Universal Press Syndicate
© 2002 PAWS, INC. All Rights Reserved.

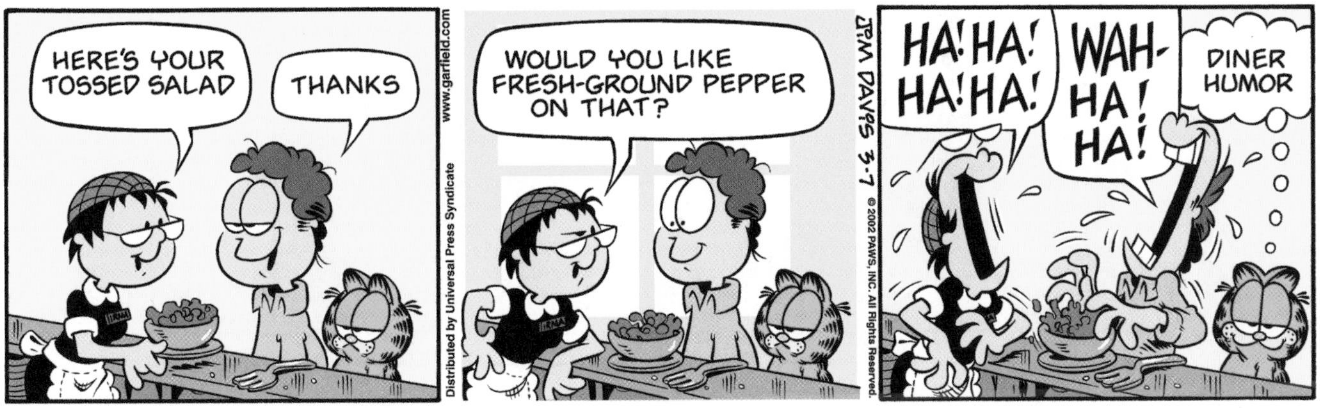
HERE'S YOUR TOSSED SALAD
THANKS
WOULD YOU LIKE FRESH-GROUND PEPPER ON THAT?
HA! HA! HA! HA!
WAH-HA! HA!
DINER HUMOR
JPM DAVIS 3-7
www.garfield.com
Distributed by Universal Press Syndicate
© 2002 PAWS, INC. All Rights Reserved.

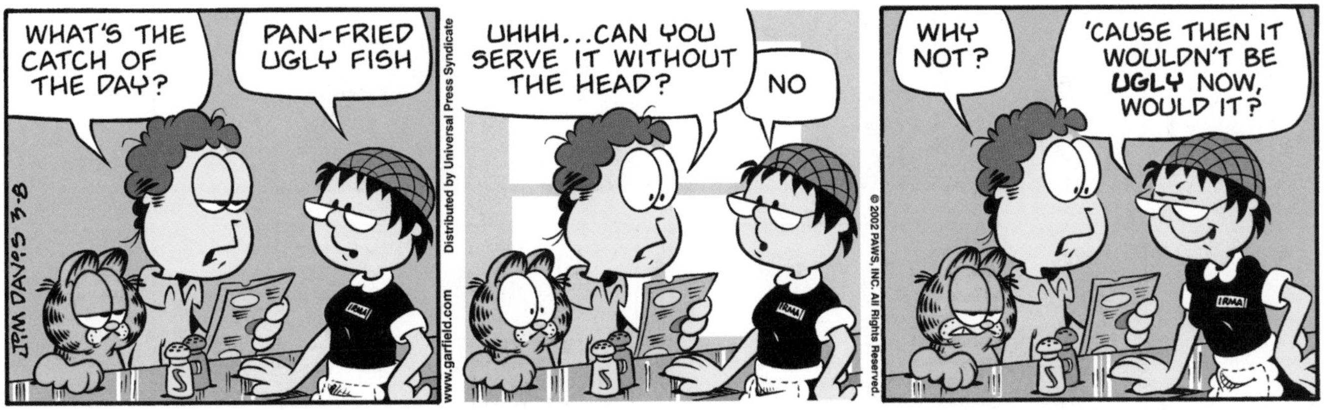
WHAT'S THE CATCH OF THE DAY?
PAN-FRIED UGLY FISH
UHHH...CAN YOU SERVE IT WITHOUT THE HEAD?
NO
WHY NOT?
'CAUSE THEN IT WOULDN'T BE UGLY NOW, WOULD IT?
JPM DAVIS 3-8
Distributed by Universal Press Syndicate
www.garfield.com
© 2002 PAWS, INC. All Rights Reserved.

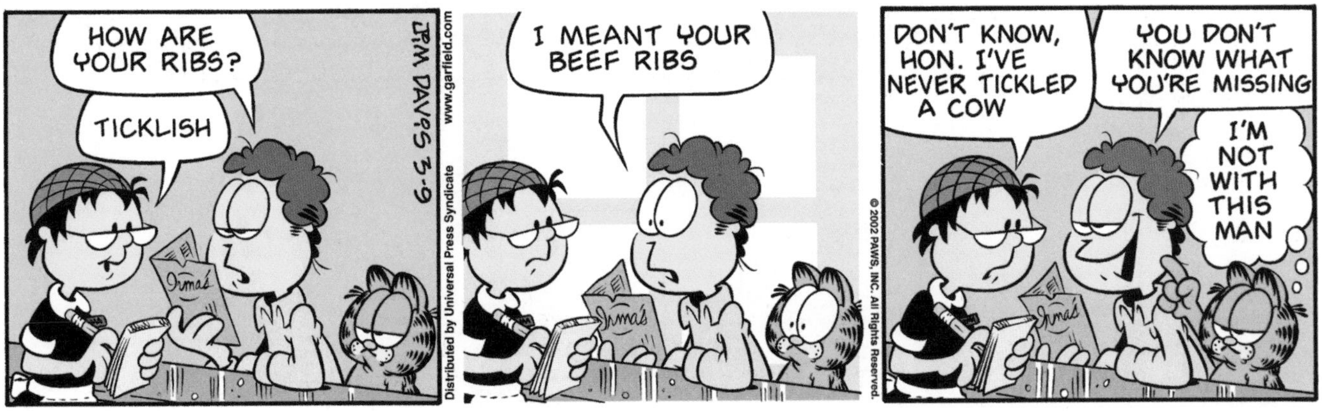
HOW ARE YOUR RIBS?
TICKLISH
I MEANT YOUR BEEF RIBS
DON'T KNOW, HON. I'VE NEVER TICKLED A COW
YOU DON'T KNOW WHAT YOU'RE MISSING
I'M NOT WITH THIS MAN
JPM DAVIS 3-9
www.garfield.com
Distributed by Universal Press Syndicate
© 2002 PAWS, INC. All Rights Reserved.

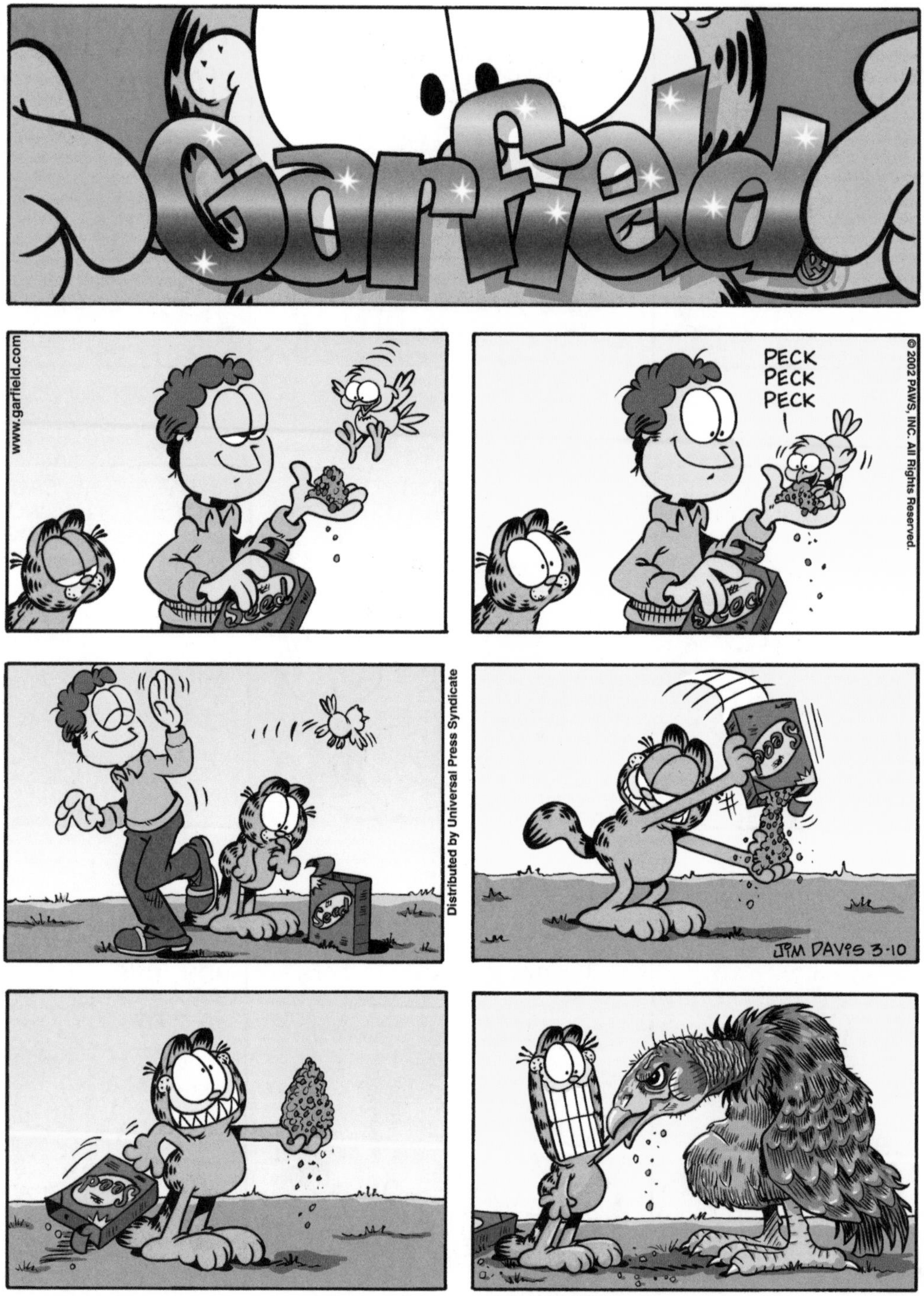
Garfield
www.garfield.com
Seed
PECK
PECK
PECK
© 2002 PAWS, INC. All Rights Reserved.
Seed
Distributed by Universal Press Syndicate
Seed
JIM DAVIS 3-10

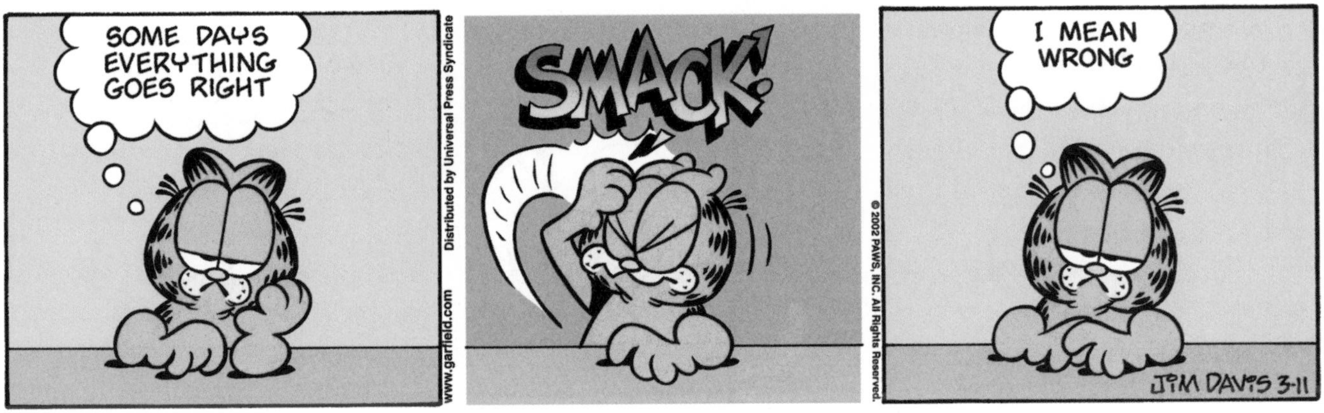
SOME DAYS EVERYTHING GOES RIGHT
Distributed by Universal Press Syndicate
www.garfield.com
SMACK!
© 2002 PAWS, INC. All Rights Reserved.
I MEAN WRONG
JIM DAVIS 3-11

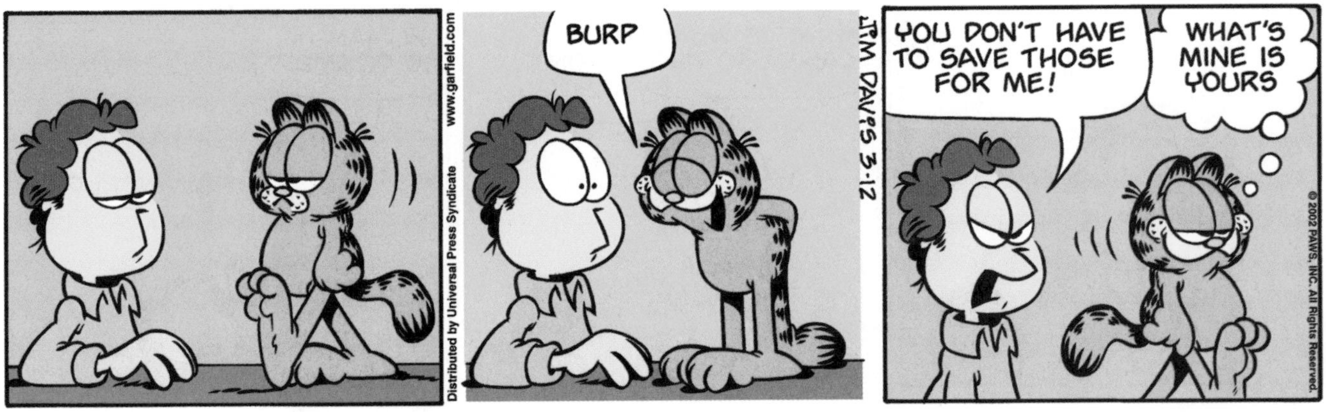
www.garfield.com
Distributed by Universal Press Syndicate
BURP
JIM DAVIS 3-12
YOU DON'T HAVE TO SAVE THOSE FOR ME!
WHAT'S MINE IS YOURS
© 2002 PAWS, INC. All Rights Reserved.

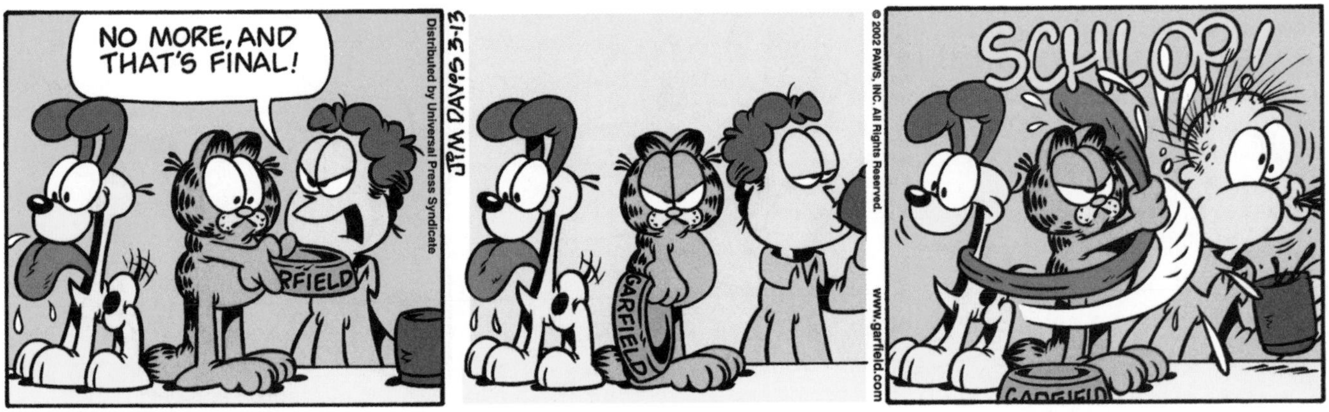
NO MORE, AND THAT'S FINAL!
Distributed by Universal Press Syndicate
JIM DAVIS 3-13
© 2002 PAWS, INC. All Rights Reserved.
www.garfield.com
SCHLOP!

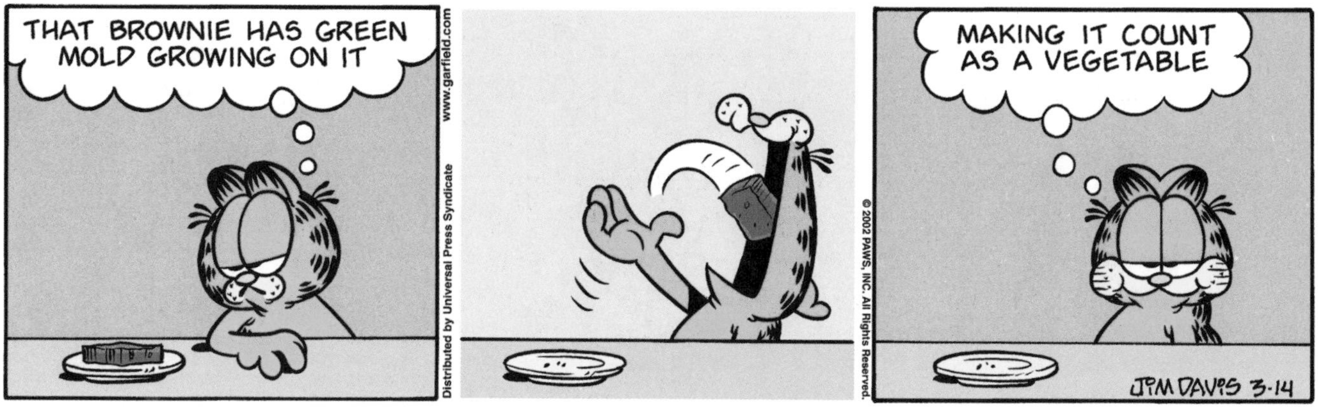
THAT BROWNIE HAS GREEN MOLD GROWING ON IT
MAKING IT COUNT AS A VEGETABLE
JIM DAVIS 3-14
www.garfield.com
Distributed by Universal Press Syndicate
© 2002 PAWS, INC. All Rights Reserved.

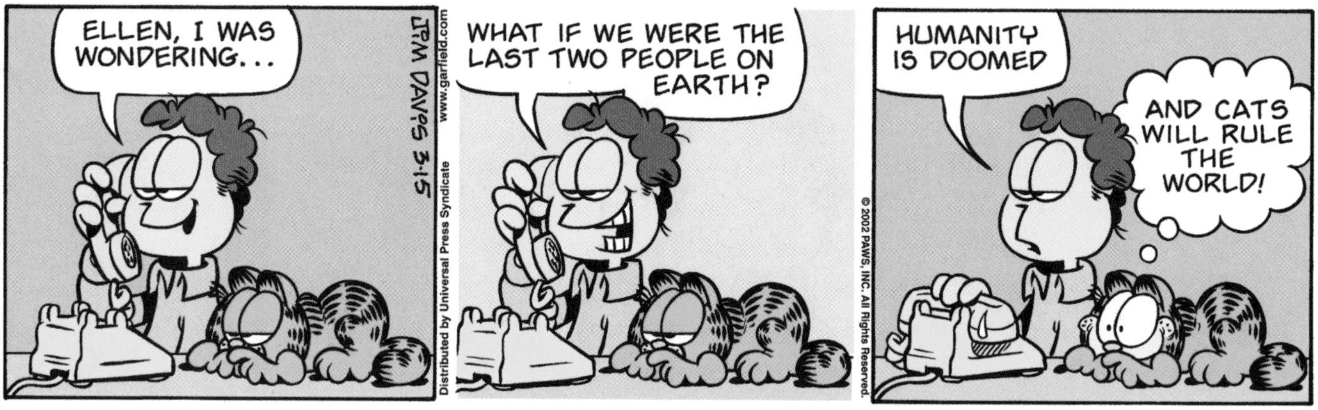
ELLEN, I WAS WONDERING...
WHAT IF WE WERE THE LAST TWO PEOPLE ON EARTH?
HUMANITY IS DOOMED
AND CATS WILL RULE THE WORLD!
JIM DAVIS 3-15
www.garfield.com
Distributed by Universal Press Syndicate
© 2002 PAWS, INC. All Rights Reserved.

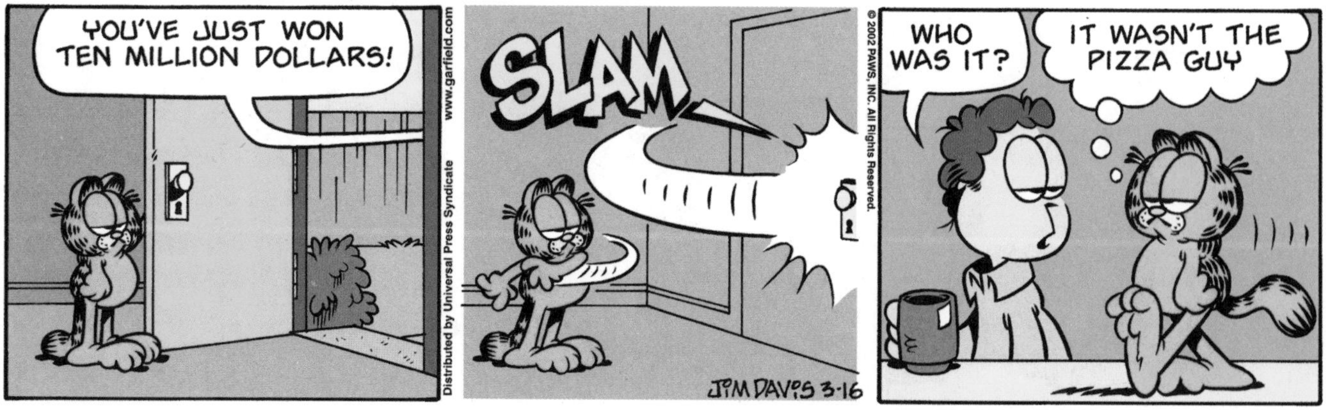
YOU'VE JUST WON TEN MILLION DOLLARS!
SLAM
WHO WAS IT?
IT WASN'T THE PIZZA GUY
JIM DAVIS 3-16
www.garfield.com
Distributed by Universal Press Syndicate
© 2002 PAWS, INC. All Rights Reserved.

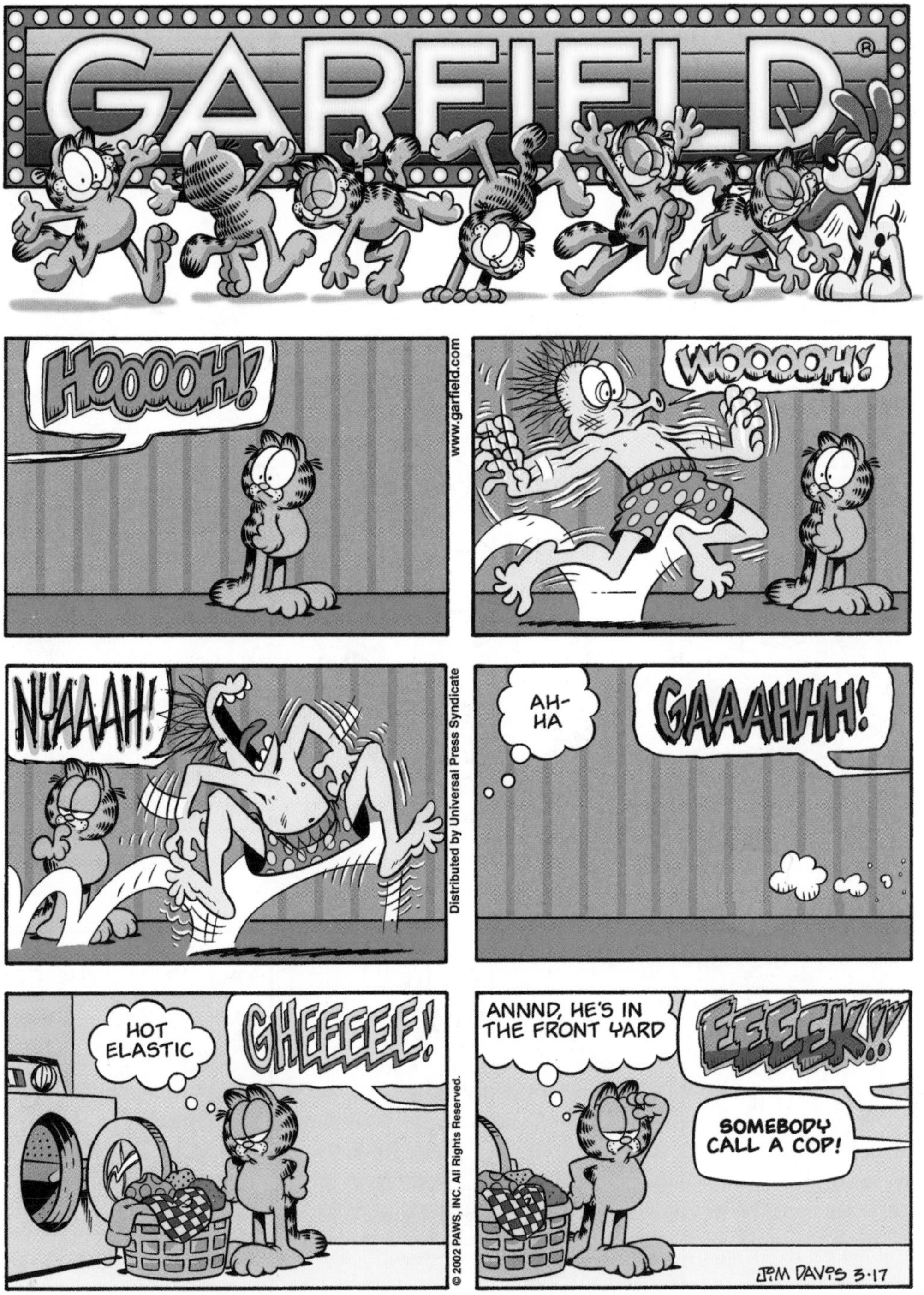
GARFIELD®
HOOOOH!
www.garfield.com
WOOOOH!
NYAAAH!
Distributed by Universal Press Syndicate
AH-HA
GAAAHHH!
HOT ELASTIC
GHEEEEE!
© 2002 PAWS, INC. All Rights Reserved.
ANNND, HE'S IN THE FRONT YARD
EEEEK!!
SOMEBODY CALL A COP!
JIM DAVIS 3-17

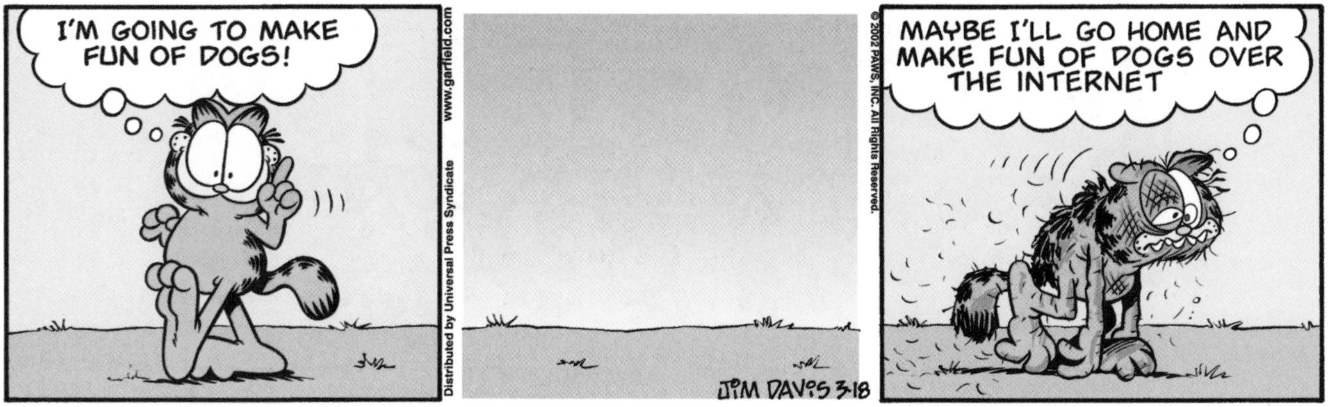
I'M GOING TO MAKE FUN OF DOGS!
www.garfield.com
Distributed by Universal Press Syndicate
JIM DAVIS 3-18
© 2002 PAWS, INC. All Rights Reserved.
MAYBE I'LL GO HOME AND MAKE FUN OF DOGS OVER THE INTERNET

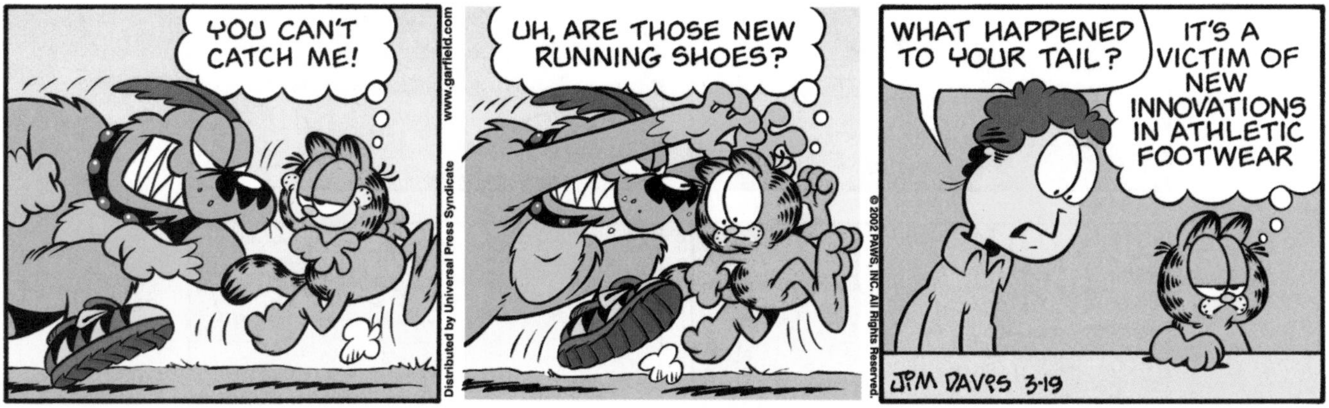
YOU CAN'T CATCH ME!
www.garfield.com
Distributed by Universal Press Syndicate
UH, ARE THOSE NEW RUNNING SHOES?
© 2002 PAWS, INC. All Rights Reserved.
WHAT HAPPENED TO YOUR TAIL?
IT'S A VICTIM OF NEW INNOVATIONS IN ATHLETIC FOOTWEAR
JIM DAVIS 3-19

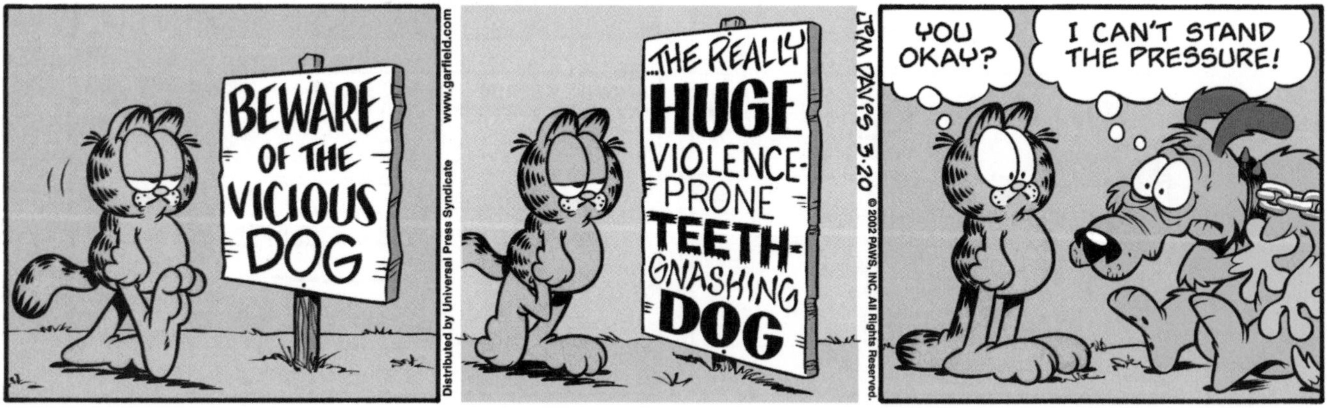
BEWARE OF THE VICIOUS DOG
www.garfield.com
Distributed by Universal Press Syndicate
...THE REALLY HUGE VIOLENCE-PRONE TEETH-GNASHING DOG
JIM DAVIS 3-20
© 2002 PAWS, INC. All Rights Reserved.
YOU OKAY?
I CAN'T STAND THE PRESSURE!

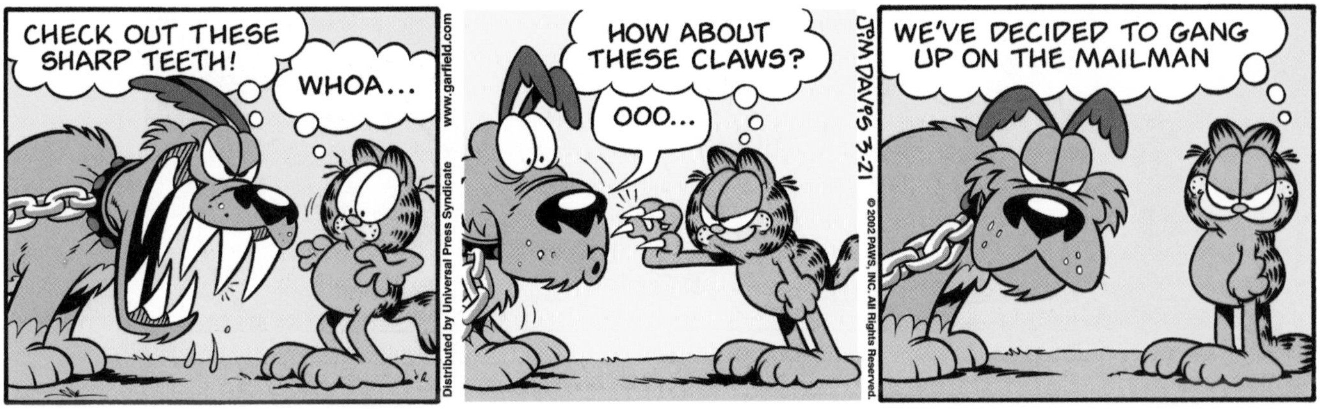
CHECK OUT THESE SHARP TEETH!
WHOA...
www.garfield.com
Distributed by Universal Press Syndicate
HOW ABOUT THESE CLAWS?
OOO...
JIM DAVIS 3-21
© 2002 PAWS, INC. All Rights Reserved.
WE'VE DECIDED TO GANG UP ON THE MAILMAN

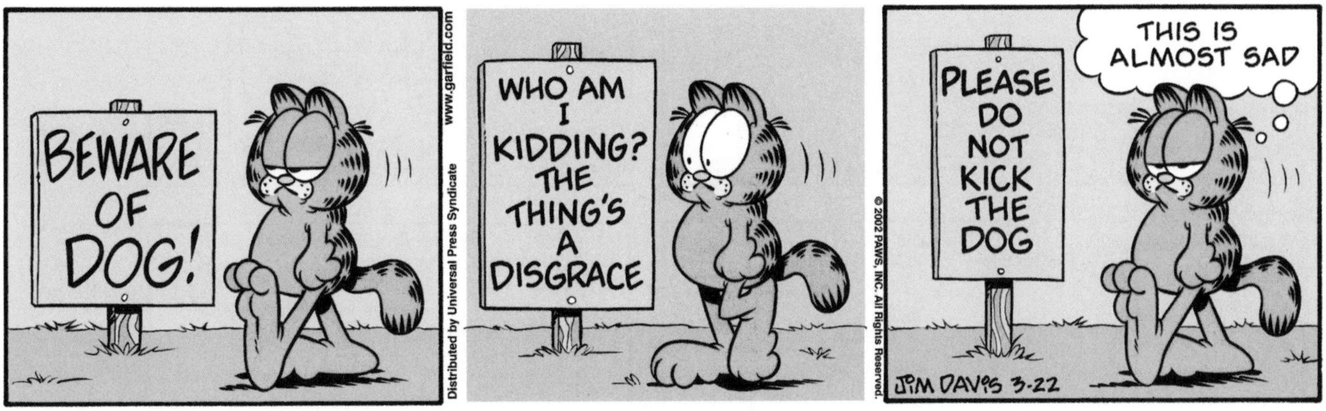
BEWARE OF DOG!
www.garfield.com
Distributed by Universal Press Syndicate
WHO AM I KIDDING? THE THING'S A DISGRACE
© 2002 PAWS, INC. All Rights Reserved.
PLEASE DO NOT KICK THE DOG
THIS IS ALMOST SAD
JIM DAVIS 3-22

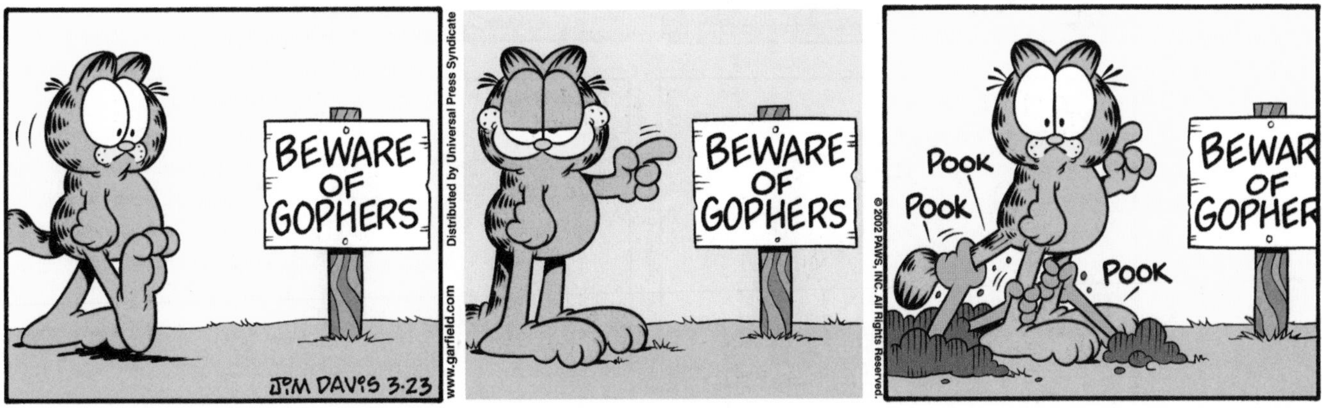
BEWARE OF GOPHERS
JIM DAVIS 3-23
Distributed by Universal Press Syndicate
www.garfield.com
BEWARE OF GOPHERS
© 2002 PAWS, INC. All Rights Reserved.
POOK
POOK
POOK
BEWAR OF GOPHER

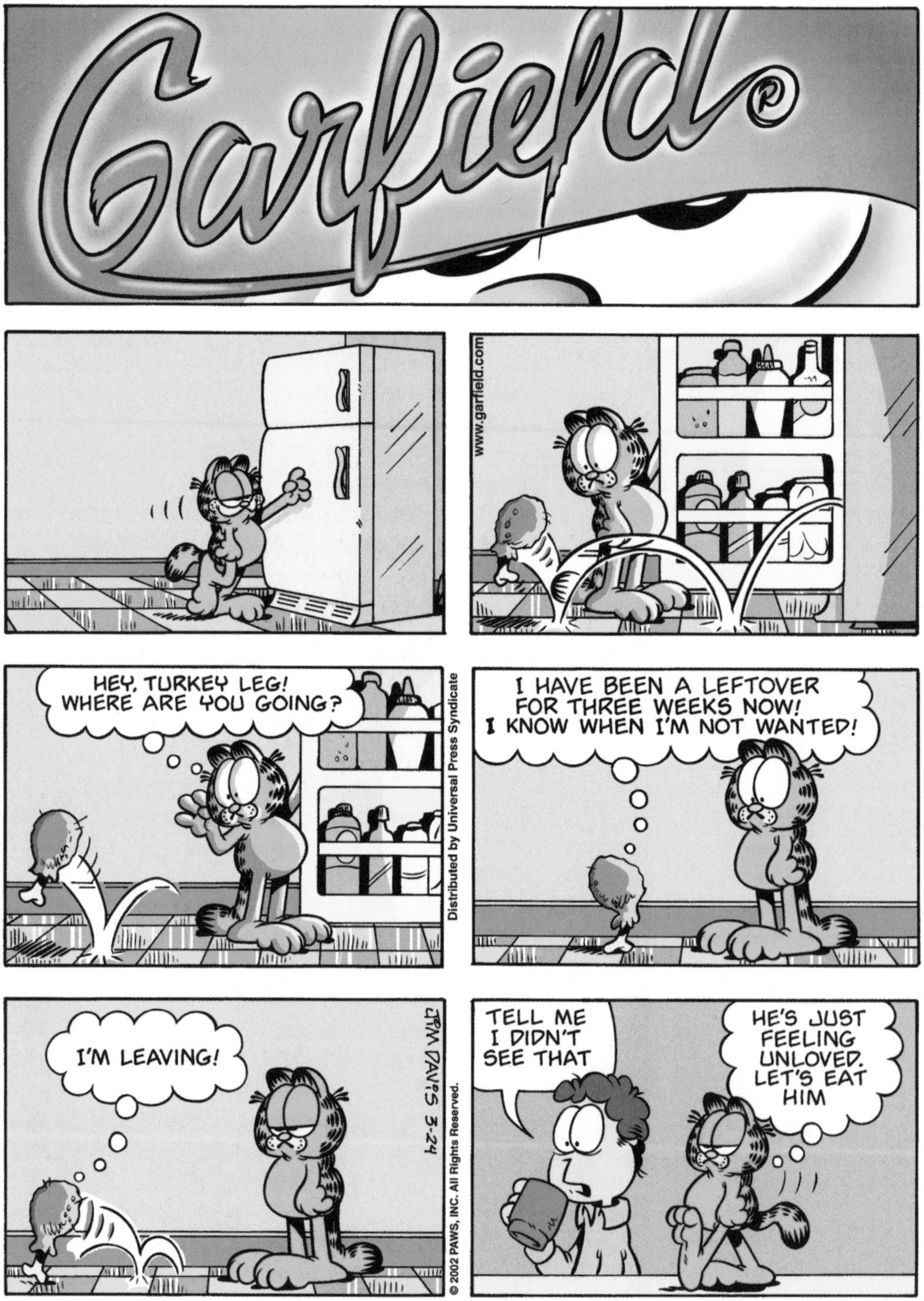
Garfield
www.garfield.com
HEY, TURKEY LEG! WHERE ARE YOU GOING?
Distributed by Universal Press Syndicate
I HAVE BEEN A LEFTOVER FOR THREE WEEKS NOW! I KNOW WHEN I'M NOT WANTED!
I'M LEAVING!
JIM DAVIS 3-24
© 2002 PAWS, INC. All Rights Reserved.
TELL ME I DIDN'T SEE THAT
HE'S JUST FEELING UNLOVED. LET'S EAT HIM

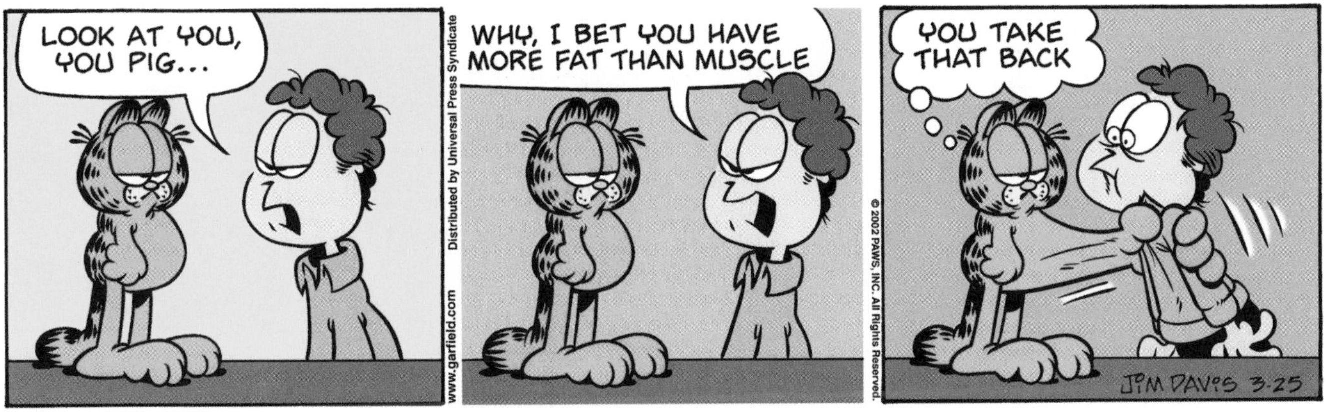
LOOK AT YOU, YOU PIG...
WHY, I BET YOU HAVE MORE FAT THAN MUSCLE
YOU TAKE THAT BACK
JIM DAVIS 3-25
www.garfield.com
Distributed by Universal Press Syndicate
© 2002 PAWS, INC. All Rights Reserved.

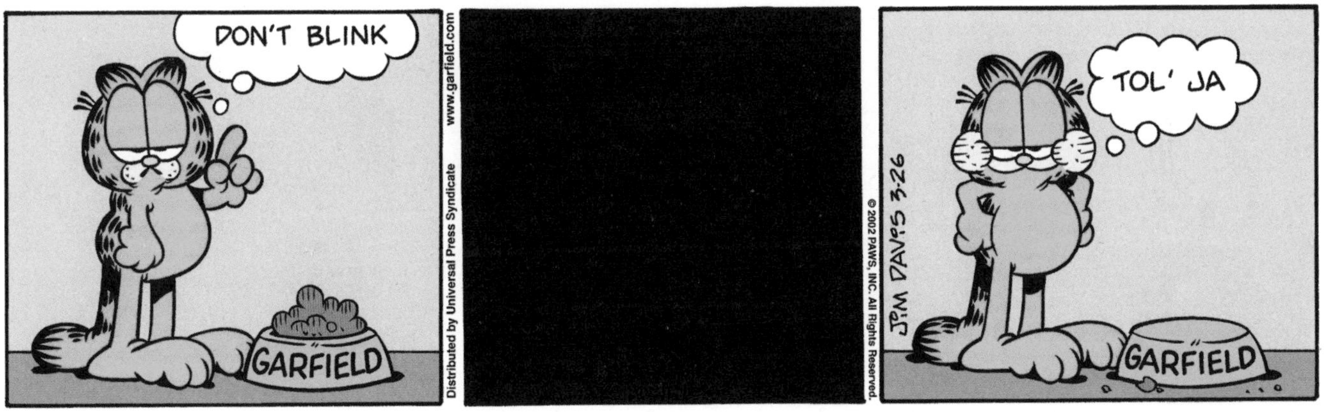
DON'T BLINK
GARFIELD
TOL' JA
GARFIELD
JIM DAVIS 3-26
www.garfield.com
Distributed by Universal Press Syndicate
© 2002 PAWS, INC. All Rights Reserved.

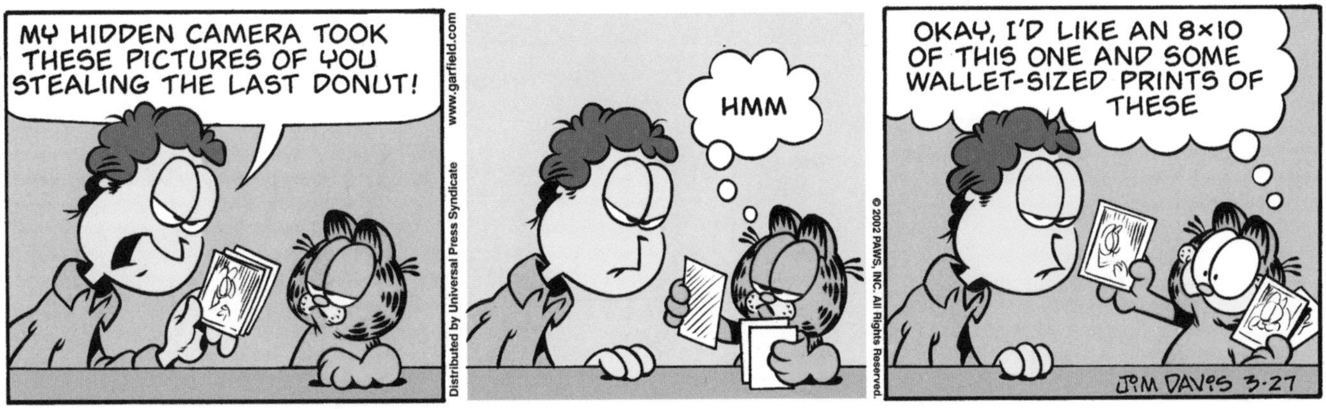
MY HIDDEN CAMERA TOOK THESE PICTURES OF YOU STEALING THE LAST DONUT!
HMM
OKAY, I'D LIKE AN 8×10 OF THIS ONE AND SOME WALLET-SIZED PRINTS OF THESE
JIM DAVIS 3-27
www.garfield.com
Distributed by Universal Press Syndicate
© 2002 PAWS, INC. All Rights Reserved.

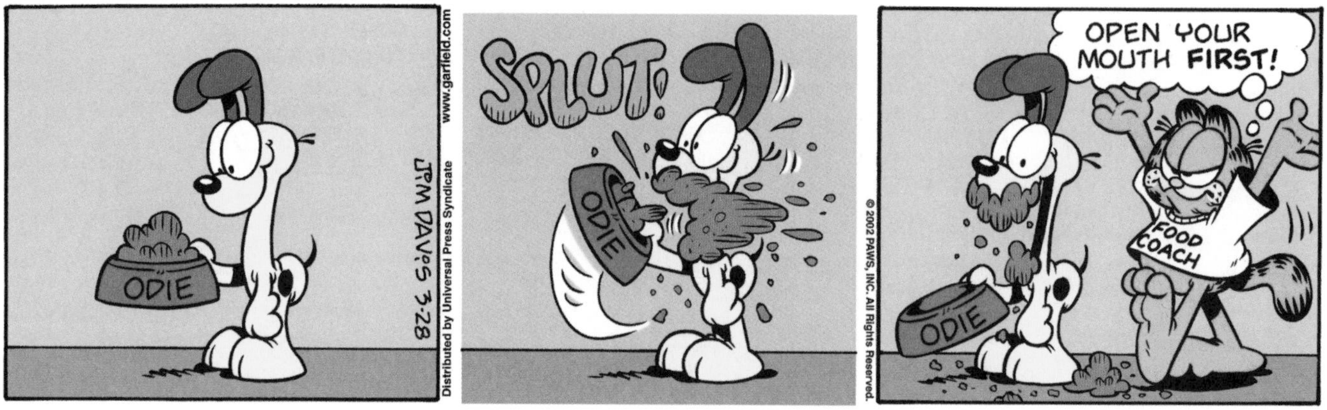
JIM DAVIS 3·28
www.garfield.com
Distributed by Universal Press Syndicate
ODIE
SPLUT!
OPEN YOUR MOUTH **FIRST!**
FOOD COACH
© 2002 PAWS, INC. All Rights Reserved.

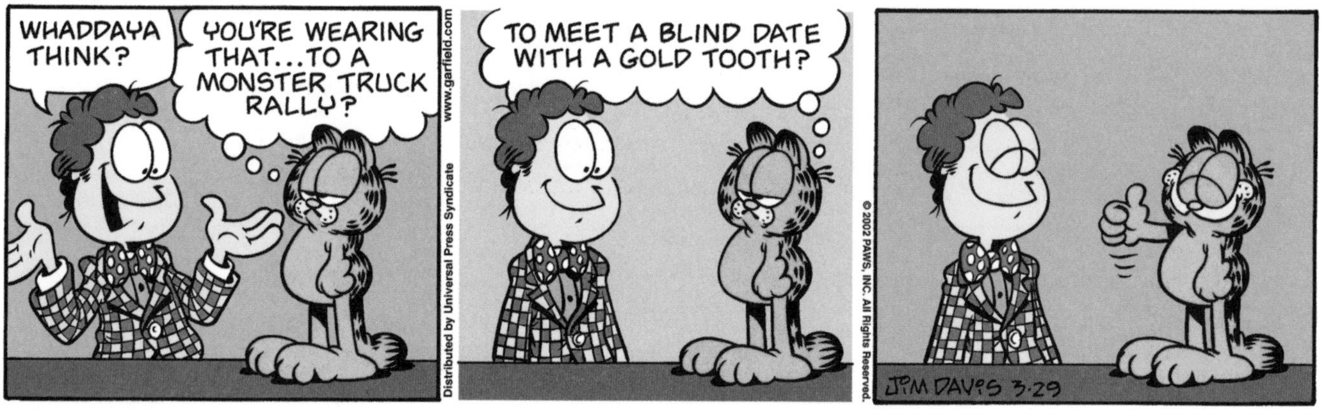
WHADDAYA THINK?
YOU'RE WEARING THAT...TO A MONSTER TRUCK RALLY?
www.garfield.com
Distributed by Universal Press Syndicate
TO MEET A BLIND DATE WITH A GOLD TOOTH?
© 2002 PAWS, INC. All Rights Reserved.
JIM DAVIS 3·29

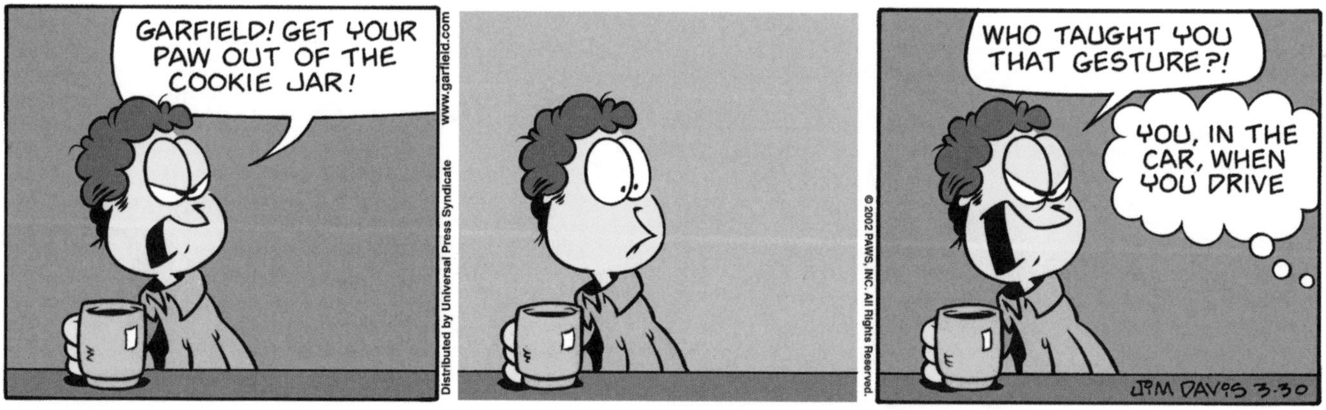
GARFIELD! GET YOUR PAW OUT OF THE COOKIE JAR!
www.garfield.com
Distributed by Universal Press Syndicate
WHO TAUGHT YOU THAT GESTURE?!
YOU, IN THE CAR, WHEN YOU DRIVE
© 2002 PAWS, INC. All Rights Reserved.
JIM DAVIS 3·30

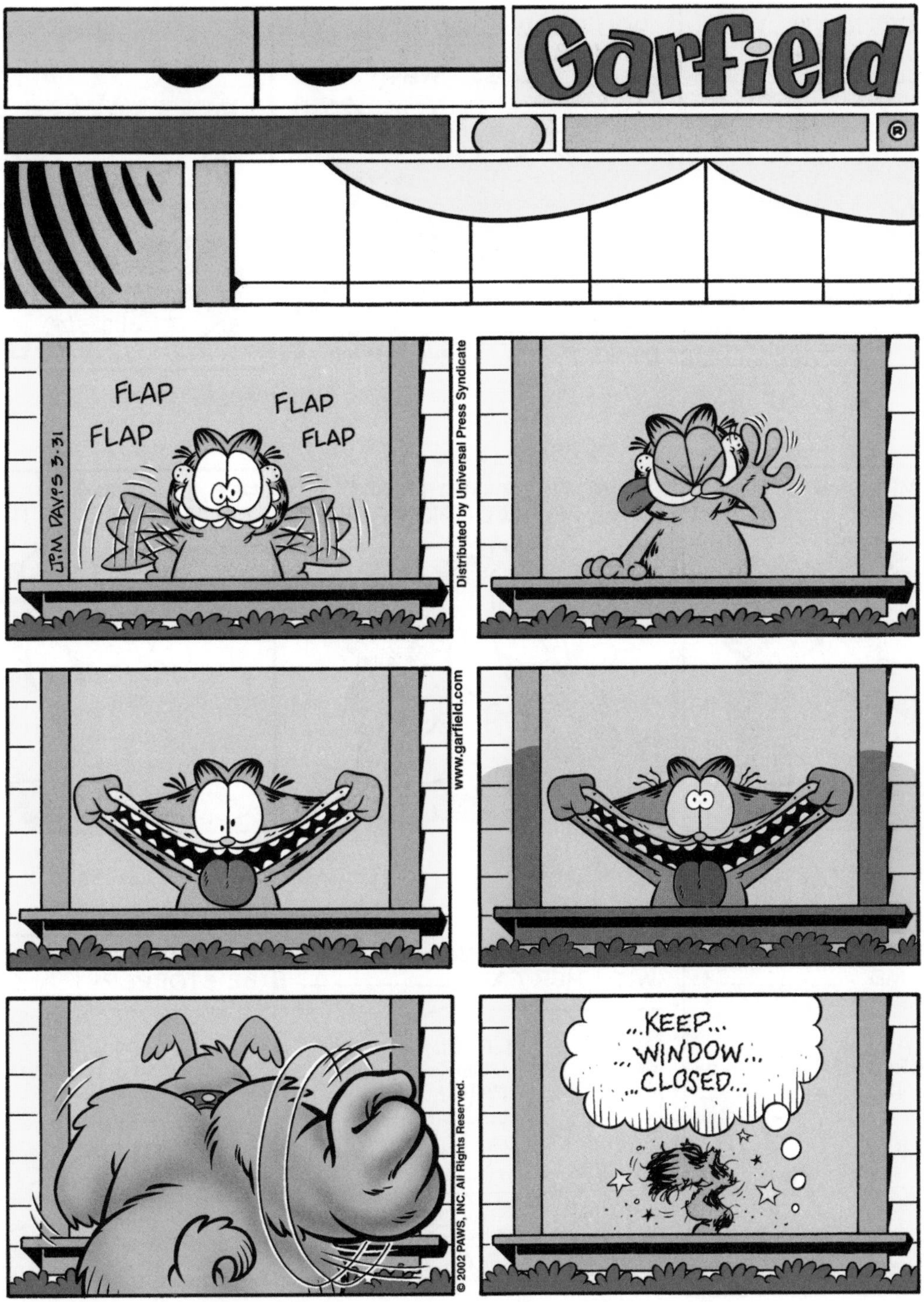
Garfield
JPM DAVPS 3-31
FLAP
FLAP
FLAP
FLAP
...KEEP...
...WINDOW...
...CLOSED...
Distributed by Universal Press Syndicate
www.garfield.com
© 2002 PAWS, INC. All Rights Reserved.

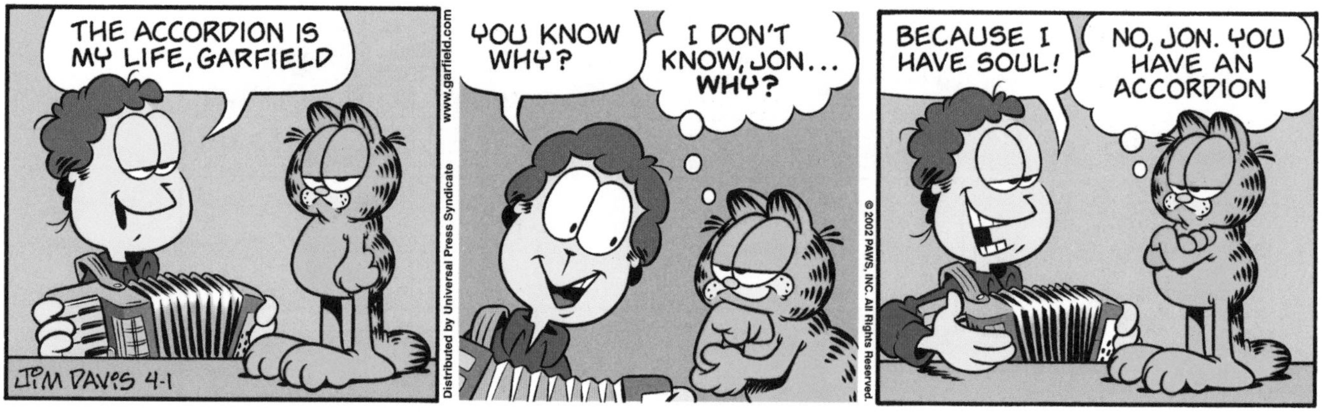
THE ACCORDION IS MY LIFE, GARFIELD
JIM DAVIS 4-1
www.garfield.com
Distributed by Universal Press Syndicate
YOU KNOW WHY?
I DON'T KNOW, JON... **WHY?**
© 2002 PAWS, INC. All Rights Reserved.
BECAUSE I HAVE SOUL!
NO, JON. YOU HAVE AN ACCORDION

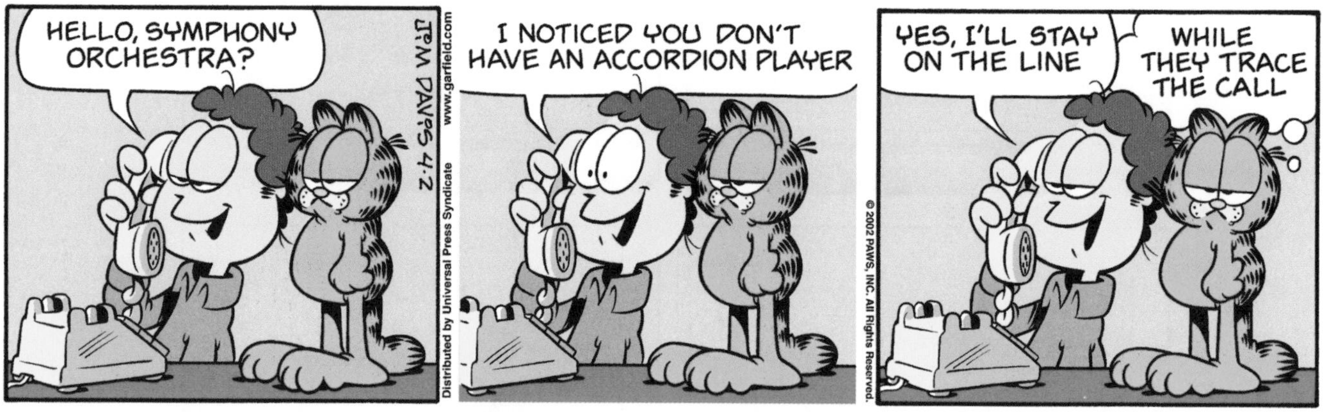
HELLO, SYMPHONY ORCHESTRA?
JIM DAVIS 4-2
www.garfield.com
Distributed by Universal Press Syndicate
I NOTICED YOU DON'T HAVE AN ACCORDION PLAYER
© 2002 PAWS, INC. All Rights Reserved.
YES, I'LL STAY ON THE LINE
WHILE THEY TRACE THE CALL

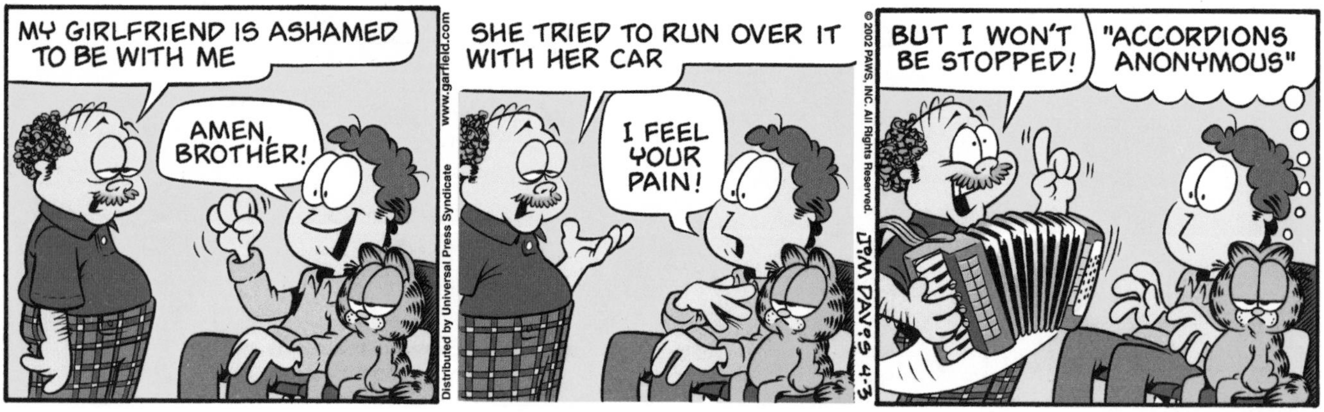
MY GIRLFRIEND IS ASHAMED TO BE WITH ME
AMEN, BROTHER!
www.garfield.com
Distributed by Universal Press Syndicate
SHE TRIED TO RUN OVER IT WITH HER CAR
I FEEL YOUR PAIN!
© 2002 PAWS, INC. All Rights Reserved.
JIM DAVIS 4-3
BUT I WON'T BE STOPPED!
"ACCORDIONS ANONYMOUS"

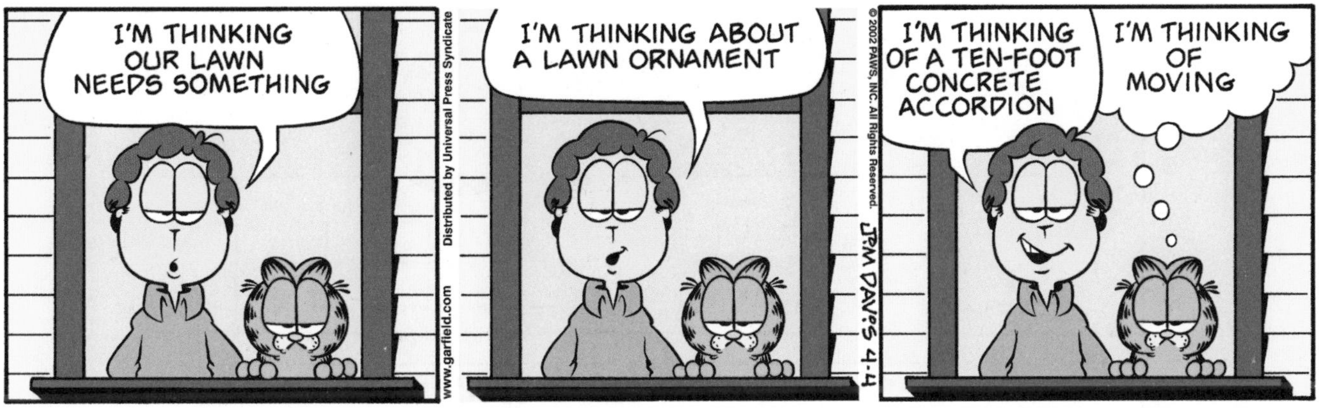
I'M THINKING OUR LAWN NEEDS SOMETHING
I'M THINKING ABOUT A LAWN ORNAMENT
I'M THINKING OF A TEN-FOOT CONCRETE ACCORDION
I'M THINKING OF MOVING
JIM DAVIS 4-4
www.garfield.com Distributed by Universal Press Syndicate
© 2002 PAWS, INC. All Rights Reserved.

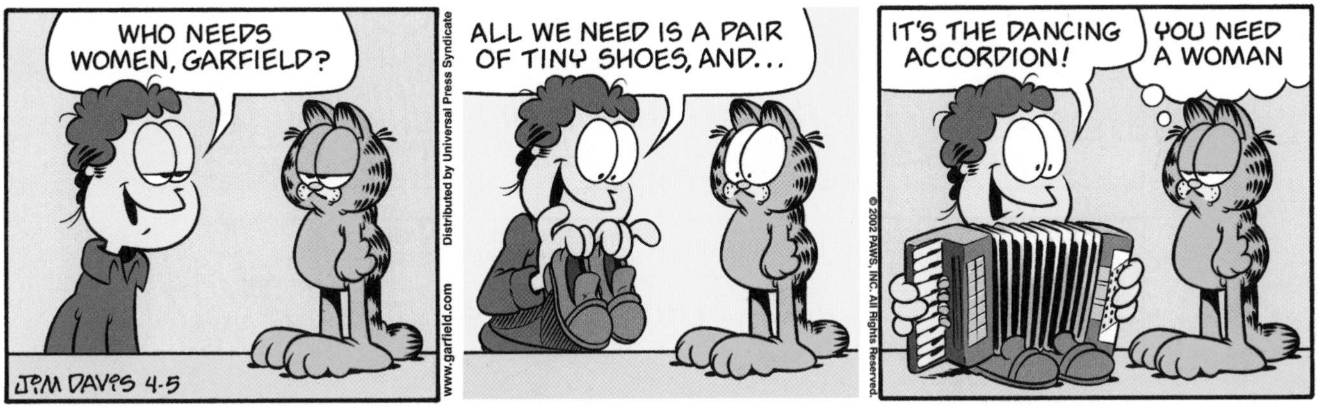
WHO NEEDS WOMEN, GARFIELD?
ALL WE NEED IS A PAIR OF TINY SHOES, AND...
IT'S THE DANCING ACCORDION!
YOU NEED A WOMAN
JIM DAVIS 4-5
www.garfield.com Distributed by Universal Press Syndicate
© 2002 PAWS, INC. All Rights Reserved.

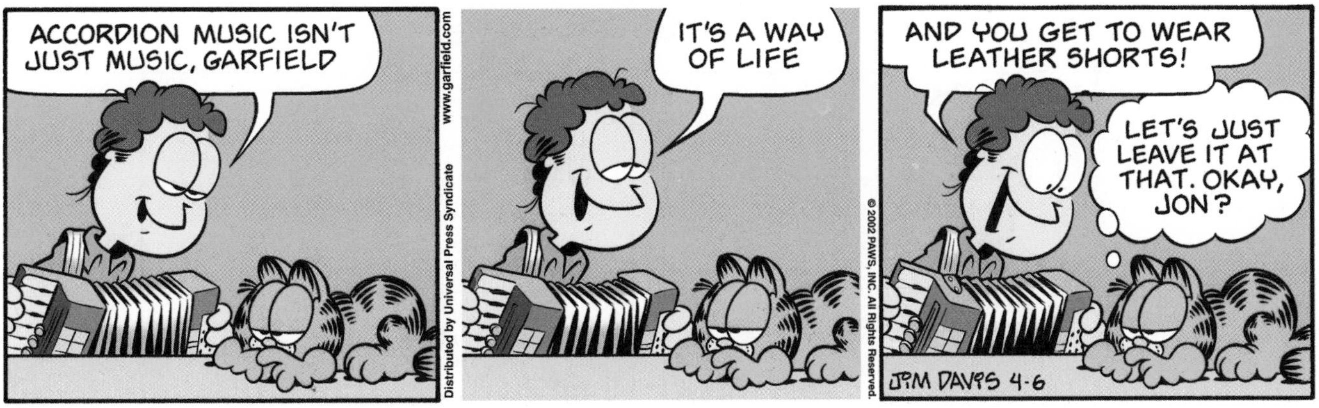
ACCORDION MUSIC ISN'T JUST MUSIC, GARFIELD
IT'S A WAY OF LIFE
AND YOU GET TO WEAR LEATHER SHORTS!
LET'S JUST LEAVE IT AT THAT. OKAY, JON?
JIM DAVIS 4-6
Distributed by Universal Press Syndicate www.garfield.com
© 2002 PAWS, INC. All Rights Reserved.

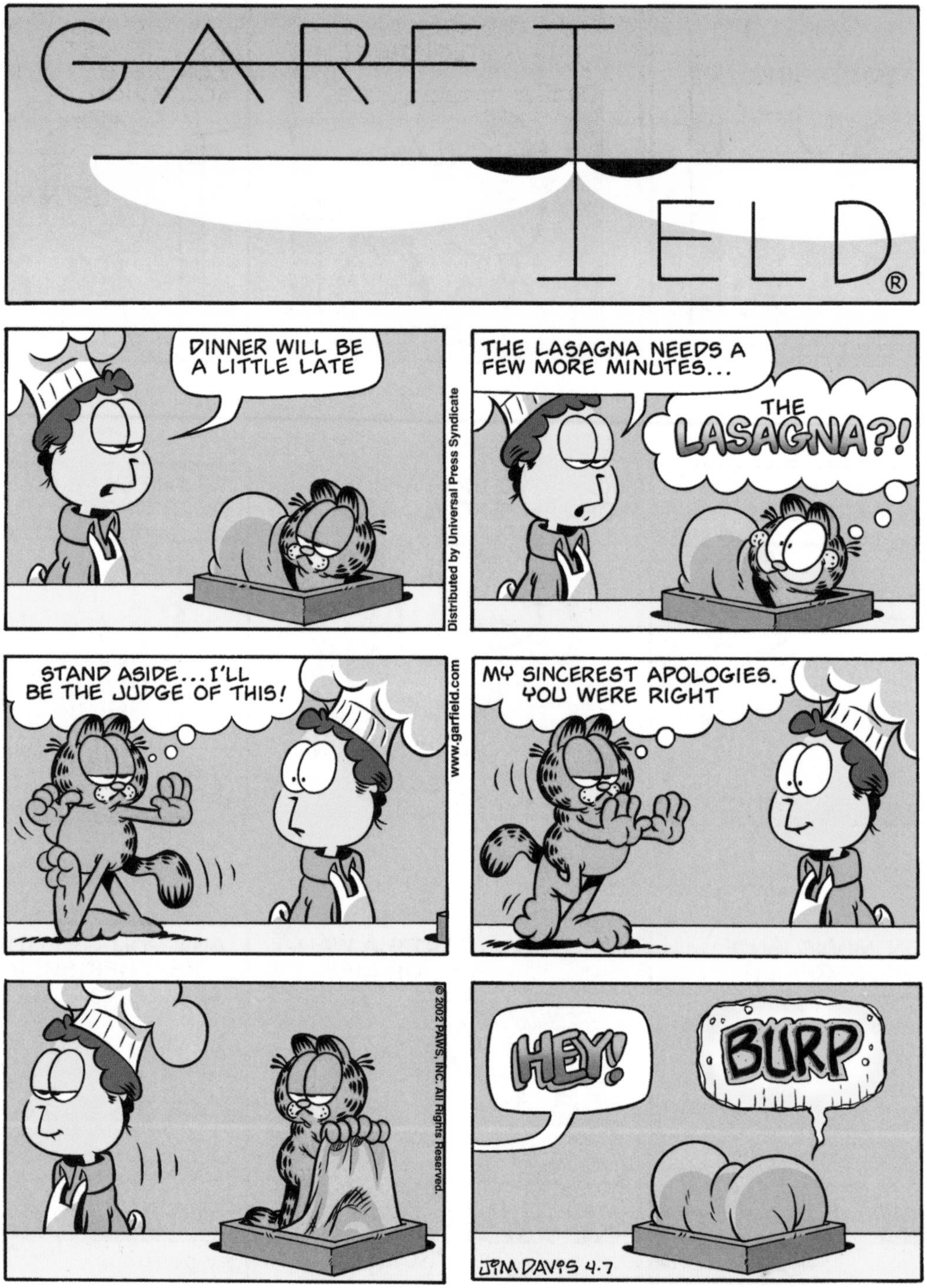
GARFIELD®
DINNER WILL BE A LITTLE LATE
THE LASAGNA NEEDS A FEW MORE MINUTES...
THE LASAGNA?!
STAND ASIDE...I'LL BE THE JUDGE OF THIS!
MY SINCEREST APOLOGIES. YOU WERE RIGHT
HEY!
BURP
JIM DAVIS 4-7
Distributed by Universal Press Syndicate
www.garfield.com
© 2002 PAWS, INC. All Rights Reserved.

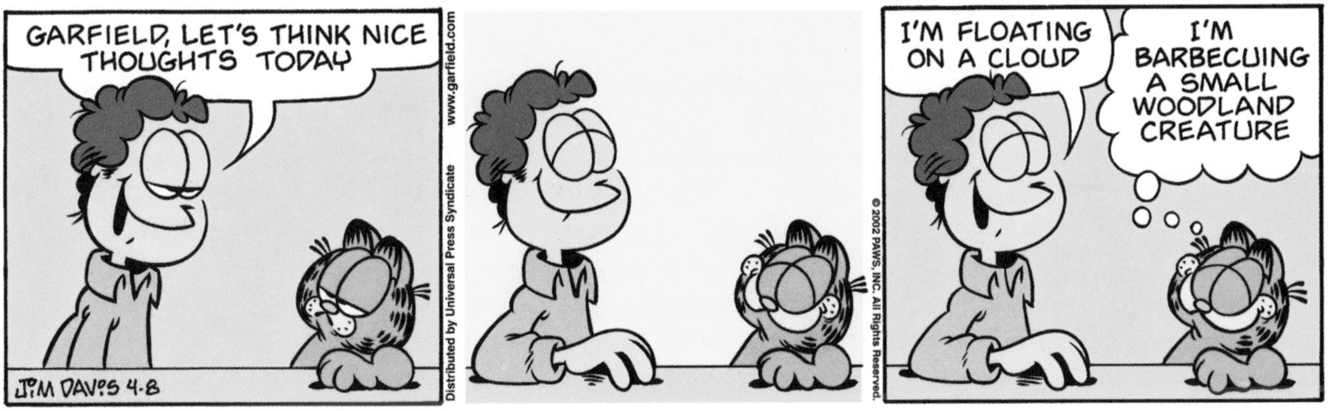
GARFIELD, LET'S THINK NICE THOUGHTS TODAY
JIM DAVIS 4-8
Distributed by Universal Press Syndicate www.garfield.com
I'M FLOATING ON A CLOUD
I'M BARBECUING A SMALL WOODLAND CREATURE
© 2002 PAWS, INC. All Rights Reserved.

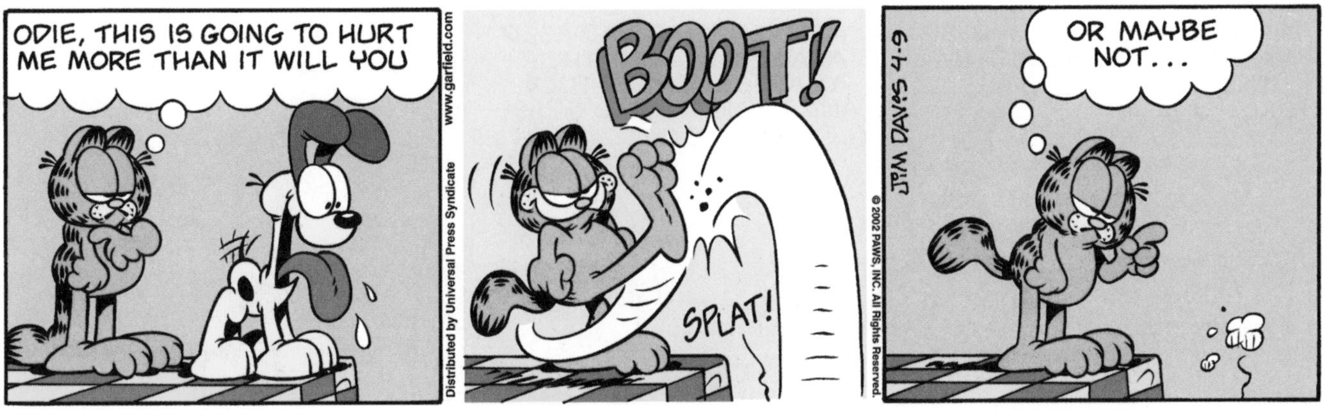
ODIE, THIS IS GOING TO HURT ME MORE THAN IT WILL YOU
Distributed by Universal Press Syndicate www.garfield.com
BOOT!
SPLAT!
© 2002 PAWS, INC. All Rights Reserved.
JIM DAVIS 4-9
OR MAYBE NOT...

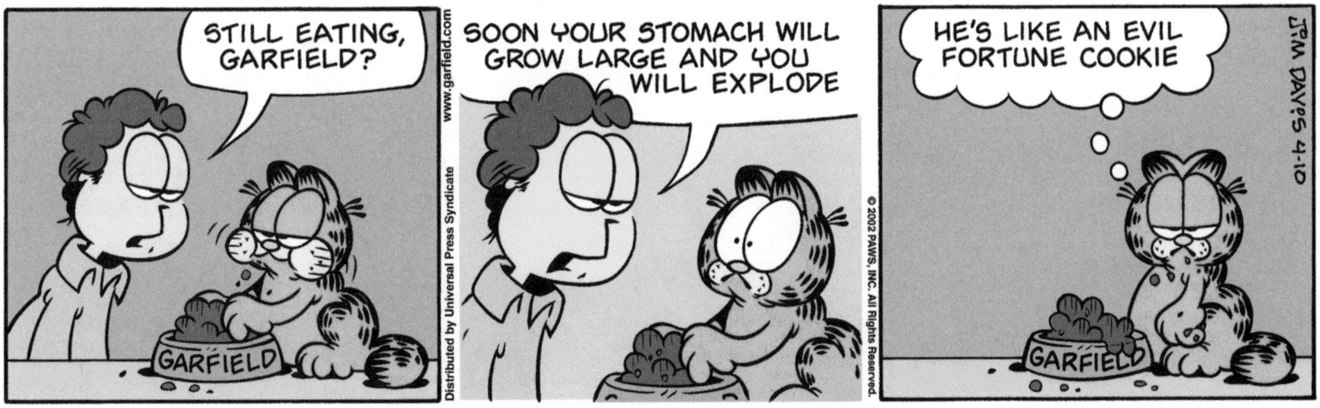
STILL EATING, GARFIELD?
GARFIELD
Distributed by Universal Press Syndicate www.garfield.com
SOON YOUR STOMACH WILL GROW LARGE AND YOU WILL EXPLODE
© 2002 PAWS, INC. All Rights Reserved.
HE'S LIKE AN EVIL FORTUNE COOKIE
JIM DAVIS 4-10
GARFIELD

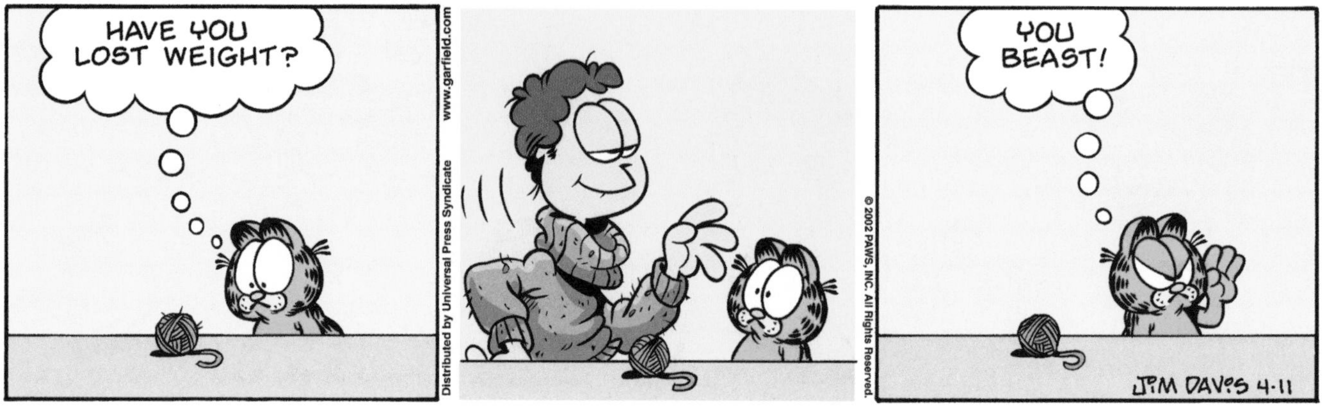
HAVE YOU LOST WEIGHT?
YOU BEAST!
JIM DAVIS 4-11
www.garfield.com
Distributed by Universal Press Syndicate
© 2002 PAWS, INC. All Rights Reserved.

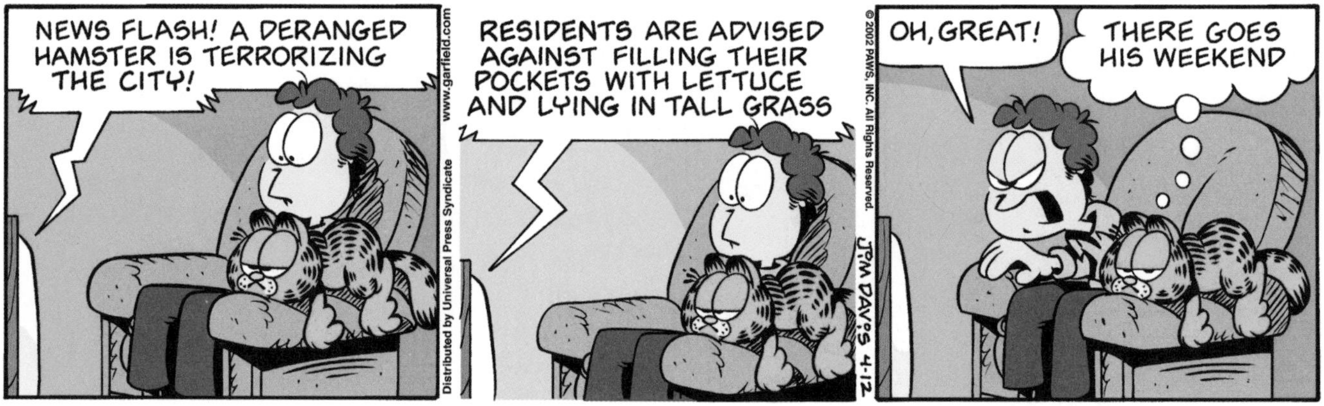
NEWS FLASH! A DERANGED HAMSTER IS TERRORIZING THE CITY!
RESIDENTS ARE ADVISED AGAINST FILLING THEIR POCKETS WITH LETTUCE AND LYING IN TALL GRASS
OH, GREAT!
THERE GOES HIS WEEKEND
JIM DAVIS 4-12
www.garfield.com
Distributed by Universal Press Syndicate
© 2002 PAWS, INC. All Rights Reserved.

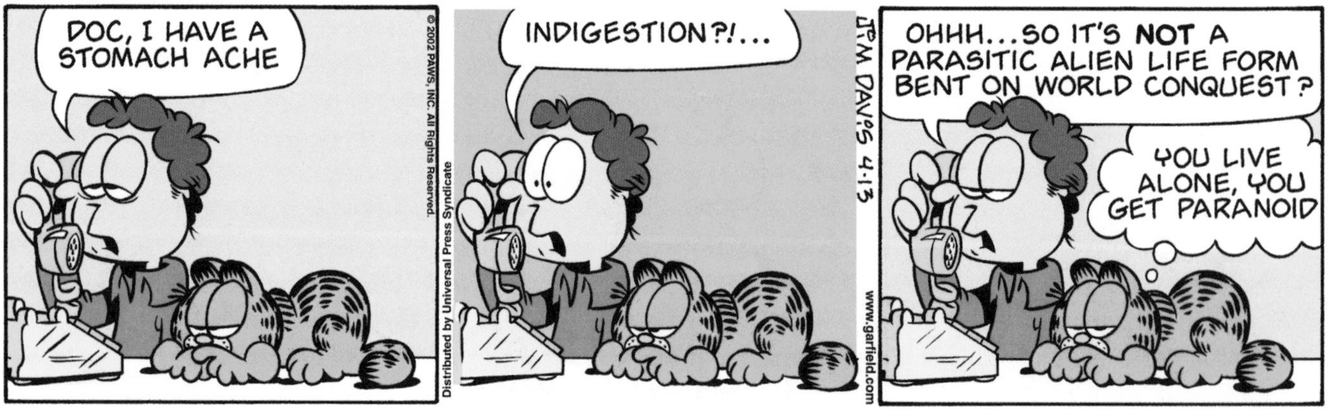
DOC, I HAVE A STOMACH ACHE
INDIGESTION?!...
OHHH...SO IT'S **NOT** A PARASITIC ALIEN LIFE FORM BENT ON WORLD CONQUEST?
YOU LIVE ALONE, YOU GET PARANOID
JIM DAVIS 4-13
© 2002 PAWS, INC. All Rights Reserved.
Distributed by Universal Press Syndicate
www.garfield.com

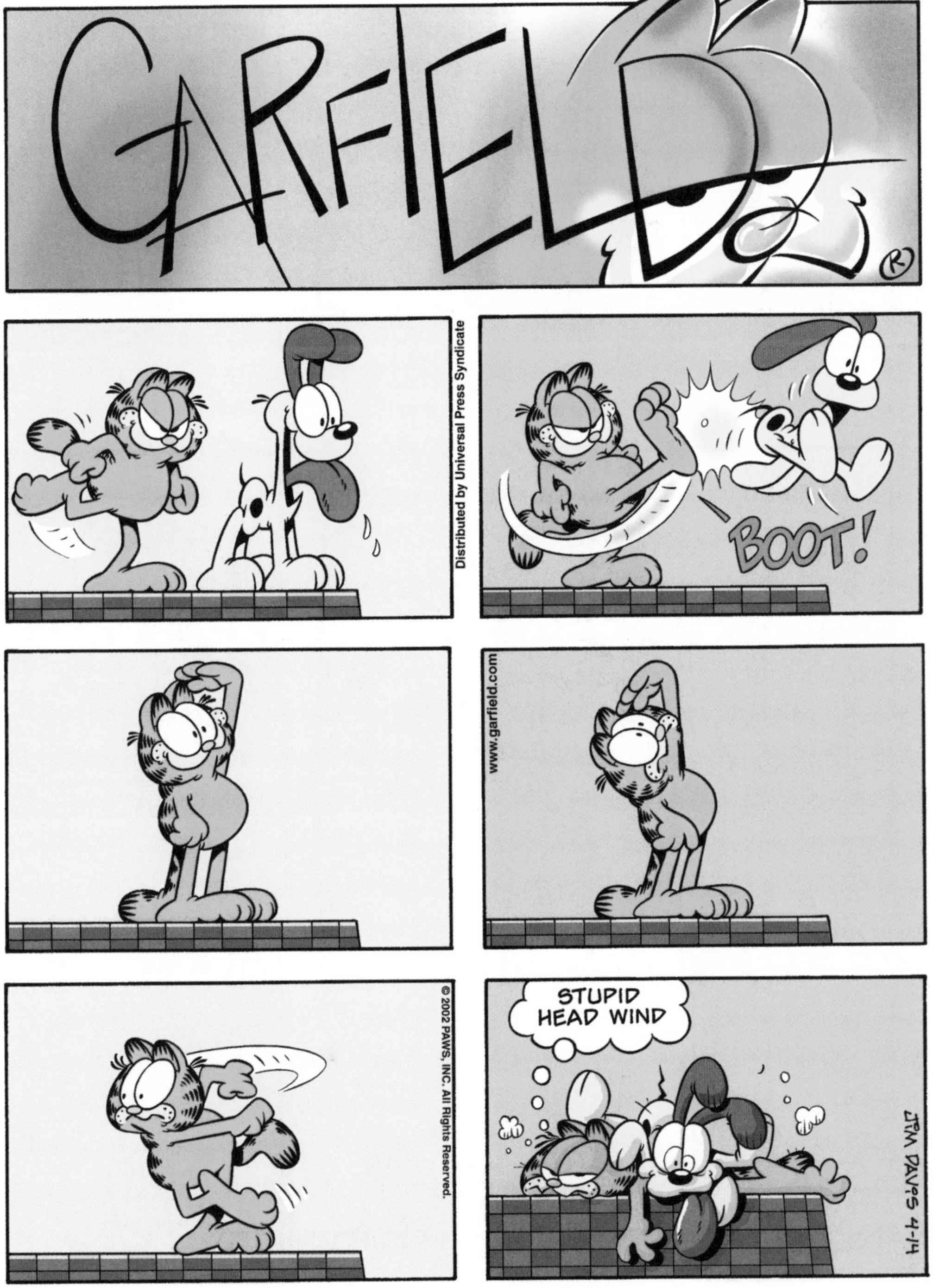
GARFIELD
Distributed by Universal Press Syndicate
BOOT!
www.garfield.com
© 2002 PAWS, INC. All Rights Reserved.
STUPID HEAD WIND
JIM DAVIS 4-14

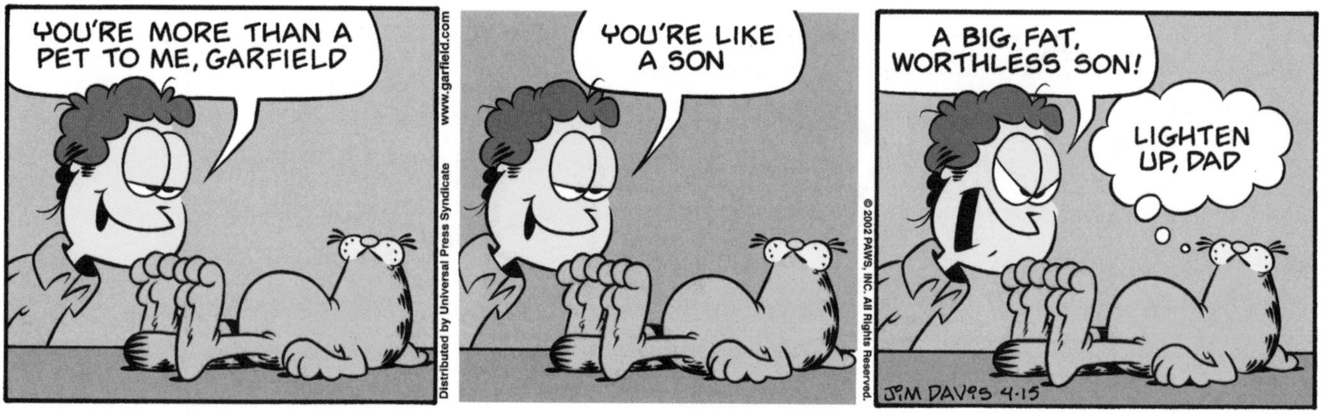
YOU'RE MORE THAN A PET TO ME, GARFIELD
YOU'RE LIKE A SON
A BIG, FAT, WORTHLESS SON!
LIGHTEN UP, DAD
JIM DAVIS 4-15
Distributed by Universal Press Syndicate www.garfield.com
© 2002 PAWS, INC. All Rights Reserved.

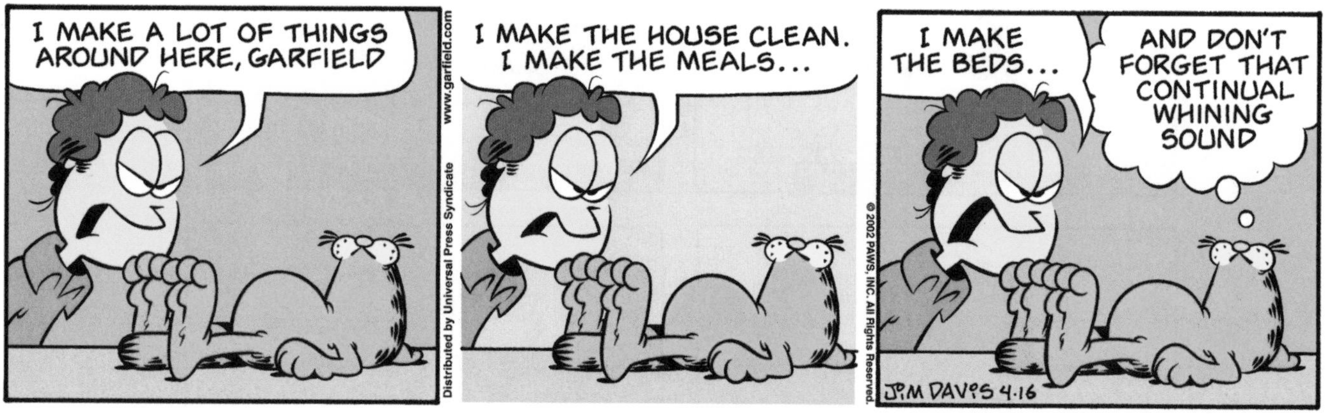
I MAKE A LOT OF THINGS AROUND HERE, GARFIELD
I MAKE THE HOUSE CLEAN. I MAKE THE MEALS...
I MAKE THE BEDS...
AND DON'T FORGET THAT CONTINUAL WHINING SOUND
JIM DAVIS 4-16
Distributed by Universal Press Syndicate www.garfield.com
© 2002 PAWS, INC. All Rights Reserved.

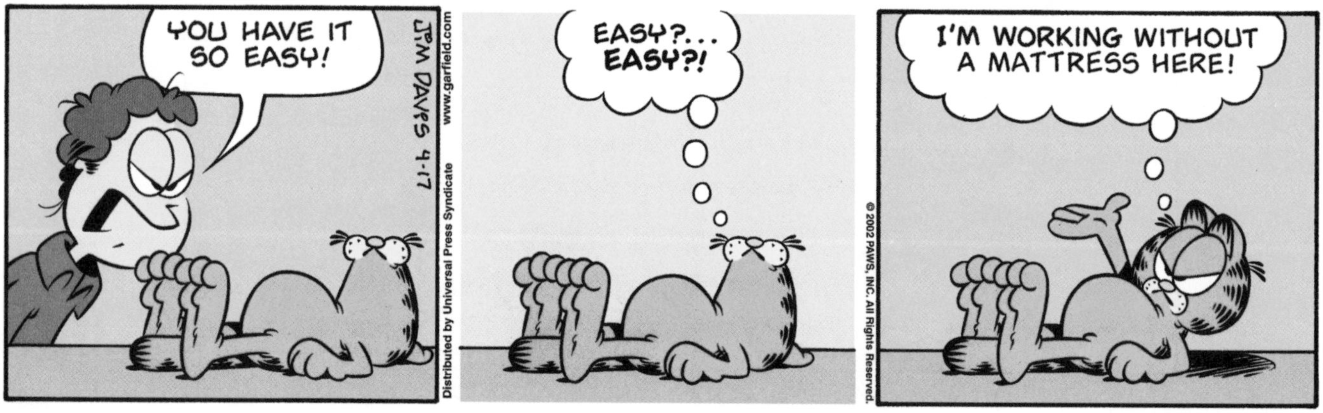
YOU HAVE IT SO EASY!
JIM DAVIS 4-17
EASY?... **EASY?!**
I'M WORKING WITHOUT A MATTRESS HERE!
Distributed by Universal Press Syndicate www.garfield.com
© 2002 PAWS, INC. All Rights Reserved.

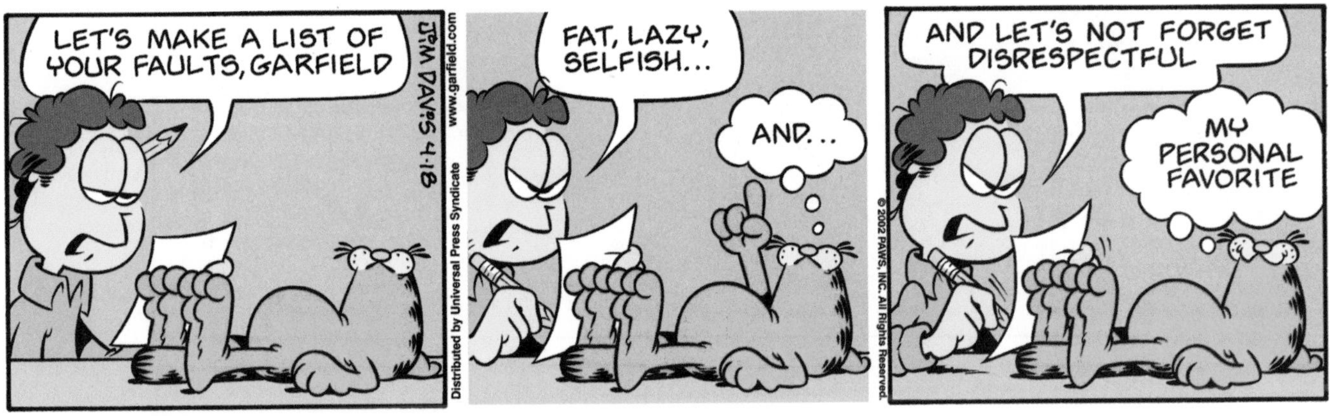
LET'S MAKE A LIST OF YOUR FAULTS, GARFIELD
JIM DAVIS 4-18
www.garfield.com
Distributed by Universal Press Syndicate
FAT, LAZY, SELFISH...
AND...
© 2002 PAWS, INC. All Rights Reserved.
AND LET'S NOT FORGET DISRESPECTFUL
MY PERSONAL FAVORITE

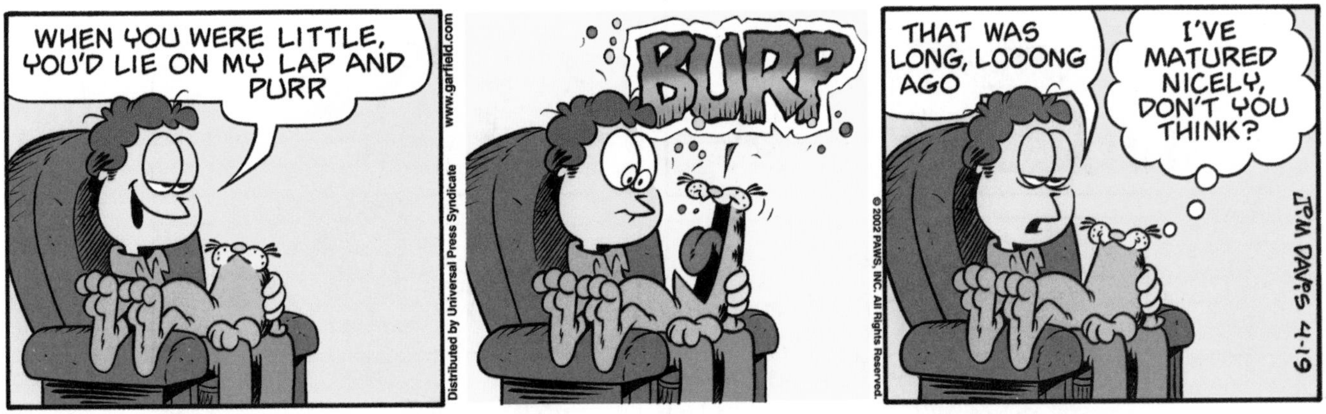
WHEN YOU WERE LITTLE, YOU'D LIE ON MY LAP AND PURR
www.garfield.com
Distributed by Universal Press Syndicate
BURP
© 2002 PAWS, INC. All Rights Reserved.
THAT WAS LONG, LOOONG AGO
I'VE MATURED NICELY, DON'T YOU THINK?
JIM DAVIS 4-19

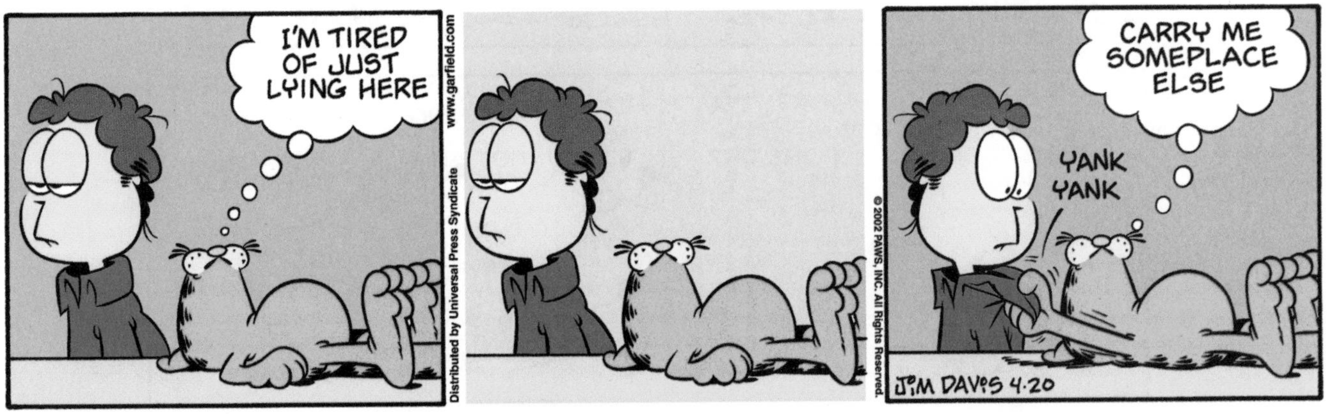
I'M TIRED OF JUST LYING HERE
www.garfield.com
Distributed by Universal Press Syndicate
© 2002 PAWS, INC. All Rights Reserved.
CARRY ME SOMEPLACE ELSE
YANK YANK
JIM DAVIS 4-20

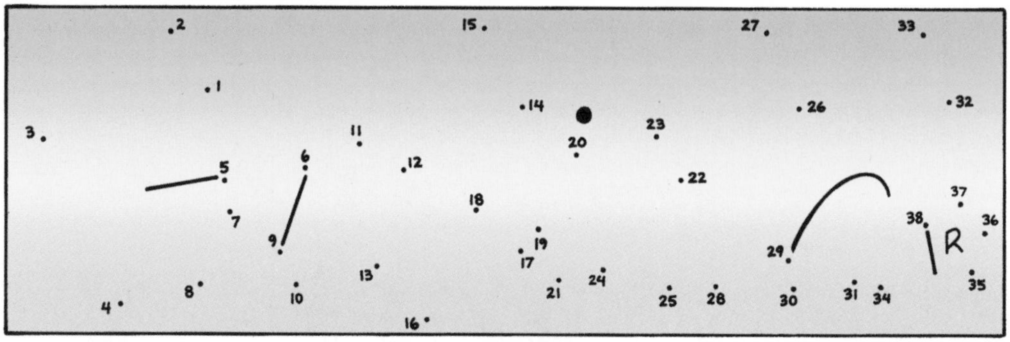

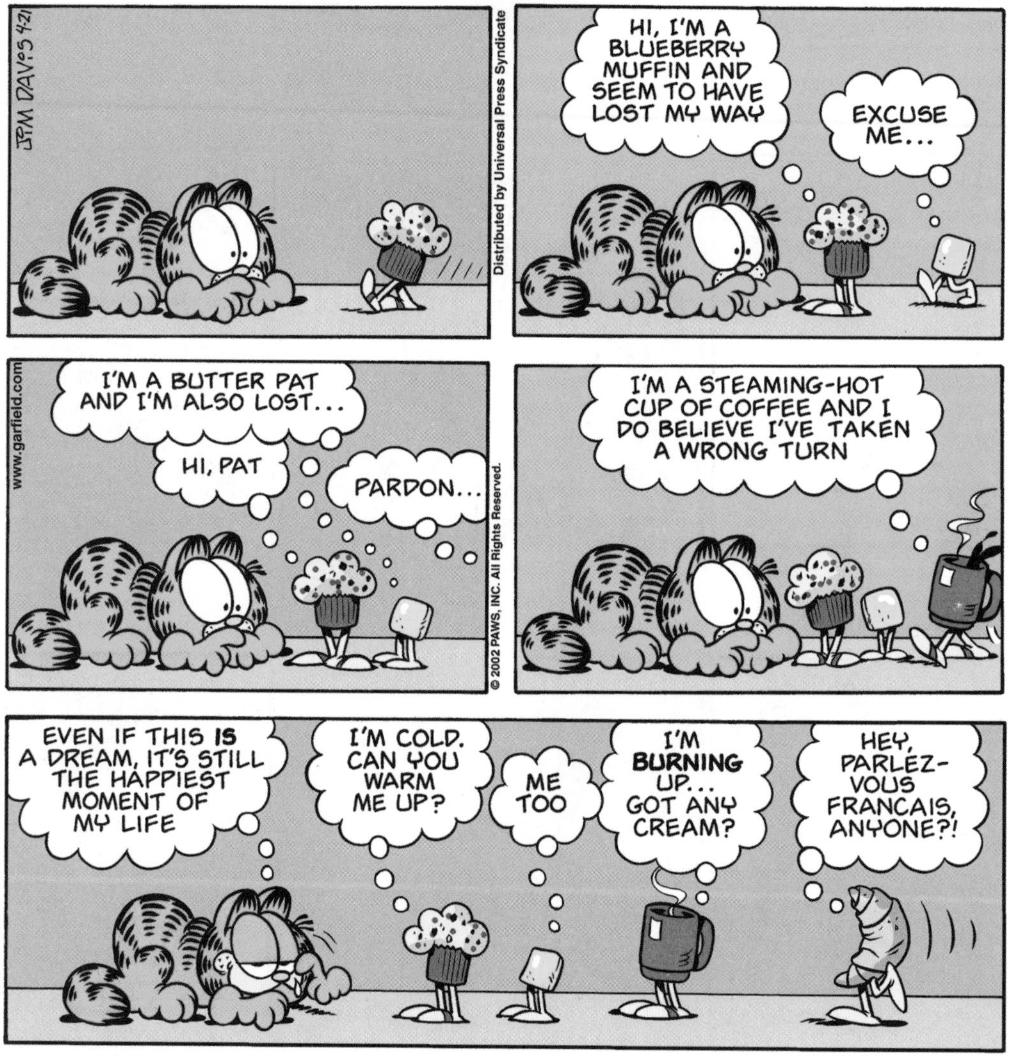
JIM DAVIS 4-21
Distributed by Universal Press Syndicate
HI, I'M A BLUEBERRY MUFFIN AND SEEM TO HAVE LOST MY WAY
EXCUSE ME...
www.garfield.com
I'M A BUTTER PAT AND I'M ALSO LOST...
HI, PAT
PARDON...
© 2002 PAWS, INC. All Rights Reserved.
I'M A STEAMING-HOT CUP OF COFFEE AND I DO BELIEVE I'VE TAKEN A WRONG TURN
EVEN IF THIS **IS** A DREAM, IT'S STILL THE HAPPIEST MOMENT OF MY LIFE
I'M COLD. CAN YOU WARM ME UP?
ME TOO
I'M **BURNING** UP... GOT ANY CREAM?
HEY, PARLEZ-VOUS FRANCAIS, ANYONE?!

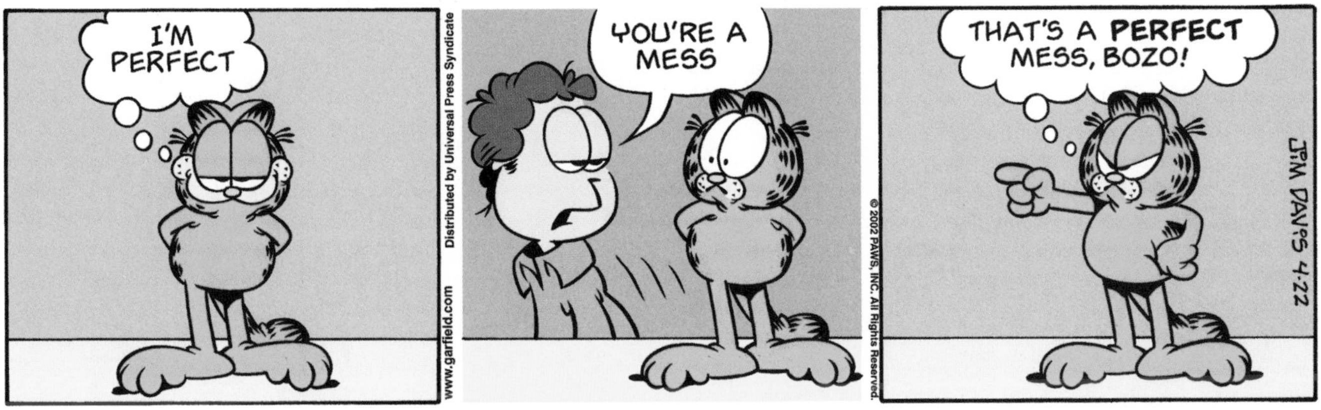
I'M PERFECT
YOU'RE A MESS
THAT'S A **PERFECT** MESS, BOZO!
JIM DAVIS 4-22
www.garfield.com Distributed by Universal Press Syndicate
© 2002 PAWS, INC. All Rights Reserved.

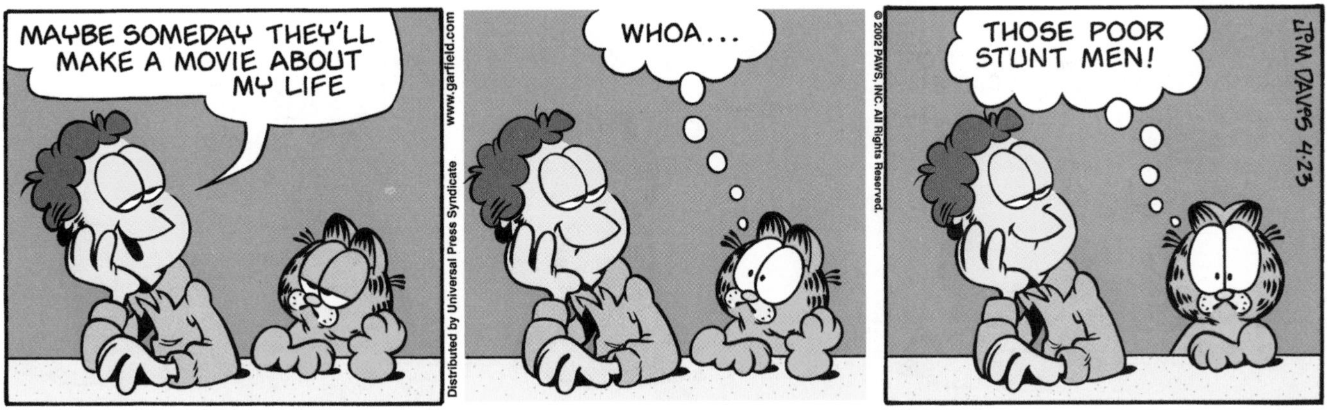
MAYBE SOMEDAY THEY'LL MAKE A MOVIE ABOUT MY LIFE
WHOA...
THOSE POOR STUNT MEN!
JIM DAVIS 4-23
www.garfield.com Distributed by Universal Press Syndicate
© 2002 PAWS, INC. All Rights Reserved.

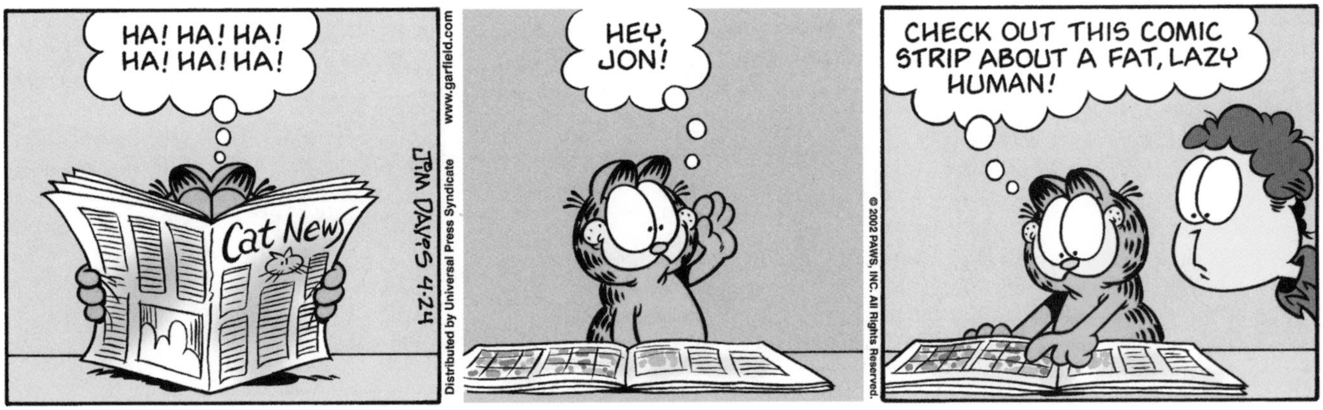
HA! HA! HA! HA! HA! HA!
Cat News
HEY, JON!
CHECK OUT THIS COMIC STRIP ABOUT A FAT, LAZY HUMAN!
JIM DAVIS 4-24
www.garfield.com Distributed by Universal Press Syndicate
© 2002 PAWS, INC. All Rights Reserved.

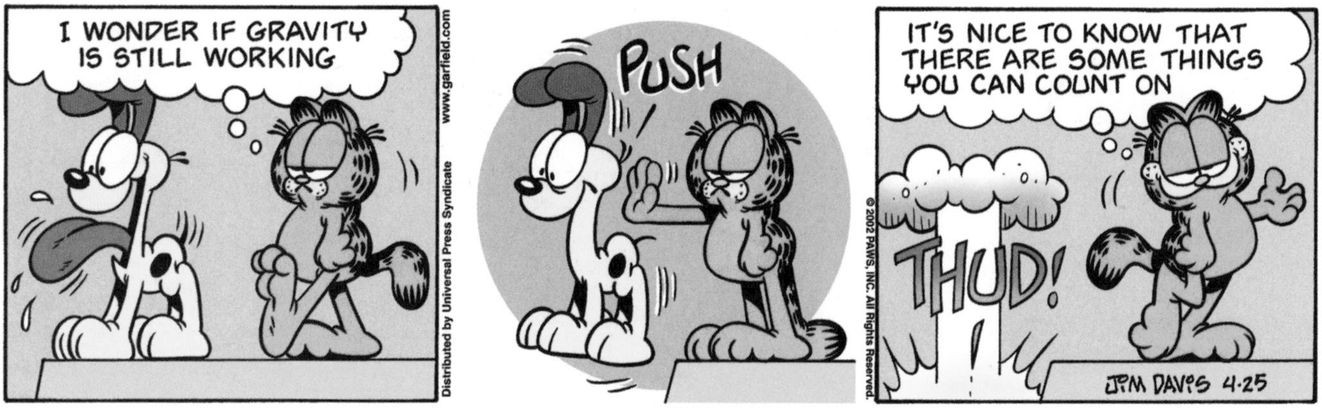
I WONDER IF GRAVITY IS STILL WORKING
www.garfield.com
Distributed by Universal Press Syndicate
PUSH
© 2002 PAWS, INC. All Rights Reserved.
IT'S NICE TO KNOW THAT THERE ARE SOME THINGS YOU CAN COUNT ON
THUD!
JIM DAVIS 4·25

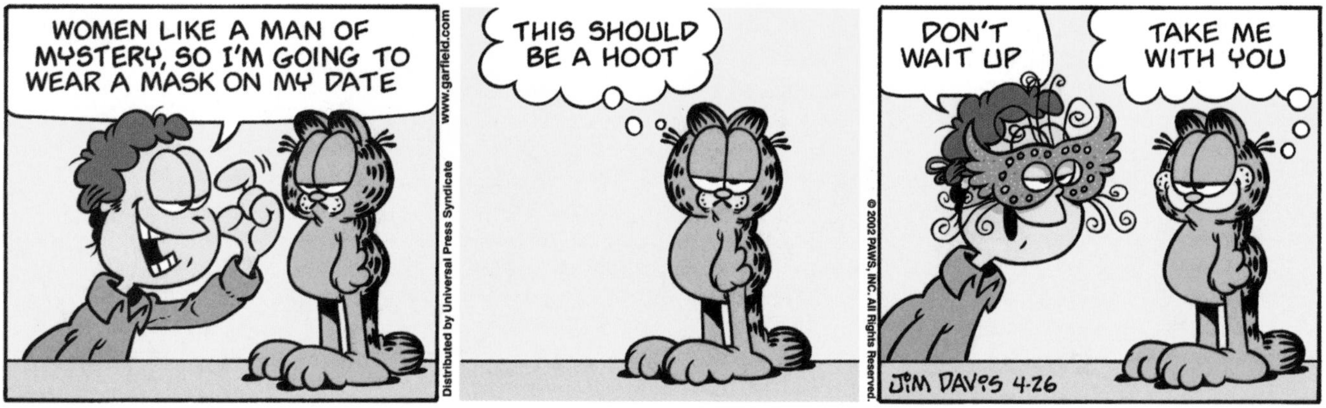
WOMEN LIKE A MAN OF MYSTERY, SO I'M GOING TO WEAR A MASK ON MY DATE
www.garfield.com
Distributed by Universal Press Syndicate
THIS SHOULD BE A HOOT
© 2002 PAWS, INC. All Rights Reserved.
DON'T WAIT UP
TAKE ME WITH YOU
JIM DAVIS 4·26

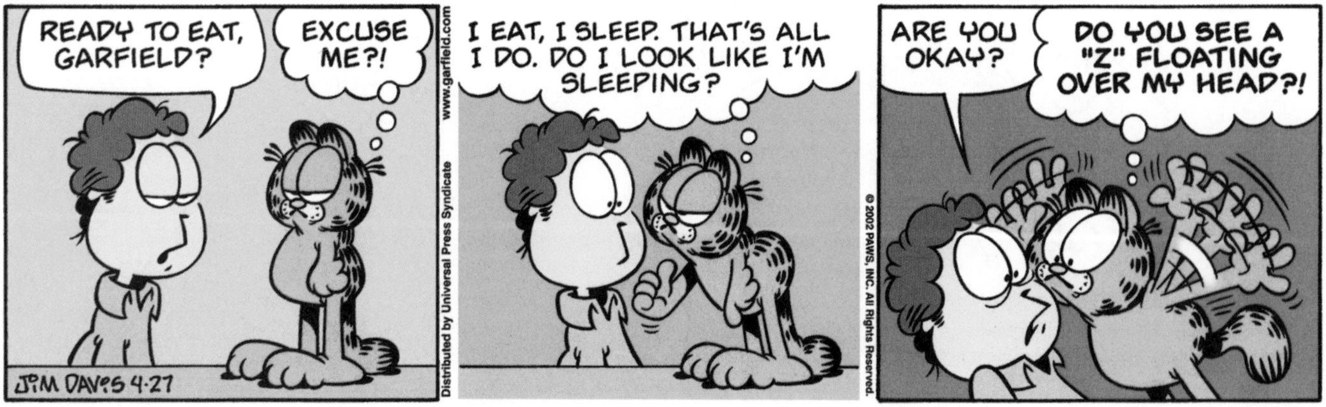
READY TO EAT, GARFIELD?
EXCUSE ME?!
JIM DAVIS 4·27
www.garfield.com
Distributed by Universal Press Syndicate
I EAT, I SLEEP. THAT'S ALL I DO. DO I LOOK LIKE I'M SLEEPING?
© 2002 PAWS, INC. All Rights Reserved.
ARE YOU OKAY?
DO YOU SEE A "Z" FLOATING OVER MY HEAD?!

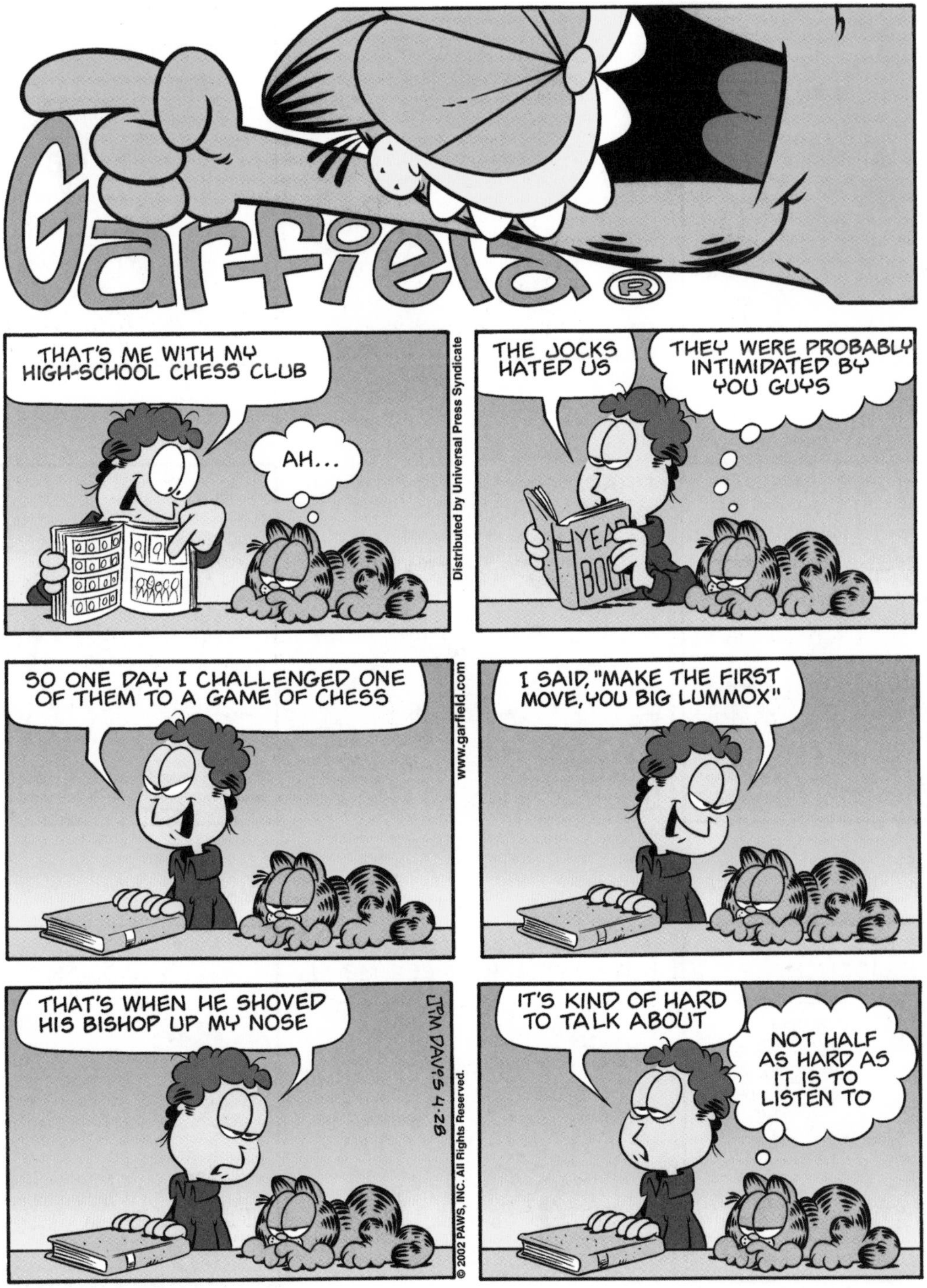
Garfield®
THAT'S ME WITH MY HIGH-SCHOOL CHESS CLUB
AH...
THE JOCKS HATED US
THEY WERE PROBABLY INTIMIDATED BY YOU GUYS
SO ONE DAY I CHALLENGED ONE OF THEM TO A GAME OF CHESS
I SAID, "MAKE THE FIRST MOVE, YOU BIG LUMMOX"
THAT'S WHEN HE SHOVED HIS BISHOP UP MY NOSE
JIM DAVIS 4-28
IT'S KIND OF HARD TO TALK ABOUT
NOT HALF AS HARD AS IT IS TO LISTEN TO

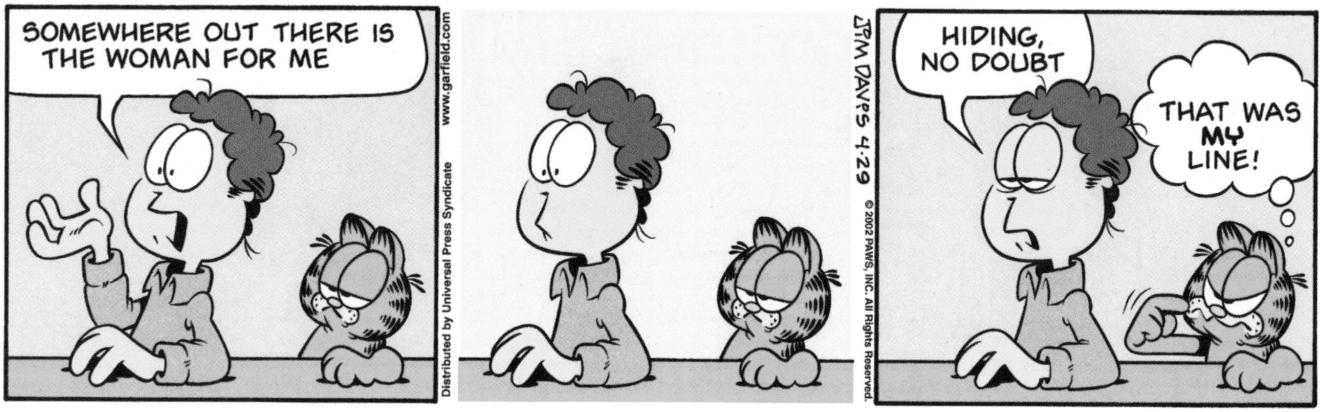
SOMEWHERE OUT THERE IS THE WOMAN FOR ME
www.garfield.com
Distributed by Universal Press Syndicate
JIM DAVIS 4-29
© 2002 PAWS, INC. All Rights Reserved.
HIDING, NO DOUBT
THAT WAS MY LINE!

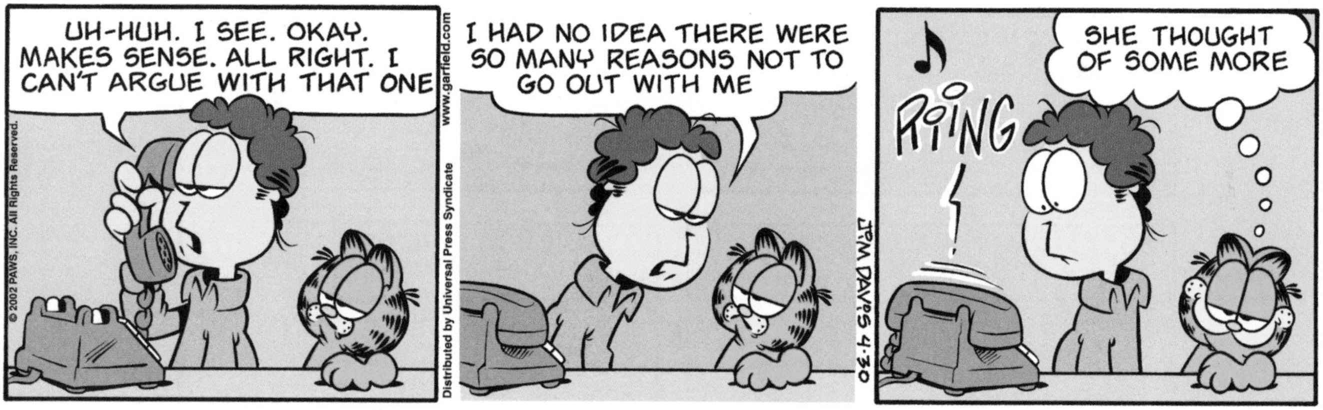
UH-HUH. I SEE. OKAY. MAKES SENSE. ALL RIGHT. I CAN'T ARGUE WITH THAT ONE
© 2002 PAWS, INC. All Rights Reserved.
www.garfield.com
Distributed by Universal Press Syndicate
I HAD NO IDEA THERE WERE SO MANY REASONS NOT TO GO OUT WITH ME
JIM DAVIS 4-30
RING
SHE THOUGHT OF SOME MORE

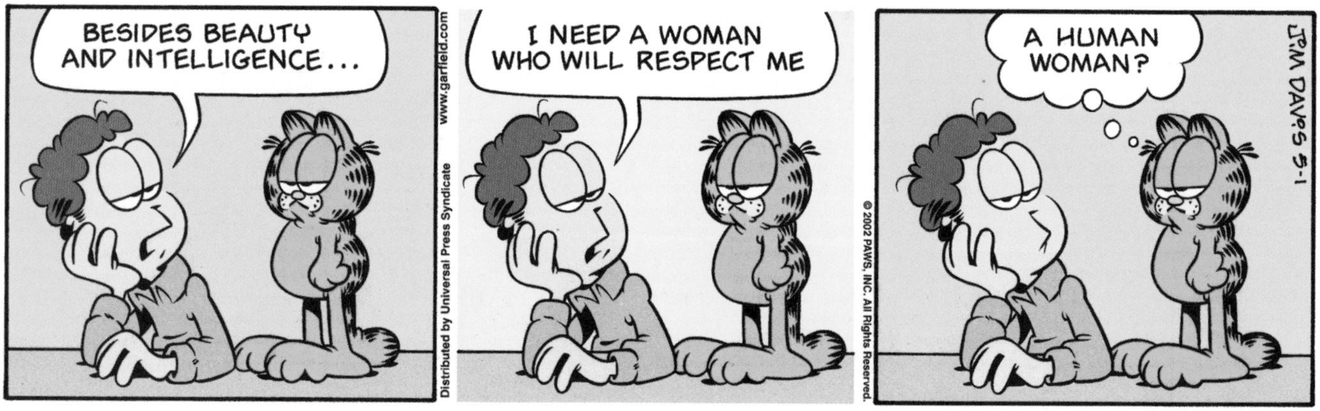
BESIDES BEAUTY AND INTELLIGENCE...
www.garfield.com
Distributed by Universal Press Syndicate
I NEED A WOMAN WHO WILL RESPECT ME
© 2002 PAWS, INC. All Rights Reserved.
A HUMAN WOMAN?
JIM DAVIS 5-1

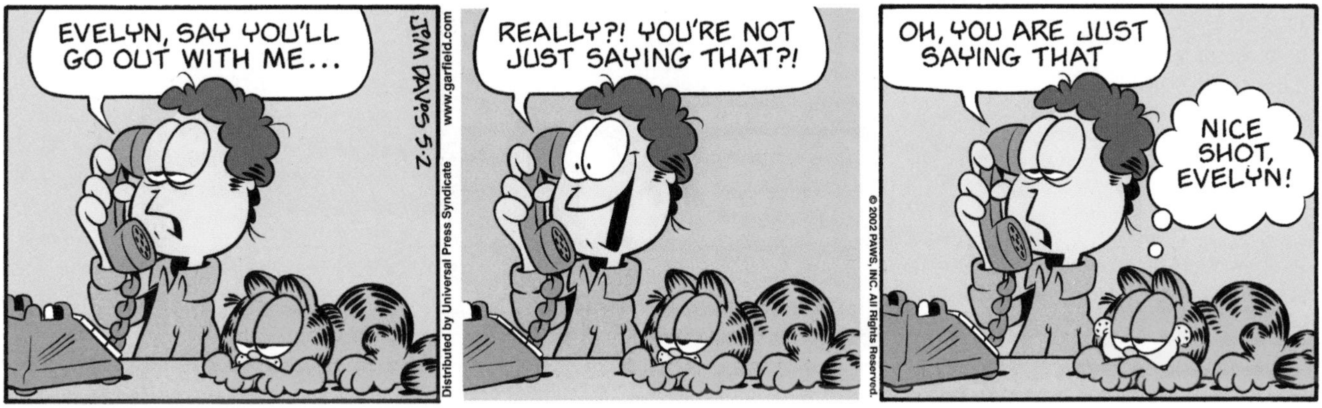
EVELYN, SAY YOU'LL GO OUT WITH ME...
JIM DAVIS 5-2
www.garfield.com
Distributed by Universal Press Syndicate
REALLY?! YOU'RE NOT JUST SAYING THAT?!
OH, YOU ARE JUST SAYING THAT
NICE SHOT, EVELYN!
© 2002 PAWS, INC. All Rights Reserved.

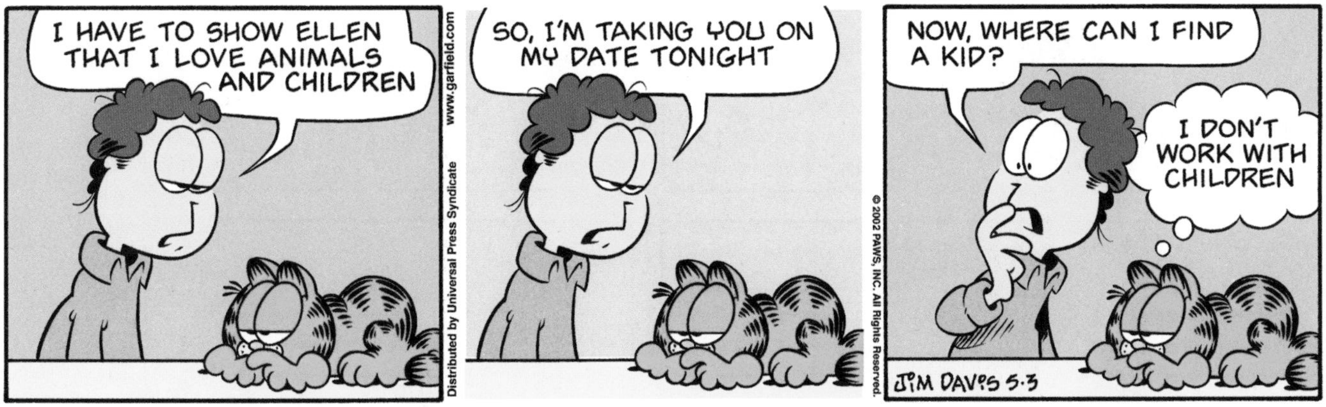
I HAVE TO SHOW ELLEN THAT I LOVE ANIMALS AND CHILDREN
www.garfield.com
Distributed by Universal Press Syndicate
SO, I'M TAKING YOU ON MY DATE TONIGHT
NOW, WHERE CAN I FIND A KID?
I DON'T WORK WITH CHILDREN
© 2002 PAWS, INC. All Rights Reserved.
JIM DAVIS 5-3

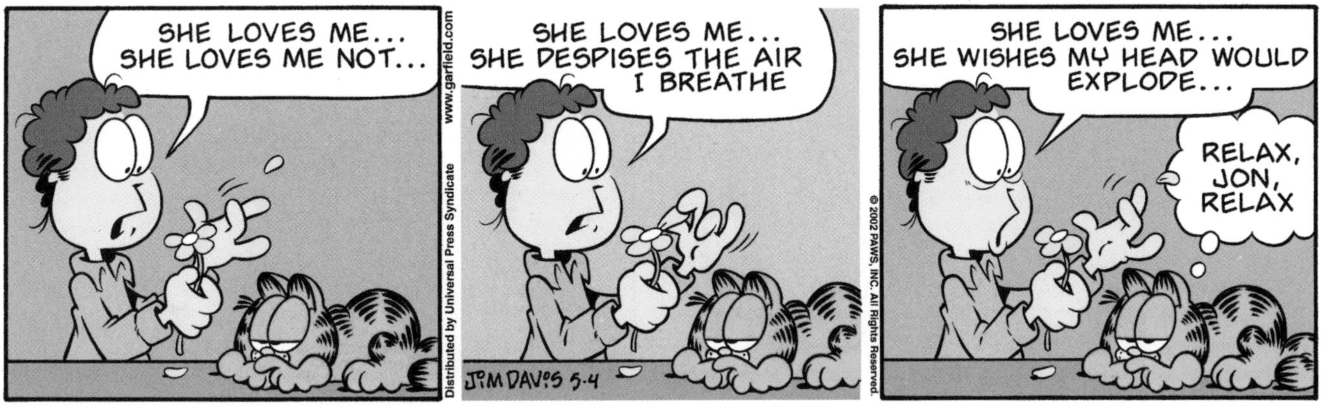
SHE LOVES ME... SHE LOVES ME NOT...
www.garfield.com
Distributed by Universal Press Syndicate
SHE LOVES ME... SHE DESPISES THE AIR I BREATHE
JIM DAVIS 5-4
SHE LOVES ME... SHE WISHES MY HEAD WOULD EXPLODE...
RELAX, JON, RELAX
© 2002 PAWS, INC. All Rights Reserved.

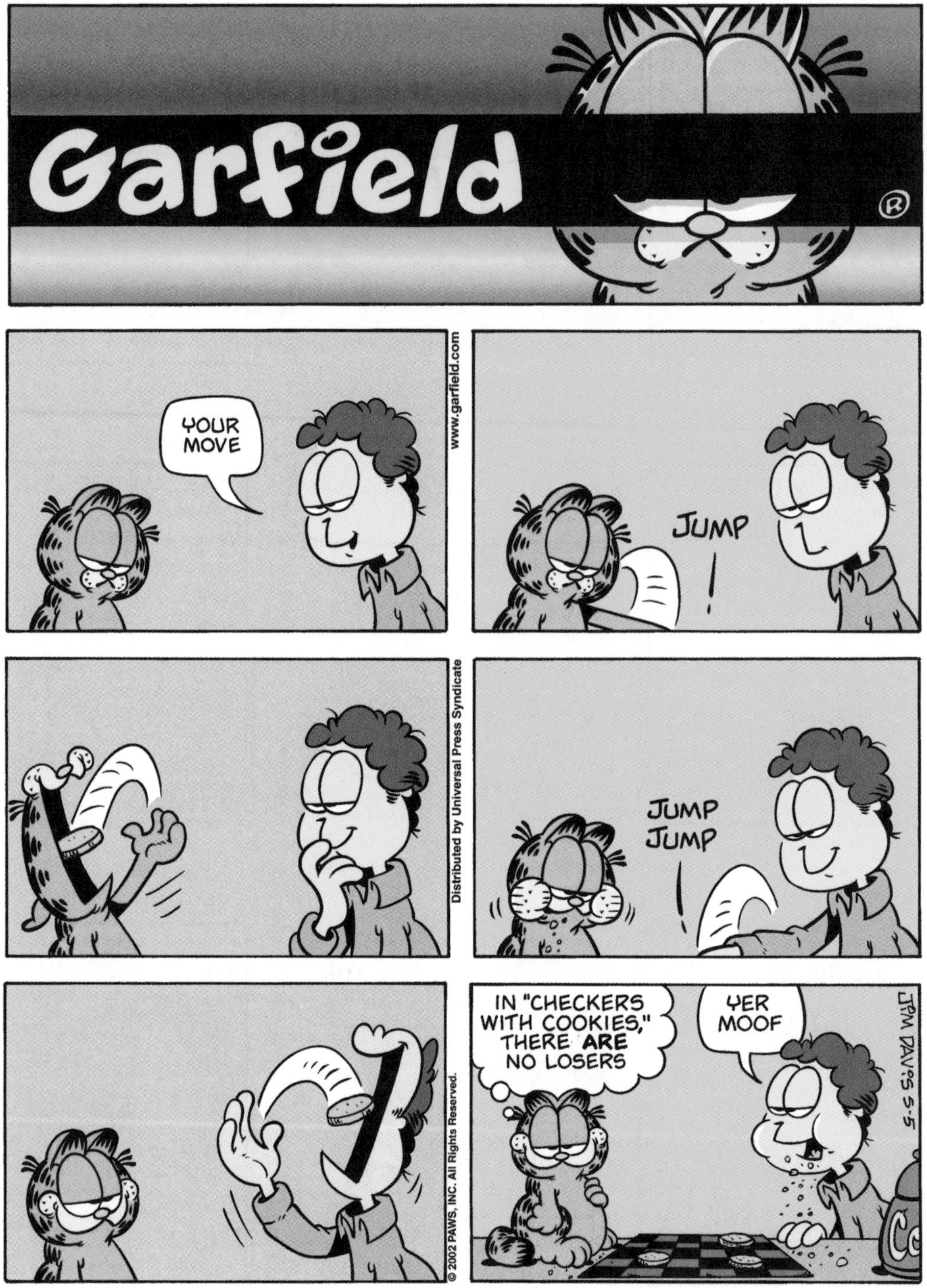
Garfield ®
www.garfield.com
YOUR MOVE
JUMP
Distributed by Universal Press Syndicate
JUMP JUMP
© 2002 PAWS, INC. All Rights Reserved.
IN "CHECKERS WITH COOKIES," THERE **ARE** NO LOSERS
YER MOOF
JIM DAVIS 5-5

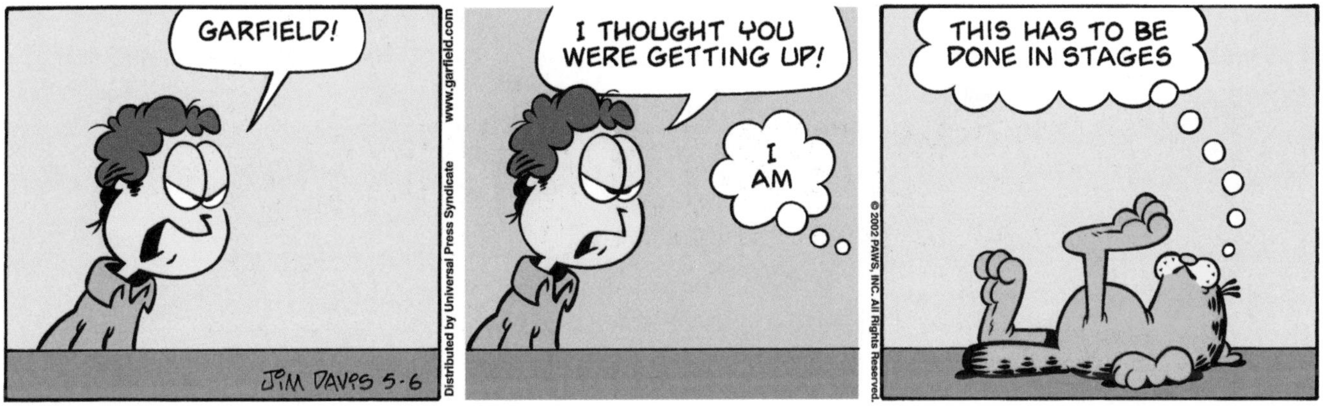
GARFIELD!
JIM DAVIS 5-6
Distributed by Universal Press Syndicate www.garfield.com
I THOUGHT YOU WERE GETTING UP!
I AM
© 2002 PAWS, INC. All Rights Reserved.
THIS HAS TO BE DONE IN STAGES

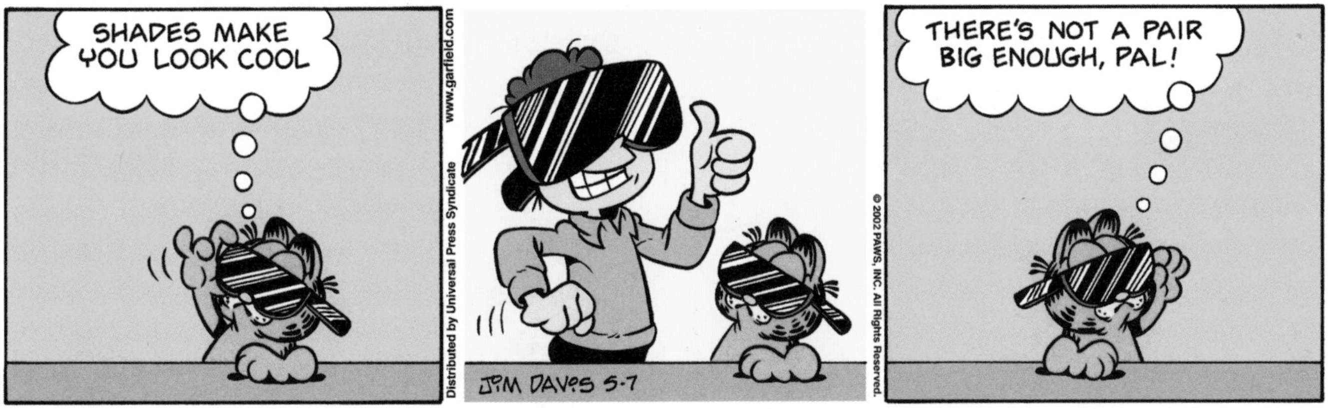
SHADES MAKE YOU LOOK COOL
Distributed by Universal Press Syndicate www.garfield.com
JIM DAVIS 5-7
© 2002 PAWS, INC. All Rights Reserved.
THERE'S NOT A PAIR BIG ENOUGH, PAL!

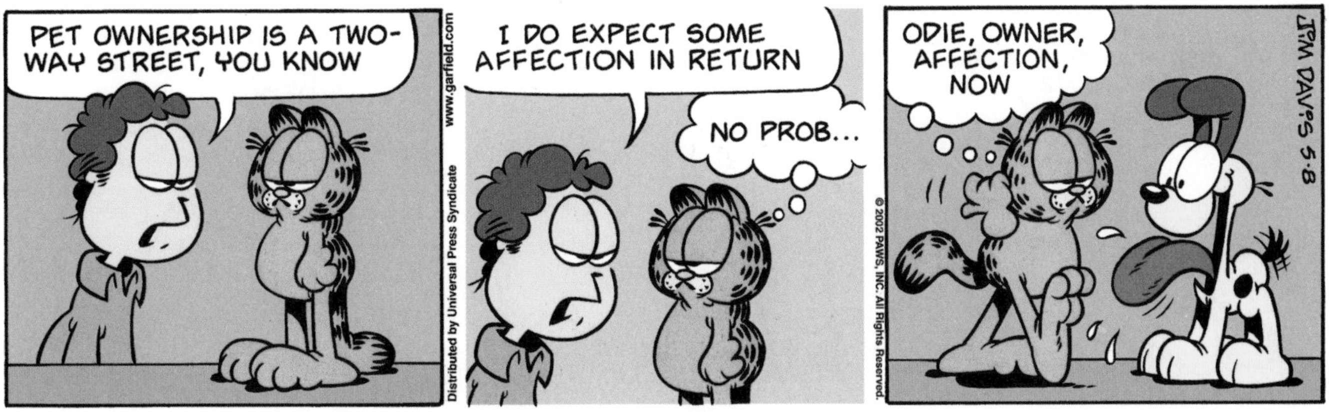
PET OWNERSHIP IS A TWO-WAY STREET, YOU KNOW
Distributed by Universal Press Syndicate www.garfield.com
I DO EXPECT SOME AFFECTION IN RETURN
NO PROB...
© 2002 PAWS, INC. All Rights Reserved.
ODIE, OWNER, AFFECTION, NOW
JIM DAVIS 5-8

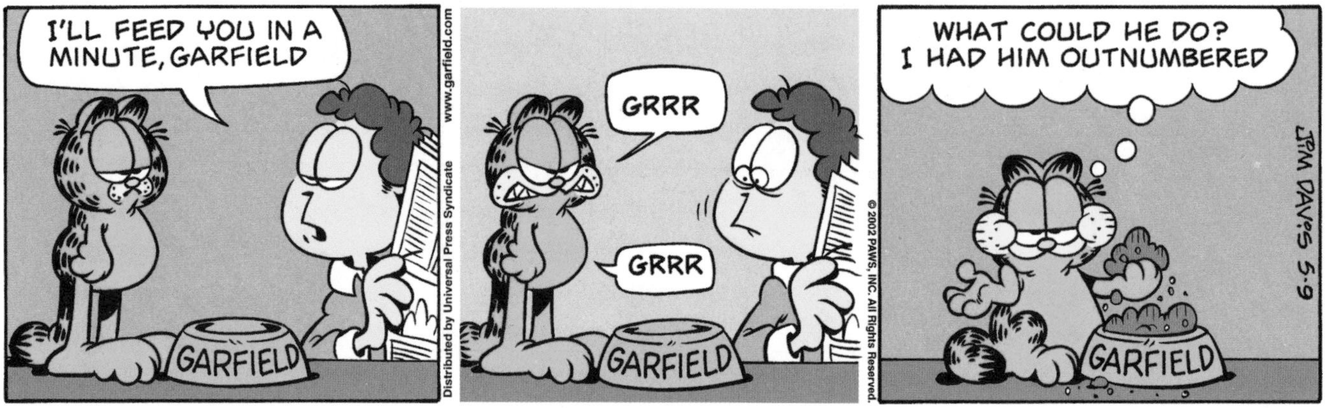
I'LL FEED YOU IN A MINUTE, GARFIELD
www.garfield.com
Distributed by Universal Press Syndicate
GARFIELD
GRRR
GRRR
GARFIELD
© 2002 PAWS, INC. All Rights Reserved.
WHAT COULD HE DO? I HAD HIM OUTNUMBERED
JIM DAVIS 5-9
GARFIELD

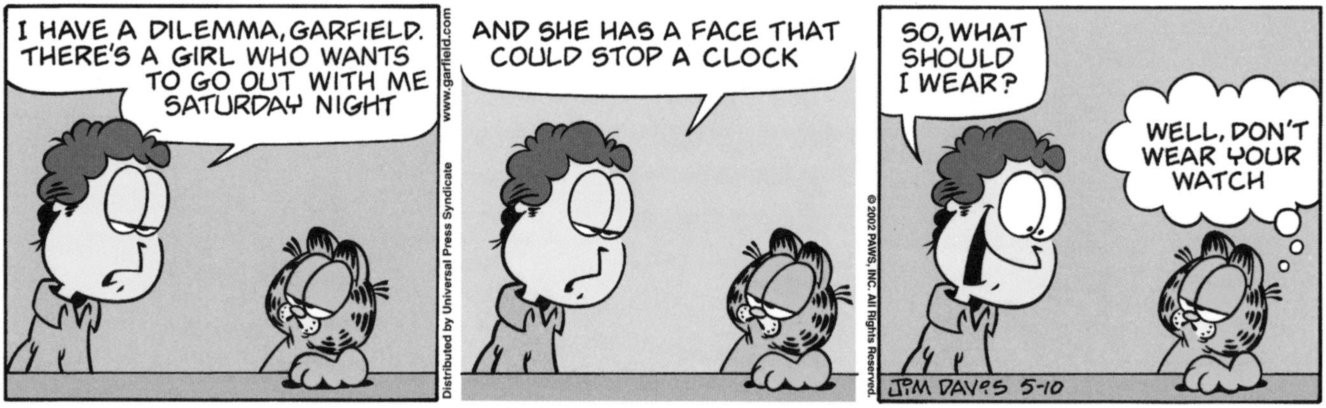
I HAVE A DILEMMA, GARFIELD. THERE'S A GIRL WHO WANTS TO GO OUT WITH ME SATURDAY NIGHT
www.garfield.com
Distributed by Universal Press Syndicate
AND SHE HAS A FACE THAT COULD STOP A CLOCK
© 2002 PAWS, INC. All Rights Reserved.
SO, WHAT SHOULD I WEAR?
WELL, DON'T WEAR YOUR WATCH
JIM DAVIS 5-10

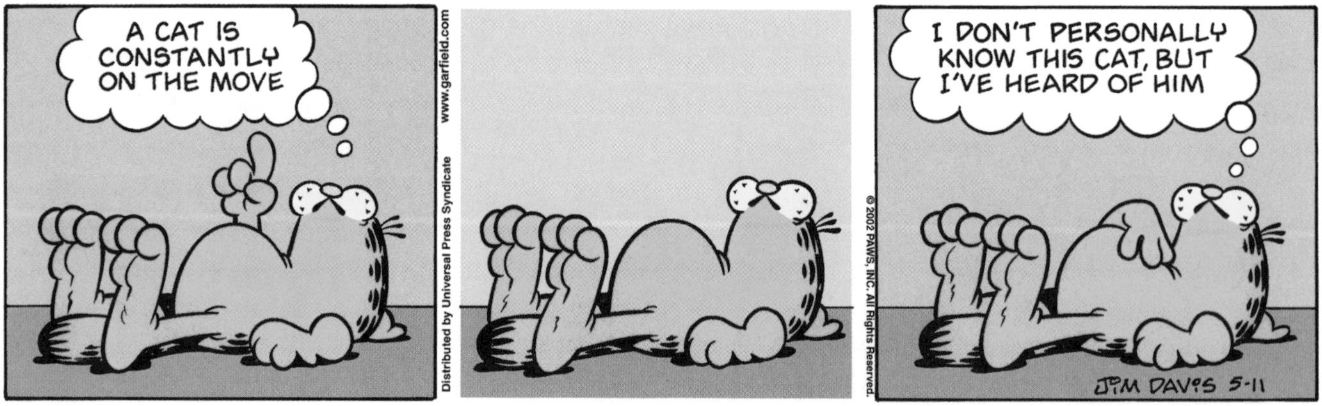
A CAT IS CONSTANTLY ON THE MOVE
www.garfield.com
Distributed by Universal Press Syndicate
© 2002 PAWS, INC. All Rights Reserved.
I DON'T PERSONALLY KNOW THIS CAT, BUT I'VE HEARD OF HIM
JIM DAVIS 5-11

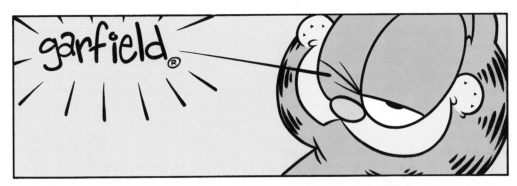

MADE YOU LOOK!

JIM DAVIS 5-12

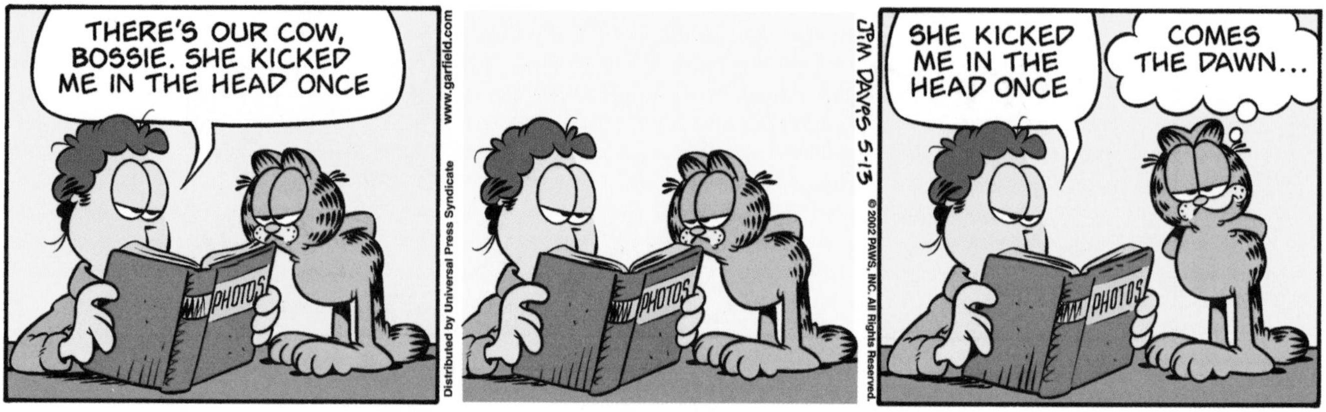
THERE'S OUR COW, BOSSIE. SHE KICKED ME IN THE HEAD ONCE
PHOTOS
www.garfield.com
Distributed by Universal Press Syndicate
PHOTOS
JIM DAVIS 5-13
© 2002 PAWS, INC. All Rights Reserved.
SHE KICKED ME IN THE HEAD ONCE
COMES THE DAWN...
PHOTOS

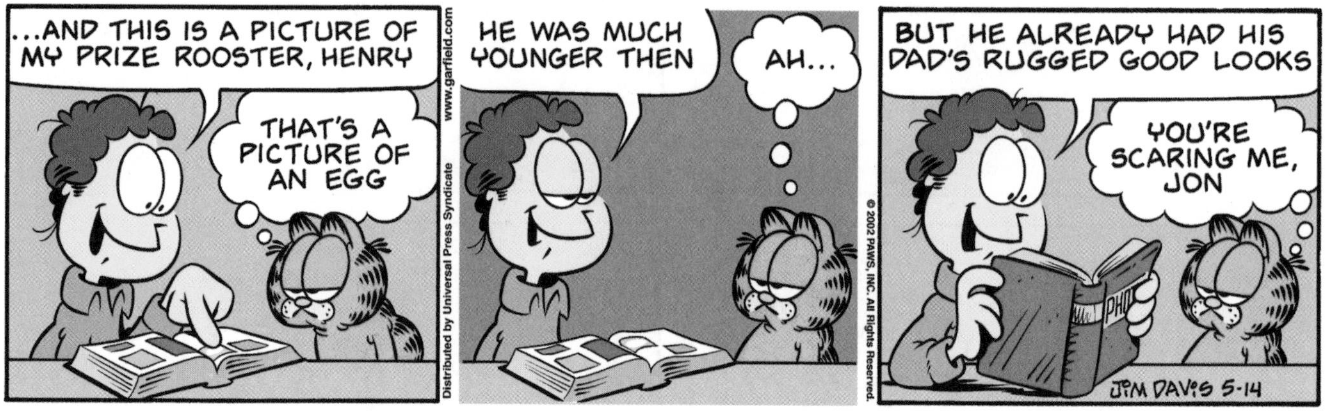
...AND THIS IS A PICTURE OF MY PRIZE ROOSTER, HENRY
THAT'S A PICTURE OF AN EGG
www.garfield.com
Distributed by Universal Press Syndicate
HE WAS MUCH YOUNGER THEN
AH...
© 2002 PAWS, INC. All Rights Reserved.
BUT HE ALREADY HAD HIS DAD'S RUGGED GOOD LOOKS
YOU'RE SCARING ME, JON
JIM DAVIS 5-14

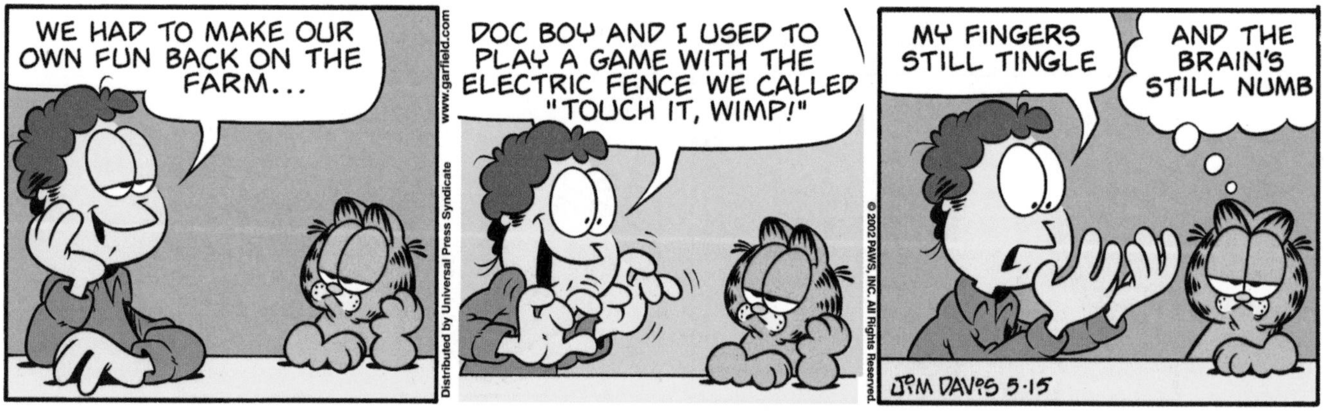
WE HAD TO MAKE OUR OWN FUN BACK ON THE FARM...
www.garfield.com
Distributed by Universal Press Syndicate
DOC BOY AND I USED TO PLAY A GAME WITH THE ELECTRIC FENCE WE CALLED "TOUCH IT, WIMP!"
© 2002 PAWS, INC. All Rights Reserved.
MY FINGERS STILL TINGLE
AND THE BRAIN'S STILL NUMB
JIM DAVIS 5-15

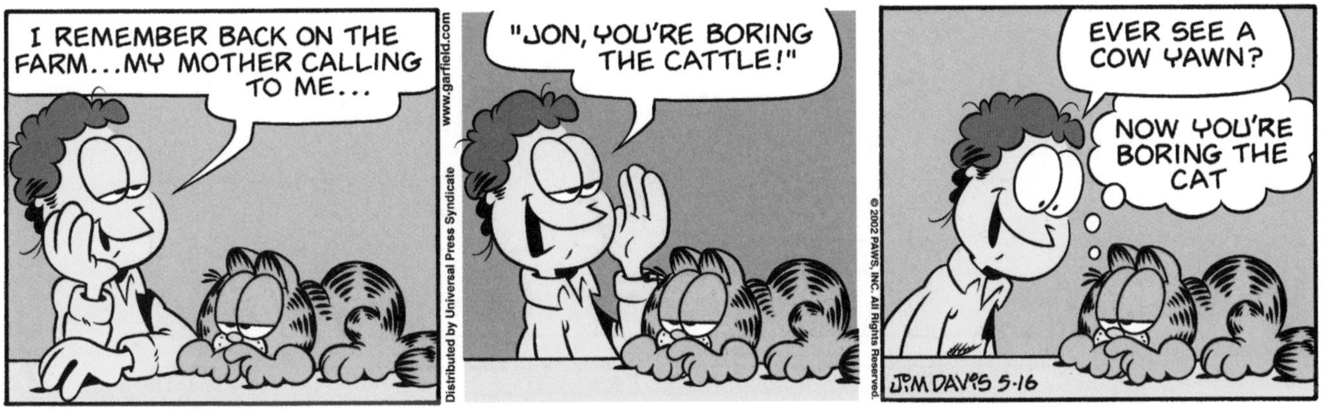
I REMEMBER BACK ON THE FARM...MY MOTHER CALLING TO ME...
Distributed by Universal Press Syndicate www.garfield.com
"JON, YOU'RE BORING THE CATTLE!"
© 2002 PAWS, INC. All Rights Reserved.
EVER SEE A COW YAWN?
NOW YOU'RE BORING THE CAT
JIM DAVIS 5-16

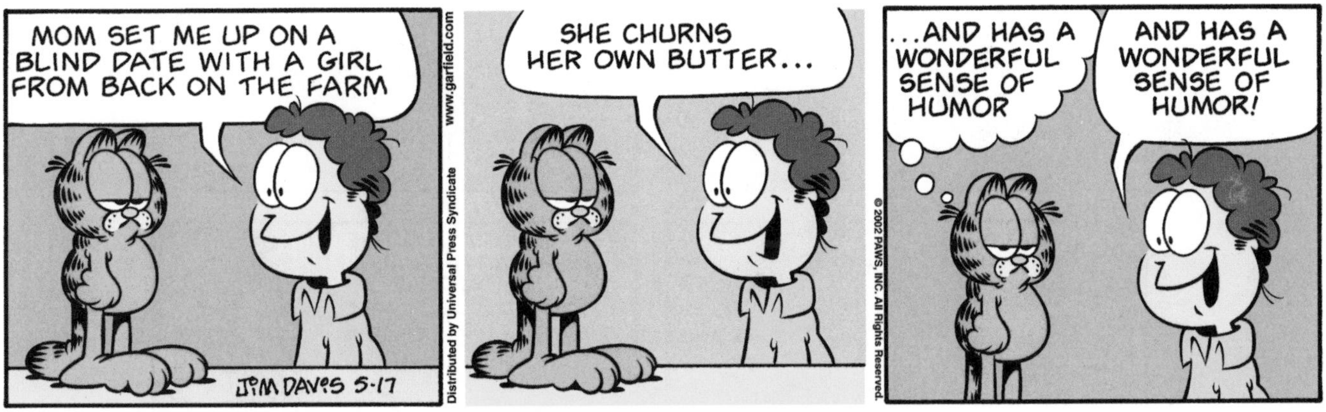
MOM SET ME UP ON A BLIND DATE WITH A GIRL FROM BACK ON THE FARM
JIM DAVIS 5-17
Distributed by Universal Press Syndicate www.garfield.com
SHE CHURNS HER OWN BUTTER...
© 2002 PAWS, INC. All Rights Reserved.
...AND HAS A WONDERFUL SENSE OF HUMOR
AND HAS A WONDERFUL SENSE OF HUMOR!

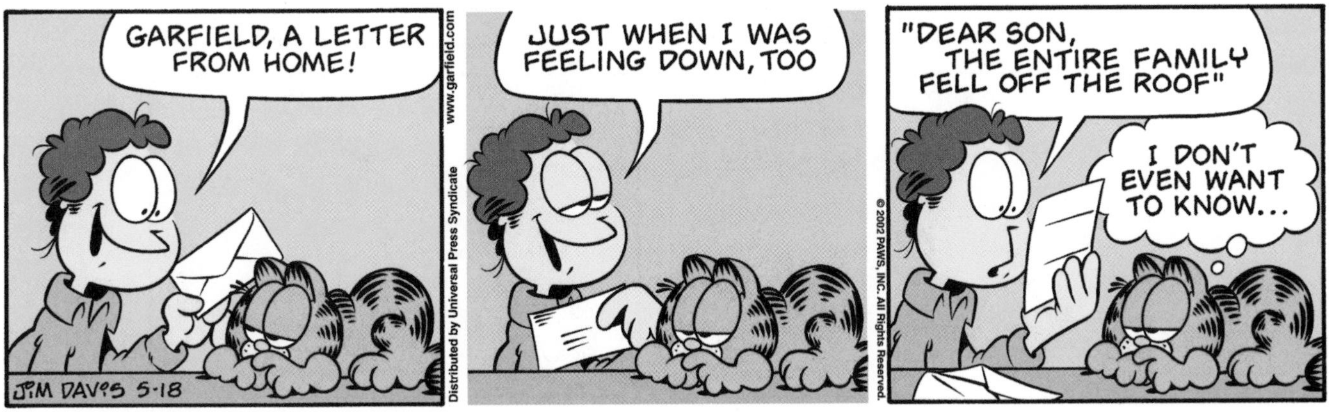
GARFIELD, A LETTER FROM HOME!
JIM DAVIS 5-18
Distributed by Universal Press Syndicate www.garfield.com
JUST WHEN I WAS FEELING DOWN, TOO
© 2002 PAWS, INC. All Rights Reserved.
"DEAR SON, THE ENTIRE FAMILY FELL OFF THE ROOF"
I DON'T EVEN WANT TO KNOW...

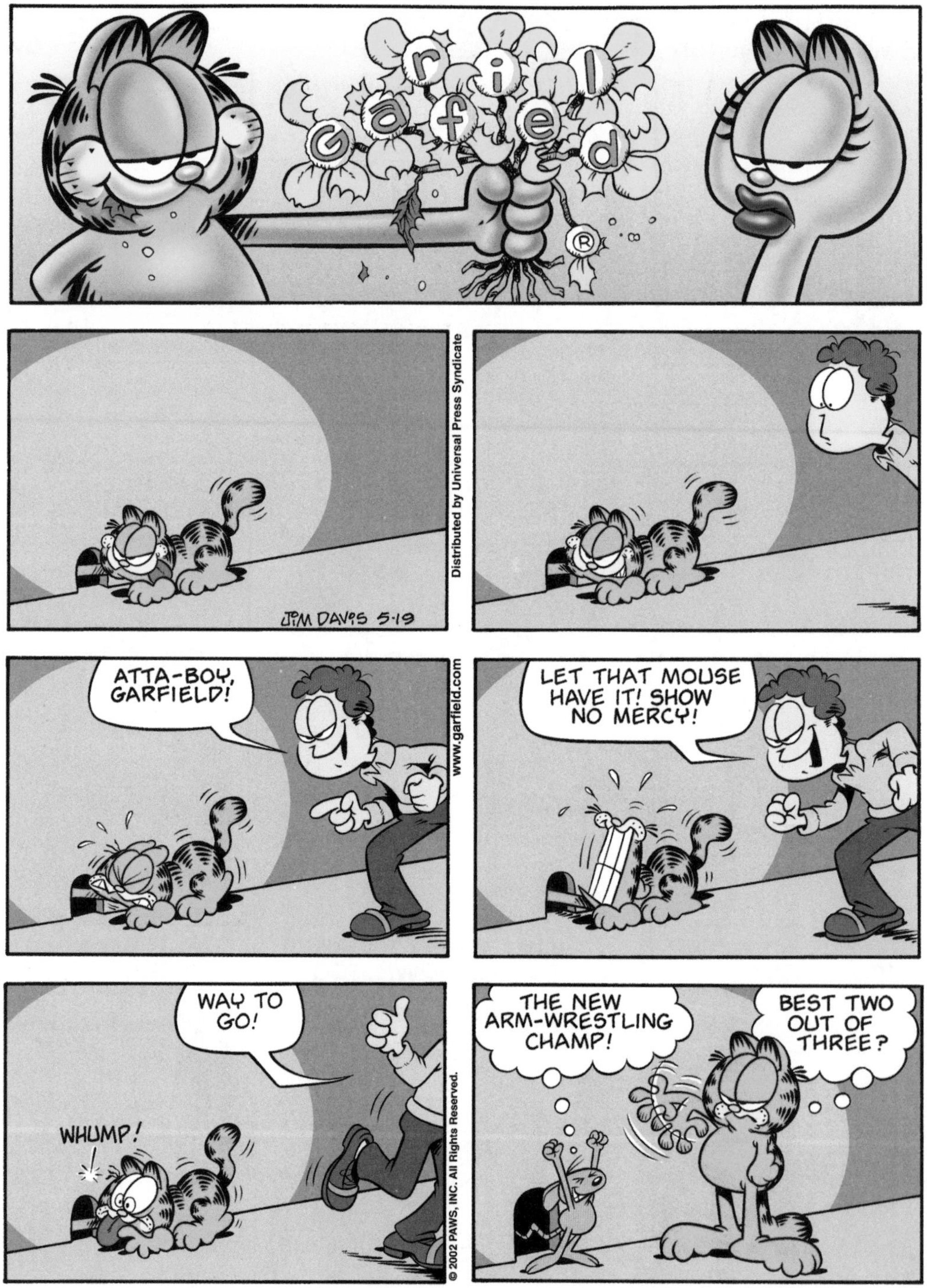
Garfield ®
JIM DAVIS 5-19
Distributed by Universal Press Syndicate
ATTA-BOY, GARFIELD!
LET THAT MOUSE HAVE IT! SHOW NO MERCY!
www.garfield.com
WAY TO GO!
WHUMP!
© 2002 PAWS, INC. All Rights Reserved.
THE NEW ARM-WRESTLING CHAMP!
BEST TWO OUT OF THREE?

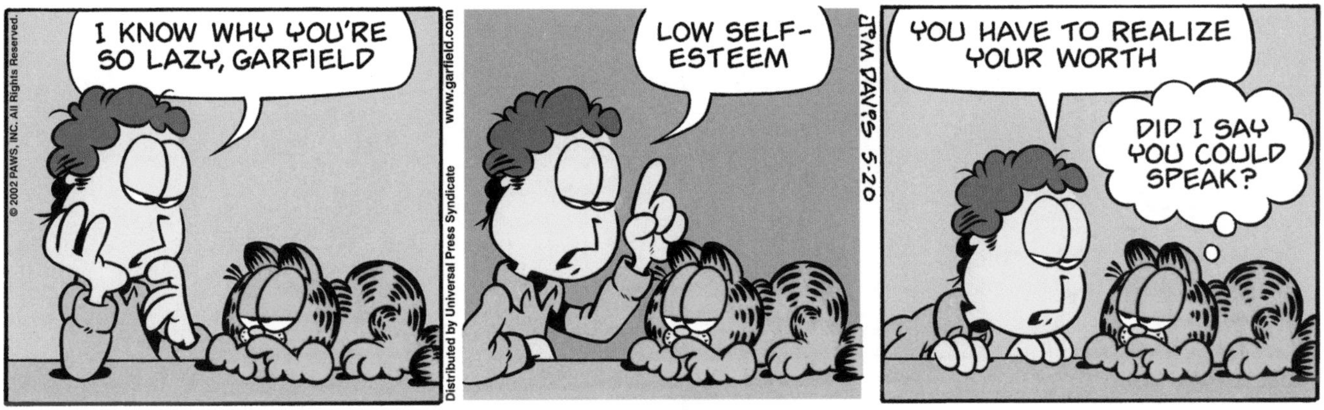
I KNOW WHY YOU'RE SO LAZY, GARFIELD
LOW SELF-ESTEEM
JIM DAVIS 5-20
YOU HAVE TO REALIZE YOUR WORTH
DID I SAY YOU COULD SPEAK?
© 2002 PAWS, INC. All Rights Reserved.
Distributed by Universal Press Syndicate
www.garfield.com

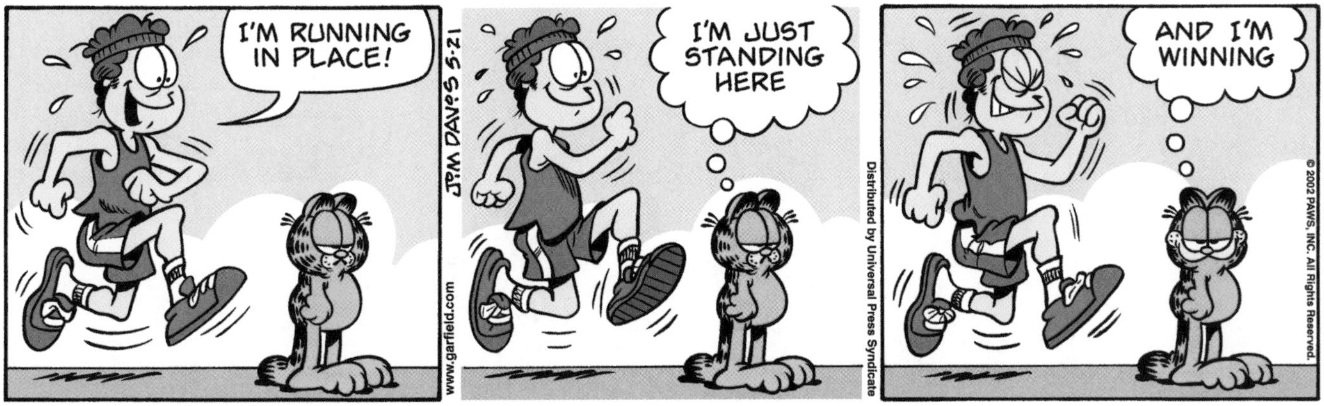
I'M RUNNING IN PLACE!
JIM DAVIS 5-21
I'M JUST STANDING HERE
AND I'M WINNING
www.garfield.com
Distributed by Universal Press Syndicate
© 2002 PAWS, INC. All Rights Reserved.

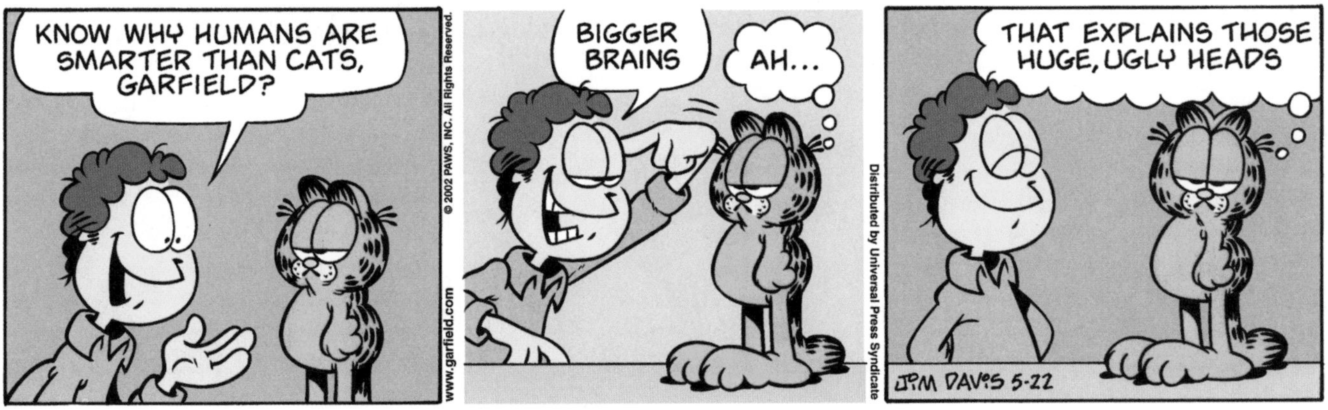
KNOW WHY HUMANS ARE SMARTER THAN CATS, GARFIELD?
BIGGER BRAINS
AH...
THAT EXPLAINS THOSE HUGE, UGLY HEADS
JIM DAVIS 5-22
© 2002 PAWS, INC. All Rights Reserved.
www.garfield.com
Distributed by Universal Press Syndicate

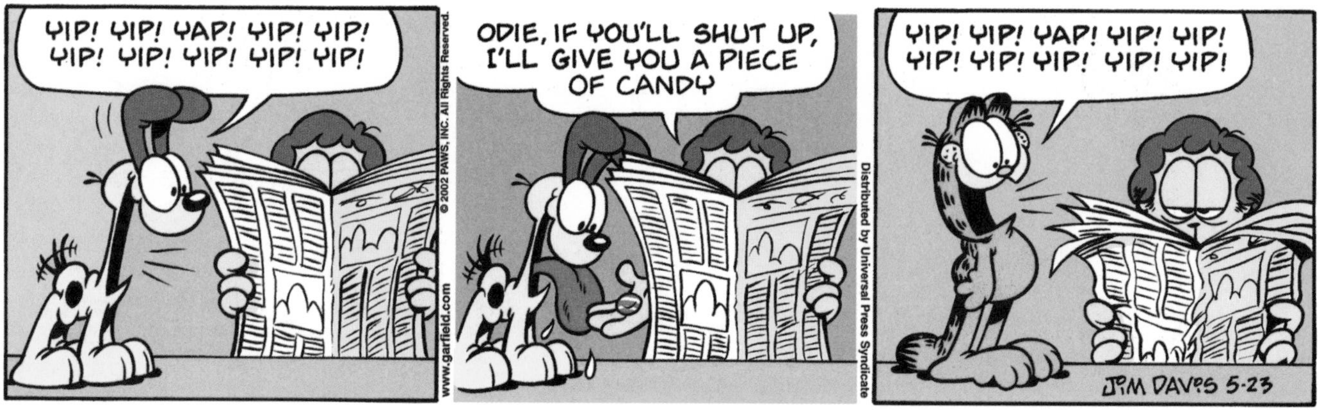
YIP! YIP! YAP! YIP! YIP! YIP! YIP! YIP! YIP! YIP!
ODIE, IF YOU'LL SHUT UP, I'LL GIVE YOU A PIECE OF CANDY
YIP! YIP! YAP! YIP! YIP! YIP! YIP! YIP! YIP! YIP!
JIM DAVIS 5-23
© 2002 PAWS, INC. All Rights Reserved.
www.garfield.com
Distributed by Universal Press Syndicate

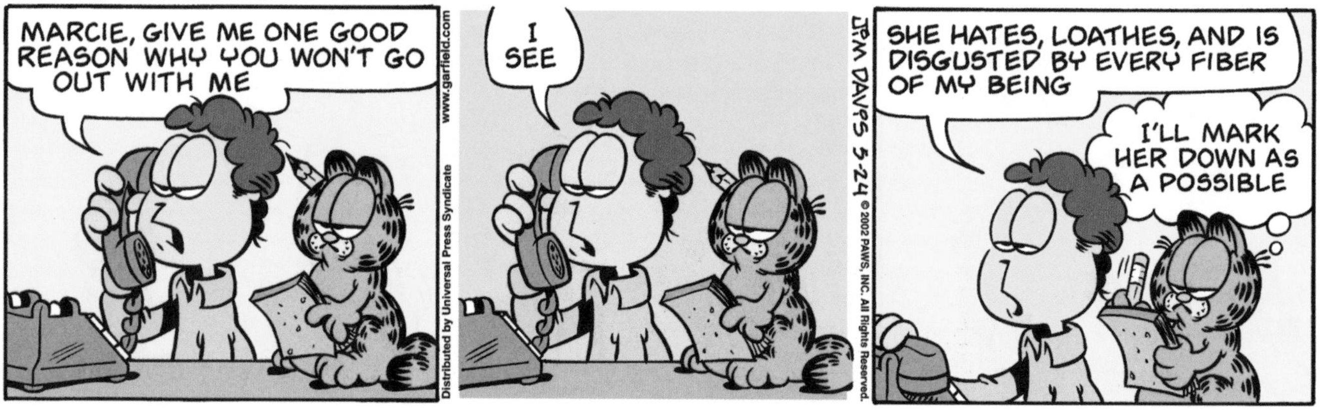
MARCIE, GIVE ME ONE GOOD REASON WHY YOU WON'T GO OUT WITH ME
I SEE
SHE HATES, LOATHES, AND IS DISGUSTED BY EVERY FIBER OF MY BEING
I'LL MARK HER DOWN AS A POSSIBLE
JIM DAVIS 5-24
© 2002 PAWS, INC. All Rights Reserved.
www.garfield.com
Distributed by Universal Press Syndicate

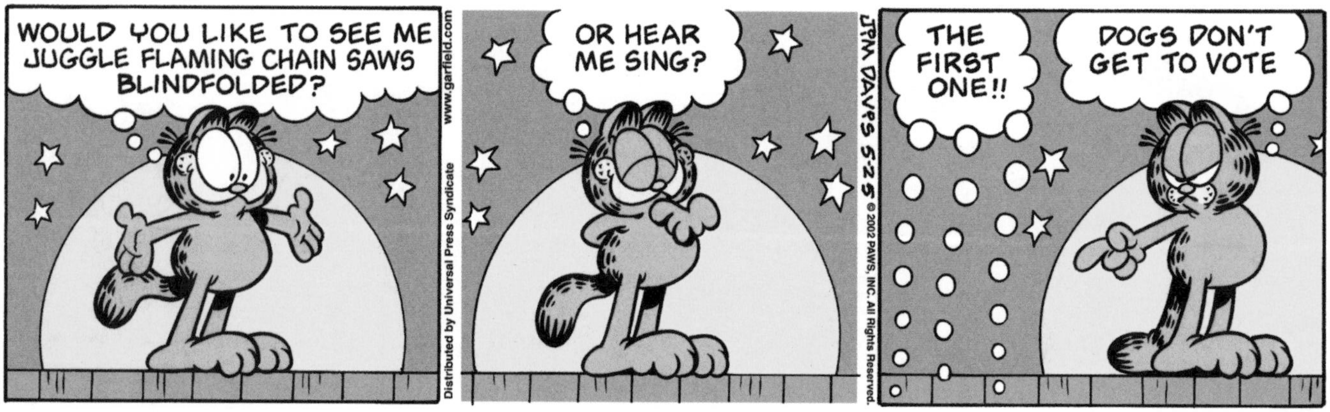
WOULD YOU LIKE TO SEE ME JUGGLE FLAMING CHAIN SAWS BLINDFOLDED?
OR HEAR ME SING?
THE FIRST ONE!!
DOGS DON'T GET TO VOTE
JIM DAVIS 5-25
© 2002 PAWS, INC. All Rights Reserved.
www.garfield.com
Distributed by Universal Press Syndicate

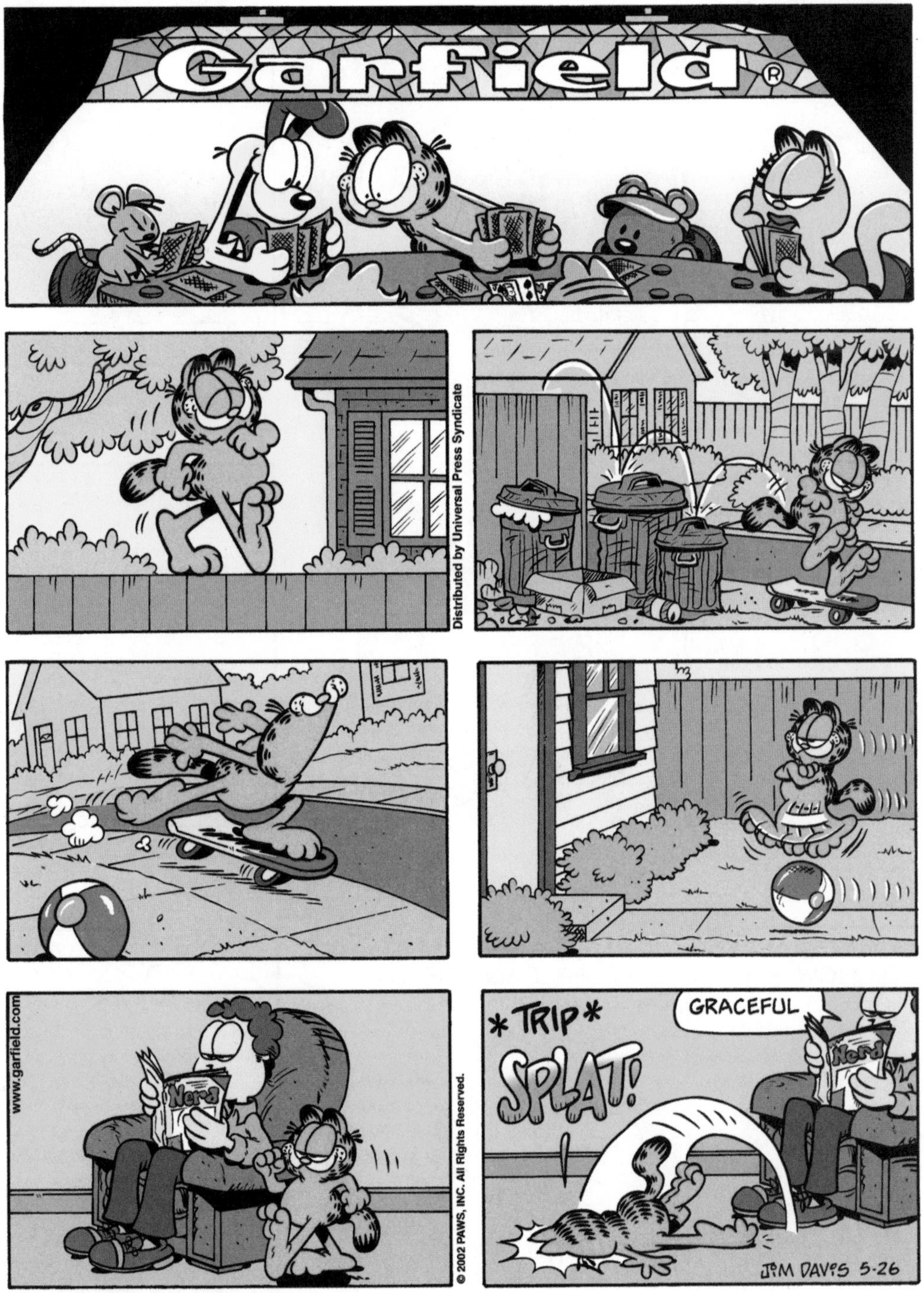
Garfield®
Distributed by Universal Press Syndicate
www.garfield.com
© 2002 PAWS, INC. All Rights Reserved.
TRIP
SPLAT!
GRACEFUL
JIM DAVIS 5-26

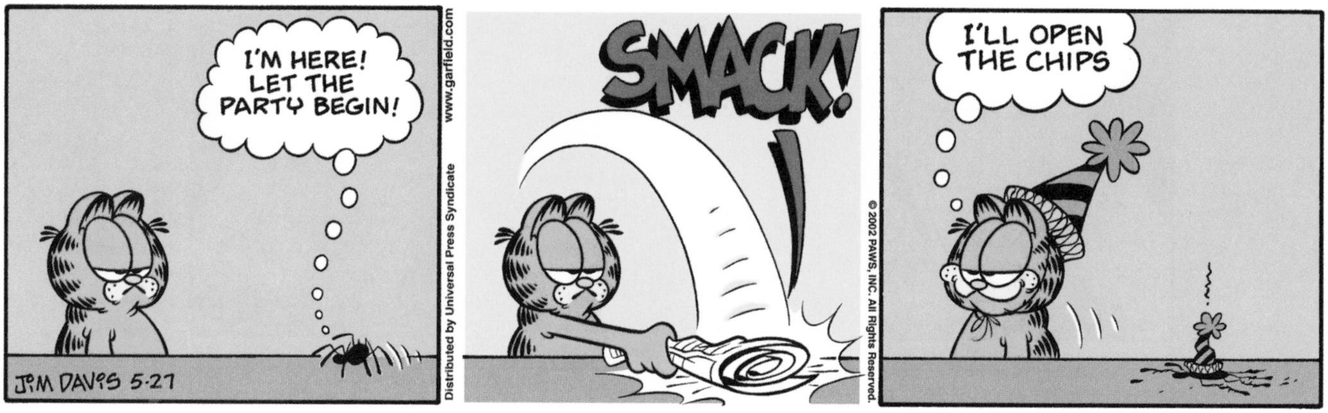
I'M HERE! LET THE PARTY BEGIN!
JIM DAVIS 5-27
Distributed by Universal Press Syndicate www.garfield.com
SMACK!
© 2002 PAWS, INC. All Rights Reserved.
I'LL OPEN THE CHIPS

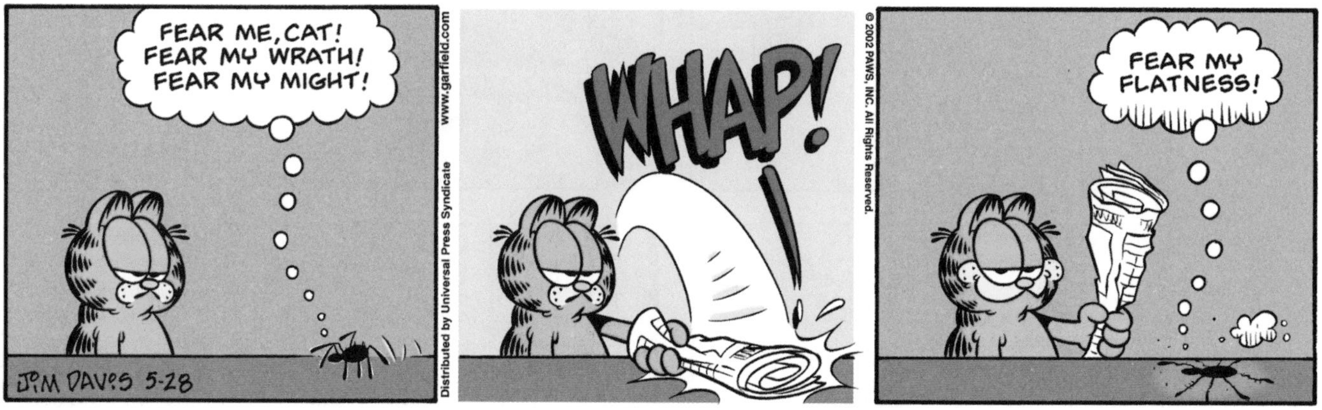
FEAR ME, CAT! FEAR MY WRATH! FEAR MY MIGHT!
JIM DAVIS 5-28
Distributed by Universal Press Syndicate www.garfield.com
WHAP!
© 2002 PAWS, INC. All Rights Reserved.
FEAR MY FLATNESS!

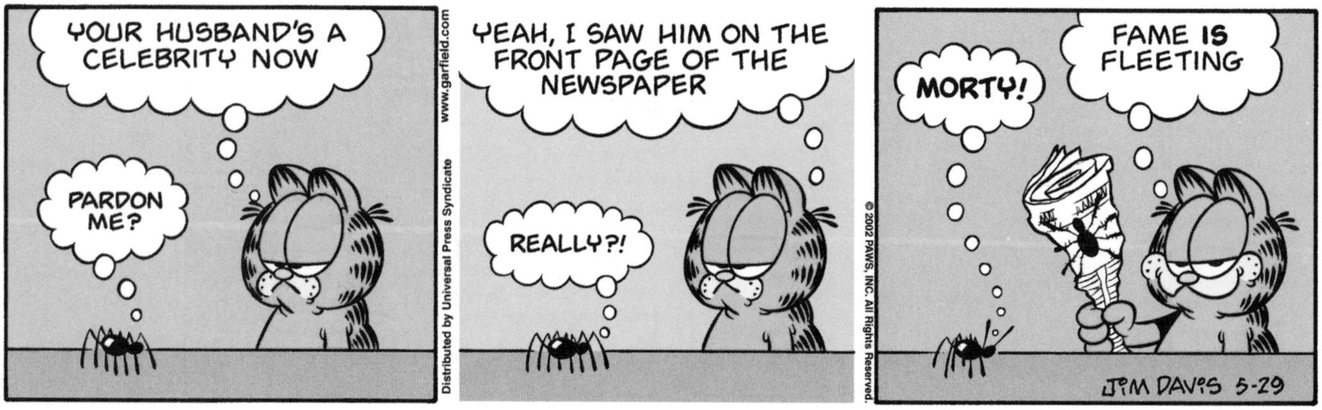
YOUR HUSBAND'S A CELEBRITY NOW
PARDON ME?
Distributed by Universal Press Syndicate www.garfield.com
YEAH, I SAW HIM ON THE FRONT PAGE OF THE NEWSPAPER
REALLY?!
© 2002 PAWS, INC. All Rights Reserved.
MORTY!
FAME IS FLEETING
JIM DAVIS 5-29

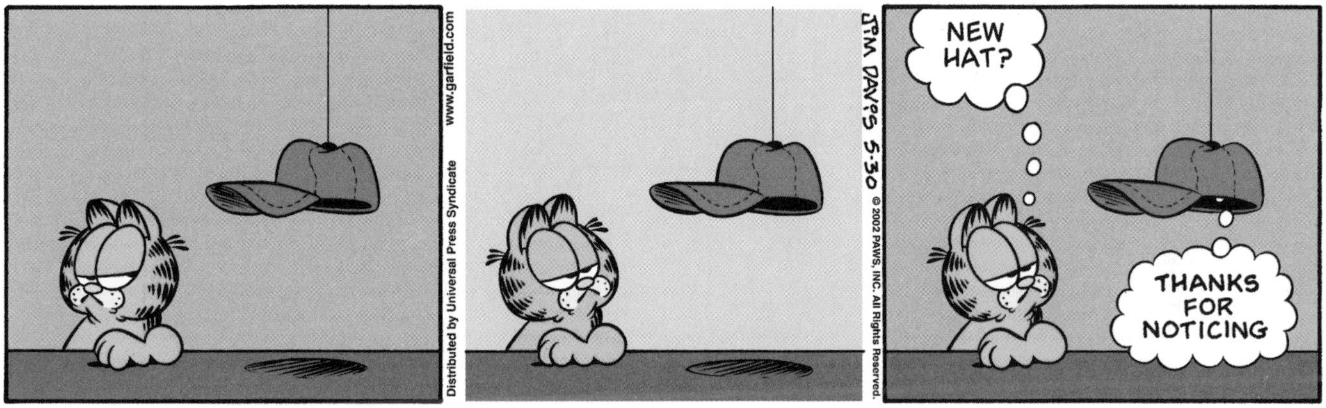
NEW HAT?
THANKS FOR NOTICING
JIM DAVIS 5-30
Distributed by Universal Press Syndicate www.garfield.com
© 2002 PAWS, INC. All Rights Reserved.

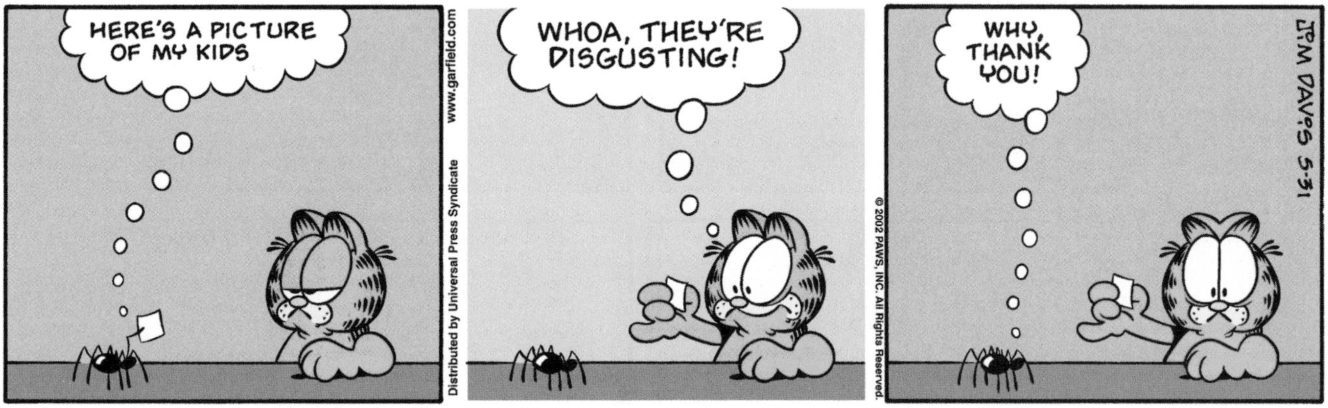
HERE'S A PICTURE OF MY KIDS
WHOA, THEY'RE DISGUSTING!
WHY, THANK YOU!
JIM DAVIS 5-31
Distributed by Universal Press Syndicate www.garfield.com
© 2002 PAWS, INC. All Rights Reserved.

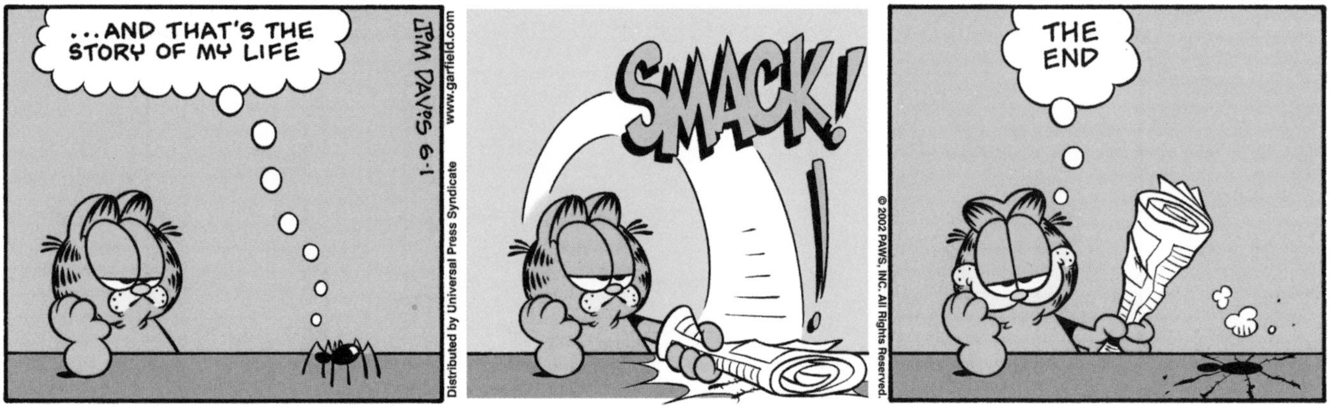
...AND THAT'S THE STORY OF MY LIFE
SMACK!
THE END
JIM DAVIS 6-1
Distributed by Universal Press Syndicate www.garfield.com
© 2002 PAWS, INC. All Rights Reserved.

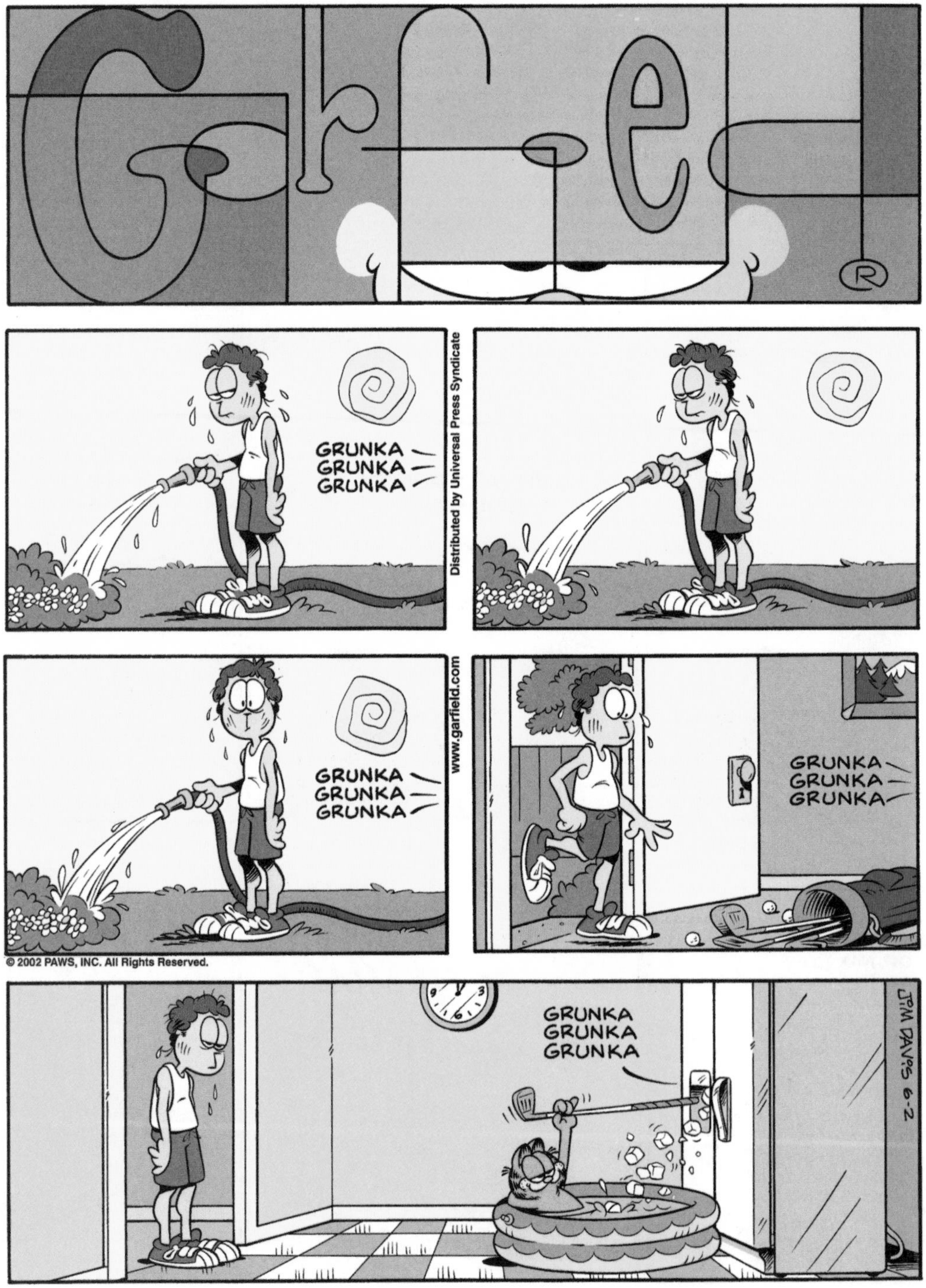
Garfield
GRUNKA GRUNKA GRUNKA
Distributed by Universal Press Syndicate
GRUNKA GRUNKA GRUNKA
GRUNKA GRUNKA GRUNKA
www.garfield.com
GRUNKA GRUNKA GRUNKA
© 2002 PAWS, INC. All Rights Reserved.
GRUNKA GRUNKA GRUNKA
JIM DAVIS 6-2

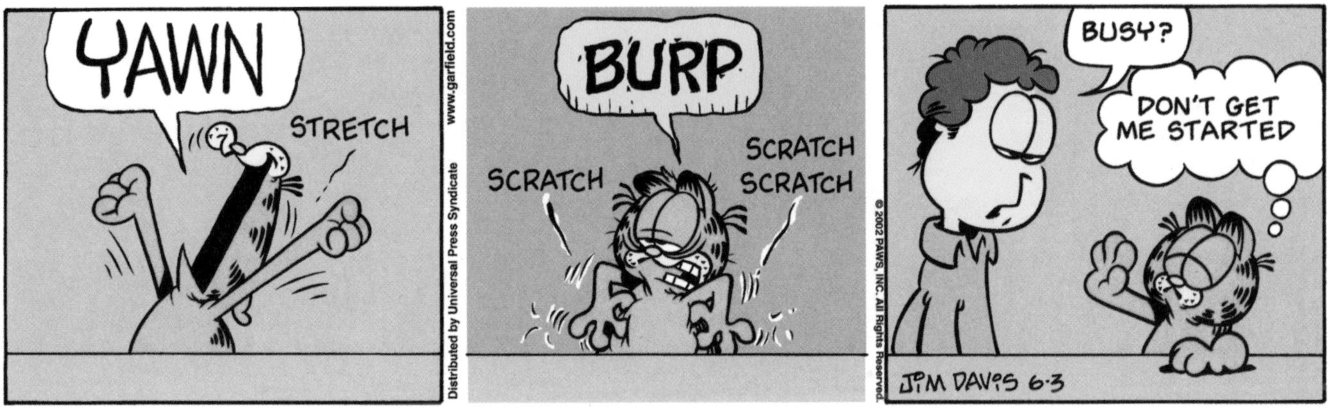
YAWN
STRETCH
BURP
SCRATCH
SCRATCH
SCRATCH
BUSY?
DON'T GET ME STARTED
JIM DAVIS 6-3
www.garfield.com
Distributed by Universal Press Syndicate
© 2002 PAWS, INC. All Rights Reserved.

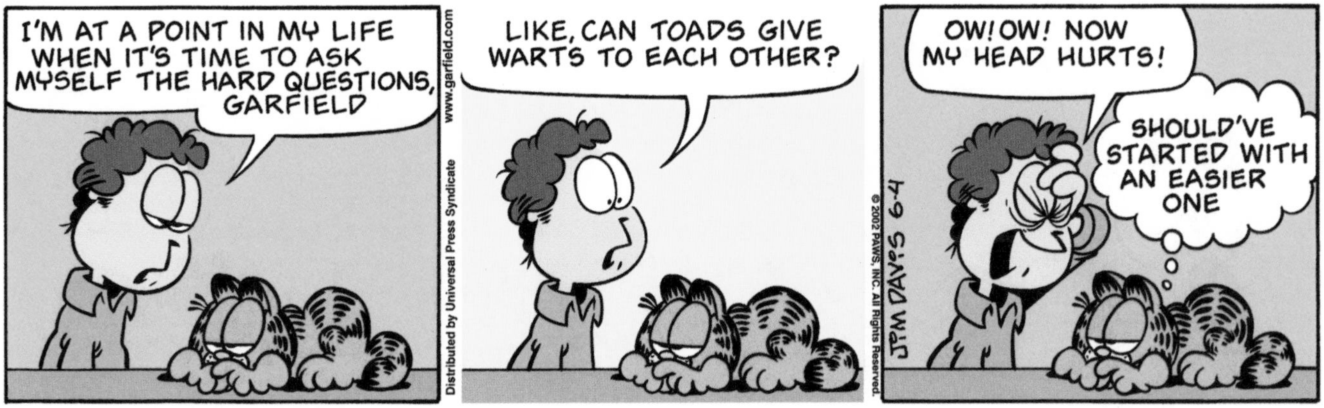
I'M AT A POINT IN MY LIFE WHEN IT'S TIME TO ASK MYSELF THE HARD QUESTIONS, GARFIELD
LIKE, CAN TOADS GIVE WARTS TO EACH OTHER?
OW! OW! NOW MY HEAD HURTS!
SHOULD'VE STARTED WITH AN EASIER ONE
JIM DAVIS 6-4
www.garfield.com
Distributed by Universal Press Syndicate
© 2002 PAWS, INC. All Rights Reserved.

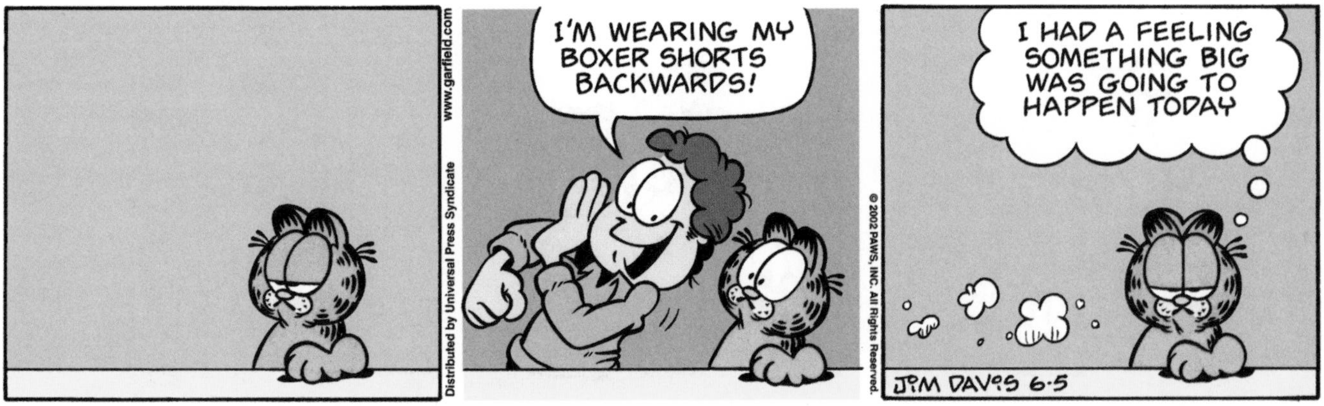
I'M WEARING MY BOXER SHORTS BACKWARDS!
I HAD A FEELING SOMETHING BIG WAS GOING TO HAPPEN TODAY
JIM DAVIS 6-5
www.garfield.com
Distributed by Universal Press Syndicate
© 2002 PAWS, INC. All Rights Reserved.

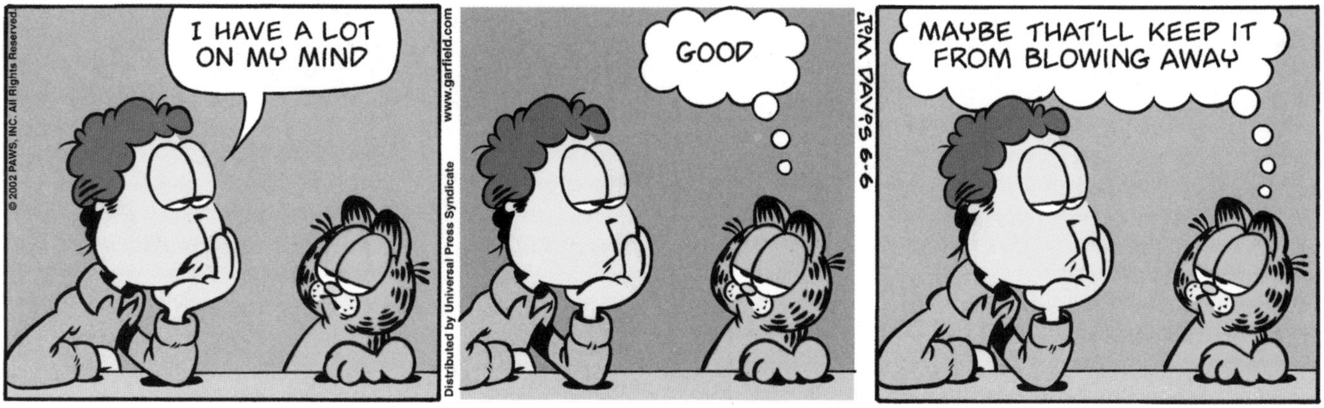
© 2002 PAWS, INC. All Rights Reserved
I HAVE A LOT ON MY MIND
Distributed by Universal Press Syndicate www.garfield.com
GOOD
JIM DAVIS 6-6
MAYBE THAT'LL KEEP IT FROM BLOWING AWAY

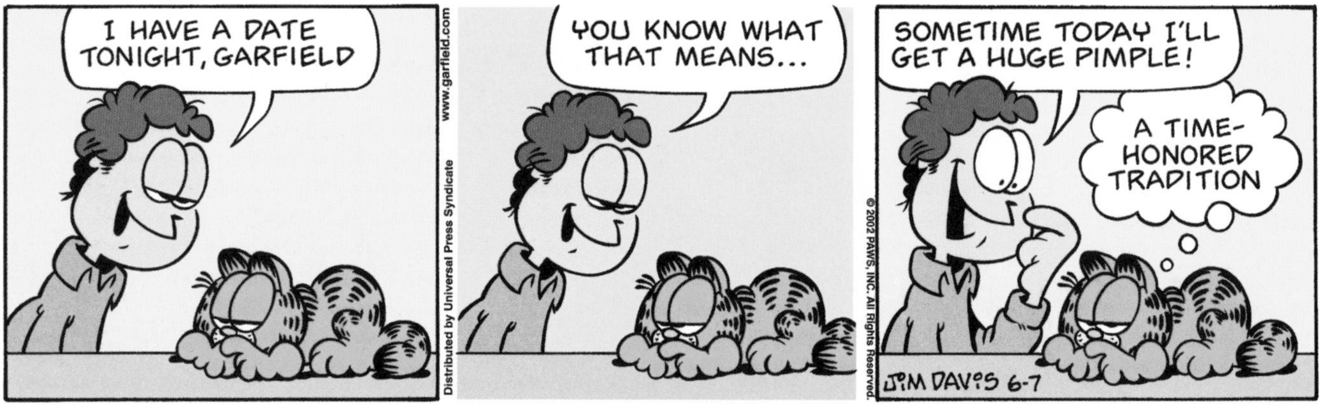
I HAVE A DATE TONIGHT, GARFIELD
Distributed by Universal Press Syndicate www.garfield.com
YOU KNOW WHAT THAT MEANS...
SOMETIME TODAY I'LL GET A HUGE PIMPLE!
A TIME-HONORED TRADITION
© 2002 PAWS, INC. All Rights Reserved.
JIM DAVIS 6-7

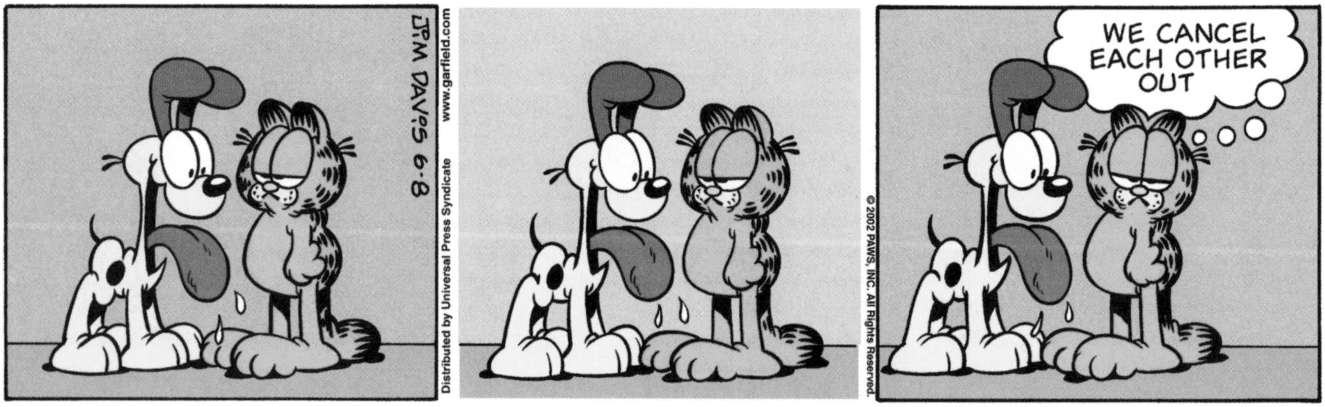
JIM DAVIS 6-8
Distributed by Universal Press Syndicate www.garfield.com
© 2002 PAWS, INC. All Rights Reserved.
WE CANCEL EACH OTHER OUT

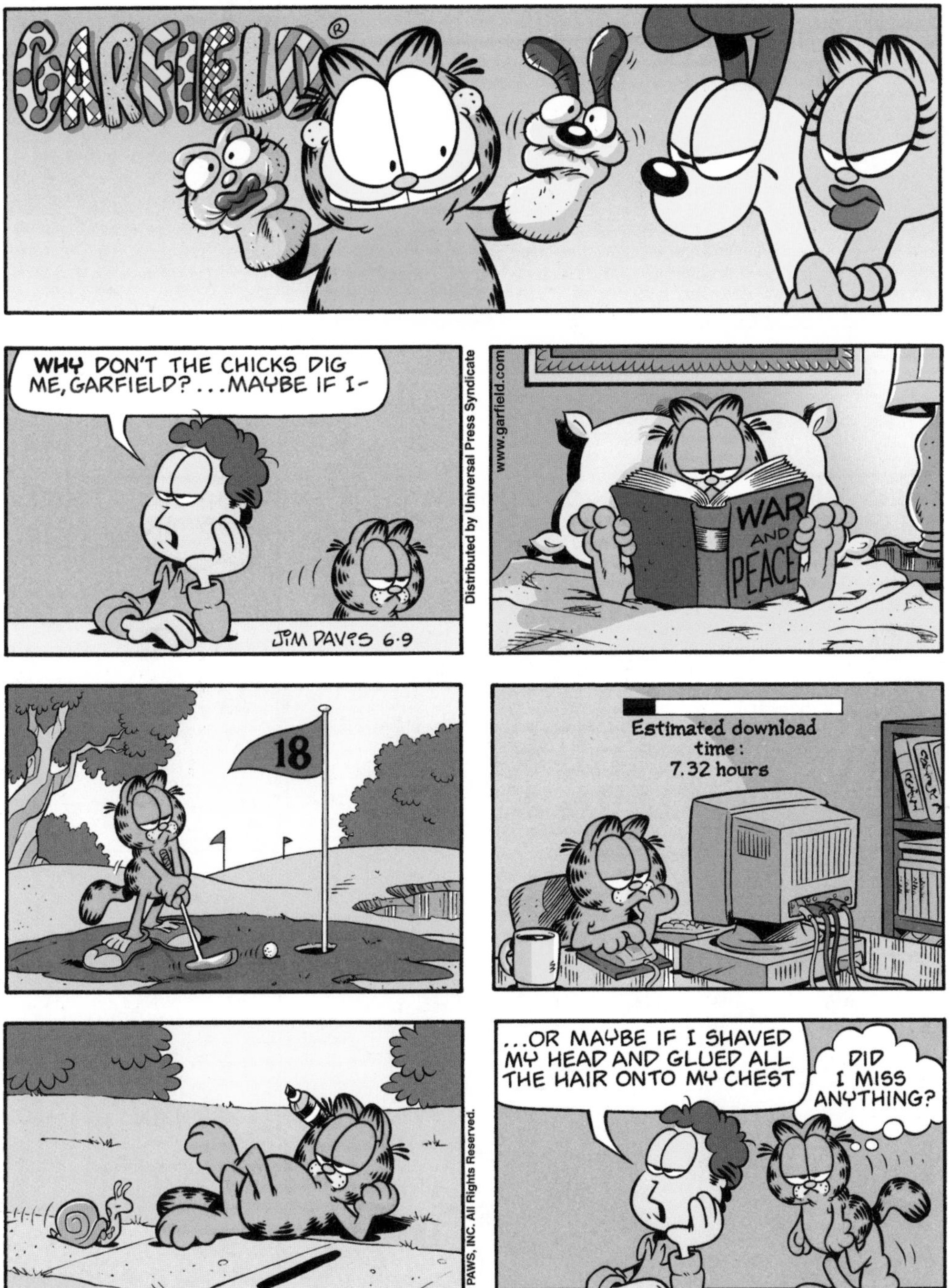
GARFIELD®
WHY DON'T THE CHICKS DIG ME, GARFIELD? . . . MAYBE IF I-
JIM DAVIS 6·9
Distributed by Universal Press Syndicate
www.garfield.com
WAR AND PEACE
18
Estimated download time : 7.32 hours
© 2002 PAWS, INC. All Rights Reserved.
. . .OR MAYBE IF I SHAVED MY HEAD AND GLUED ALL THE HAIR ONTO MY CHEST
DID I MISS ANYTHING?

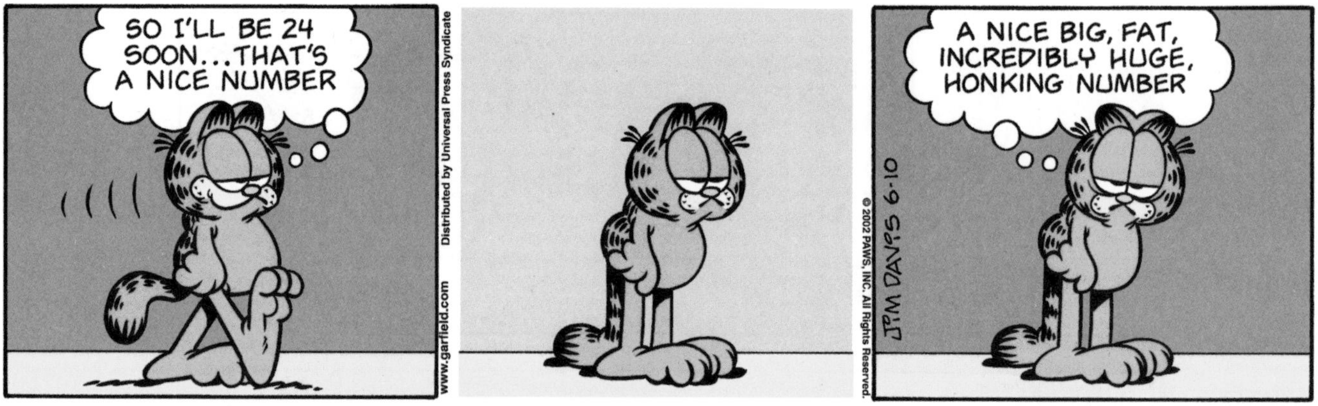
SO I'LL BE 24 SOON...THAT'S A NICE NUMBER
www.garfield.com Distributed by Universal Press Syndicate
A NICE BIG, FAT, INCREDIBLY HUGE, HONKING NUMBER
JIM DAVIS 6-10
© 2002 PAWS, INC. All Rights Reserved.

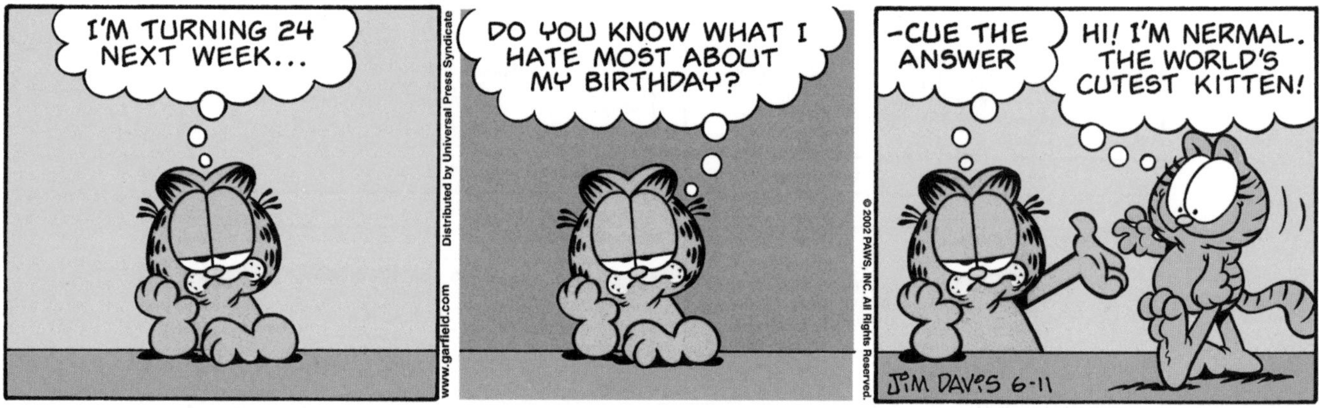
I'M TURNING 24 NEXT WEEK...
www.garfield.com Distributed by Universal Press Syndicate
DO YOU KNOW WHAT I HATE MOST ABOUT MY BIRTHDAY?
-CUE THE ANSWER
HI! I'M NERMAL. THE WORLD'S CUTEST KITTEN!
© 2002 PAWS, INC. All Rights Reserved.
JIM DAVIS 6-11

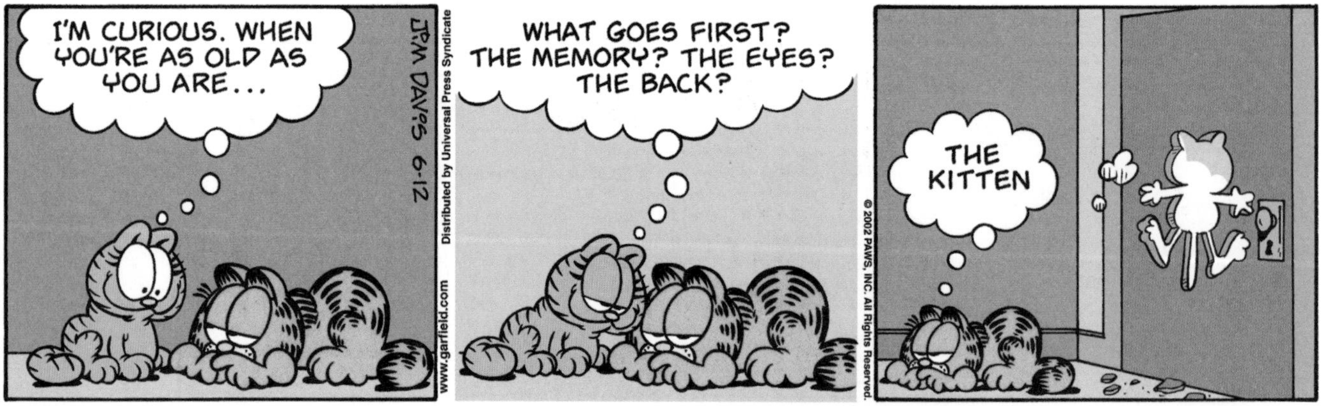
I'M CURIOUS. WHEN YOU'RE AS OLD AS YOU ARE...
JIM DAVIS 6-12
www.garfield.com Distributed by Universal Press Syndicate
WHAT GOES FIRST? THE MEMORY? THE EYES? THE BACK?
THE KITTEN
© 2002 PAWS, INC. All Rights Reserved.

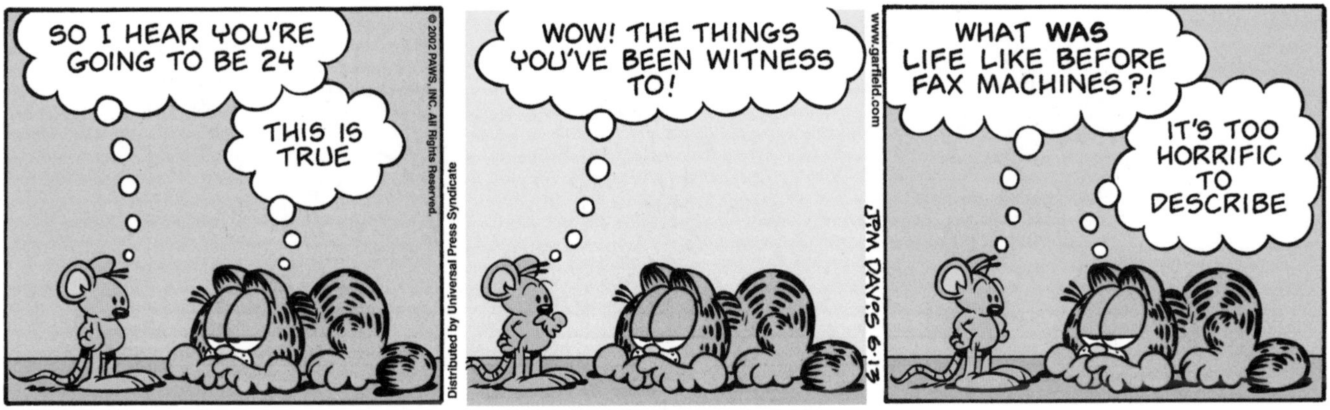
SO I HEAR YOU'RE GOING TO BE 24
THIS IS TRUE
WOW! THE THINGS YOU'VE BEEN WITNESS TO!
WHAT WAS LIFE LIKE BEFORE FAX MACHINES?!
IT'S TOO HORRIFIC TO DESCRIBE
JIM DAVIS 6-13
© 2002 PAWS, INC. All Rights Reserved.
Distributed by Universal Press Syndicate
www.garfield.com

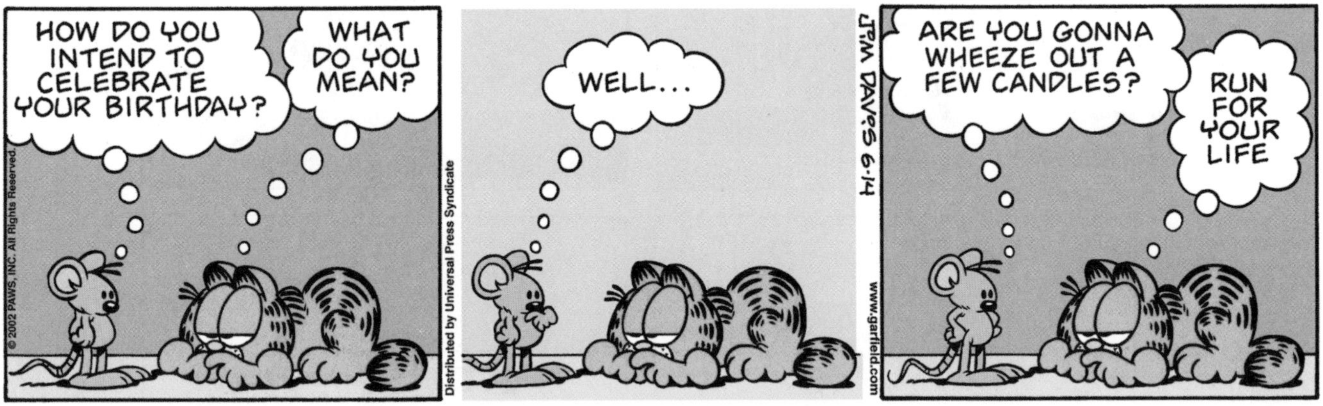
HOW DO YOU INTEND TO CELEBRATE YOUR BIRTHDAY?
WHAT DO YOU MEAN?
WELL...
ARE YOU GONNA WHEEZE OUT A FEW CANDLES?
RUN FOR YOUR LIFE
JIM DAVIS 6-14
© 2002 PAWS, INC. All Rights Reserved.
Distributed by Universal Press Syndicate
www.garfield.com

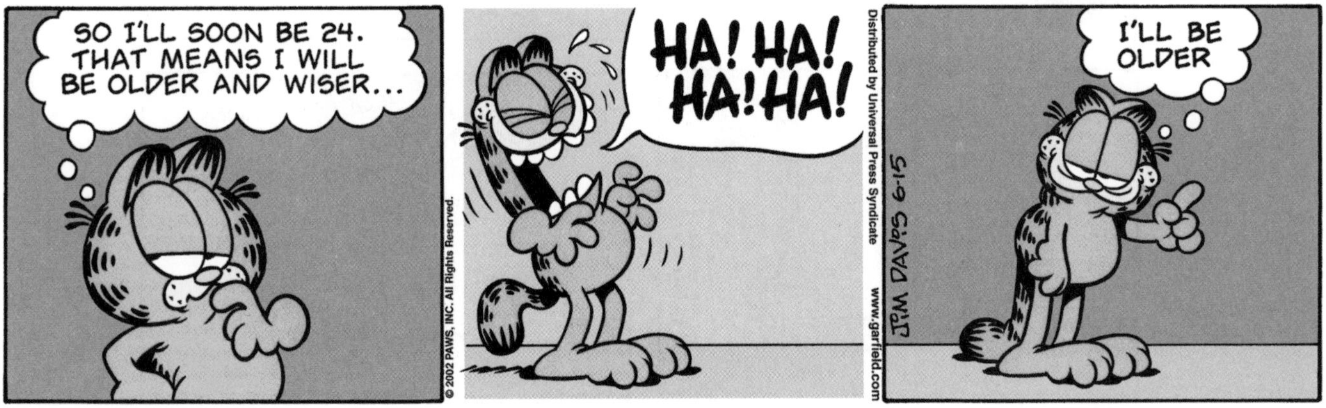
SO I'LL SOON BE 24. THAT MEANS I WILL BE OLDER AND WISER...
HA! HA! HA! HA!
I'LL BE OLDER
JIM DAVIS 6-15
© 2002 PAWS, INC. All Rights Reserved.
Distributed by Universal Press Syndicate
www.garfield.com

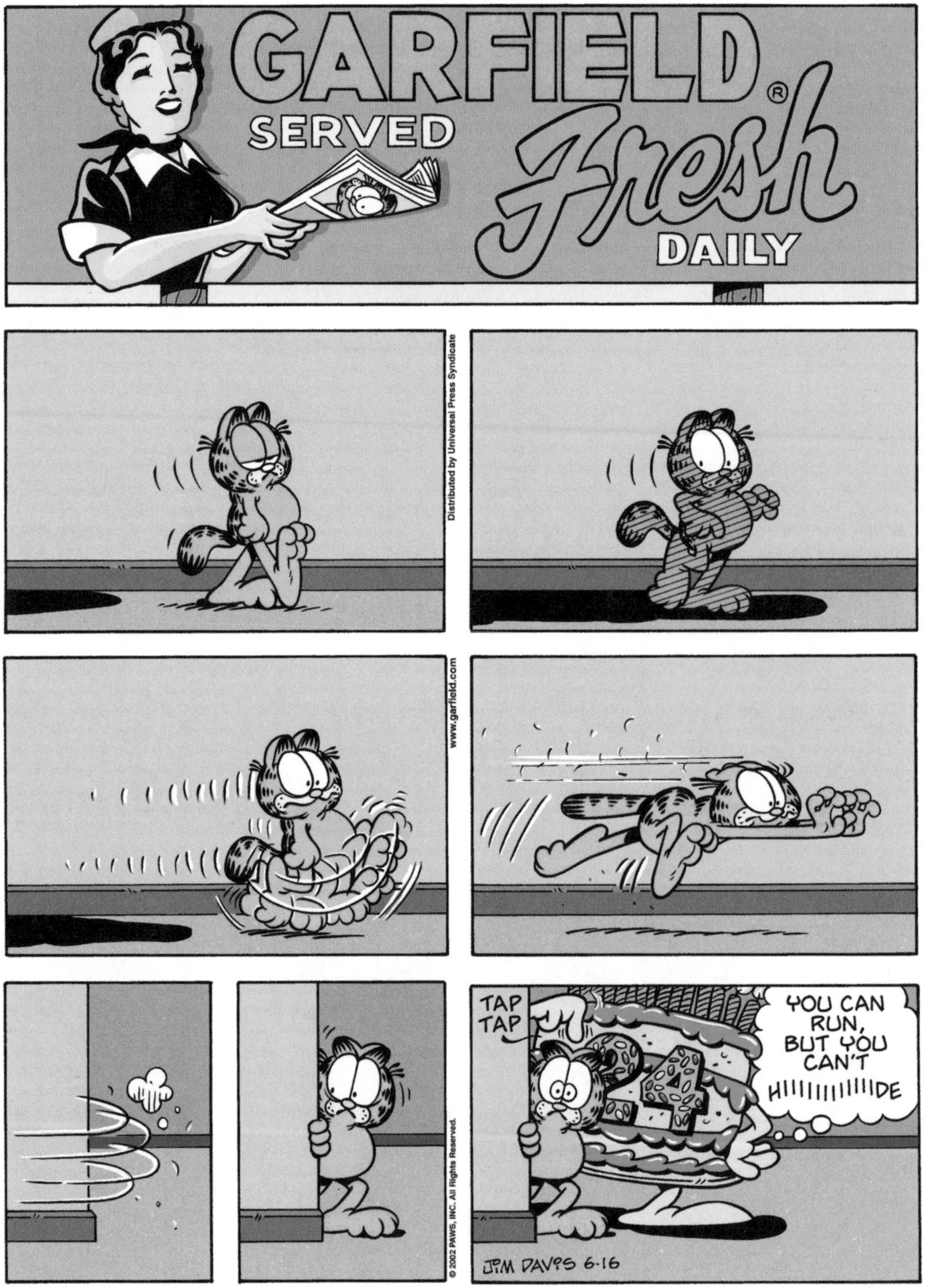
GARFIELD®
SERVED
Fresh
DAILY
Distributed by Universal Press Syndicate
www.garfield.com
© 2002 PAWS, INC. All Rights Reserved.
TAP TAP
YOU CAN RUN, BUT YOU CAN'T HIIIIIIIIIIIIDE
JIM DAVIS 6-16

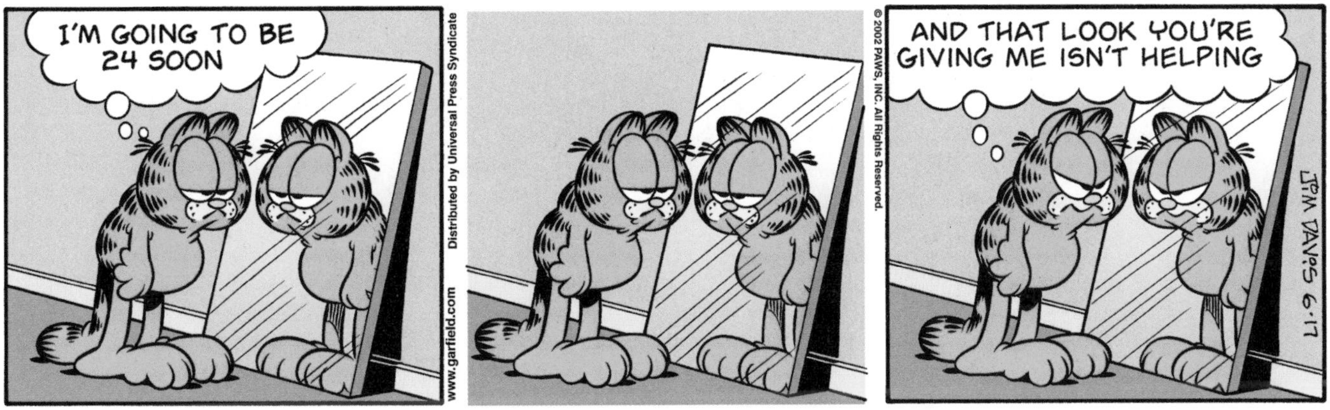
I'M GOING TO BE 24 SOON
AND THAT LOOK YOU'RE GIVING ME ISN'T HELPING
JIM DAVIS 6-17
www.garfield.com Distributed by Universal Press Syndicate
© 2002 PAWS, INC. All Rights Reserved.

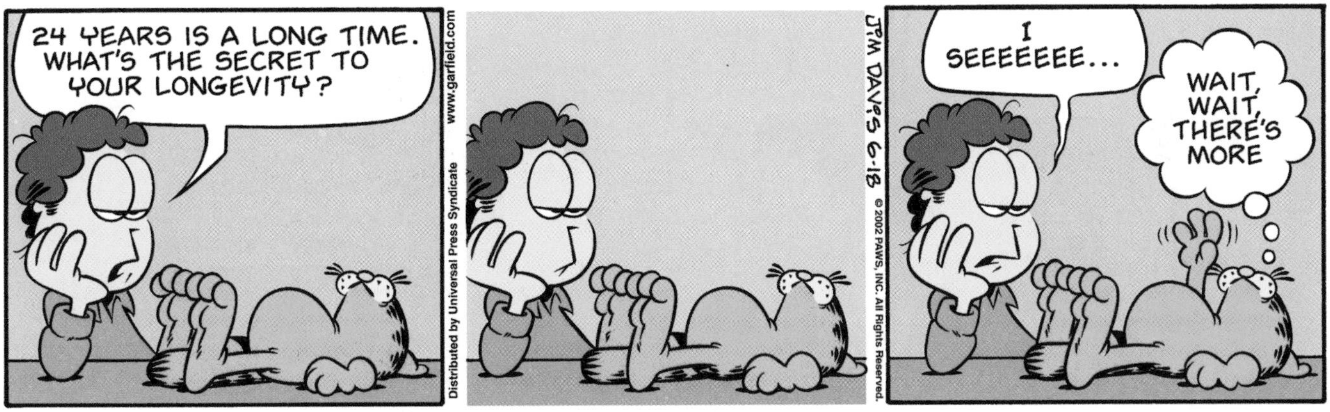
24 YEARS IS A LONG TIME. WHAT'S THE SECRET TO YOUR LONGEVITY?
I SEEEEEEE...
WAIT, WAIT, THERE'S MORE
JIM DAVIS 6-18
Distributed by Universal Press Syndicate www.garfield.com
© 2002 PAWS, INC. All Rights Reserved.

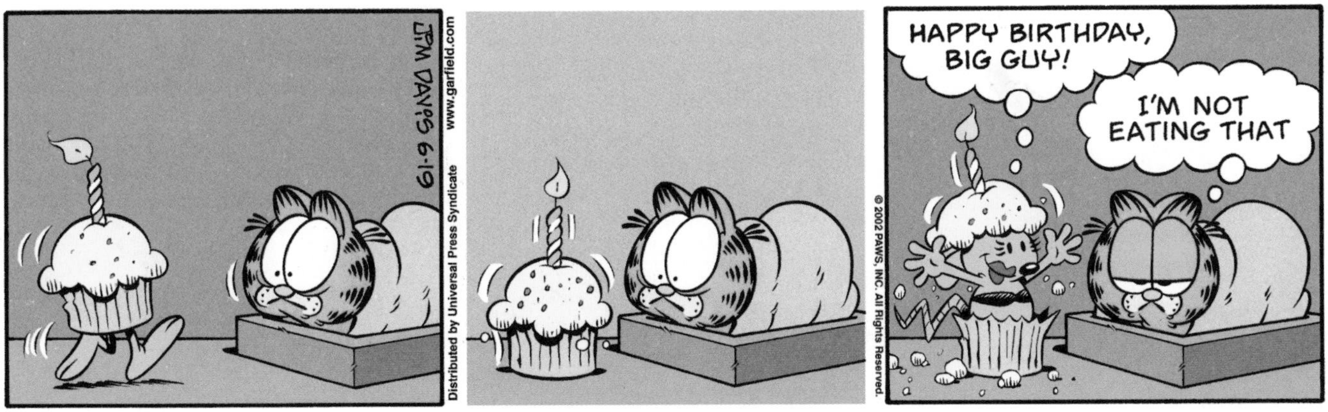
HAPPY BIRTHDAY, BIG GUY!
I'M NOT EATING THAT
JIM DAVIS 6-19
Distributed by Universal Press Syndicate www.garfield.com
© 2002 PAWS, INC. All Rights Reserved.

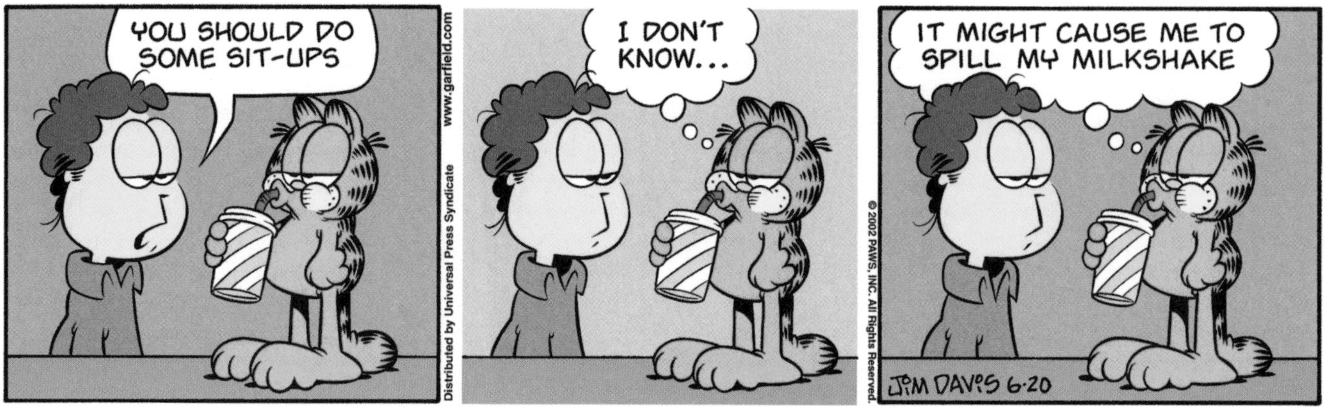
YOU SHOULD DO SOME SIT-UPS
I DON'T KNOW...
IT MIGHT CAUSE ME TO SPILL MY MILKSHAKE
JIM DAVIS 6-20
www.garfield.com
Distributed by Universal Press Syndicate
© 2002 PAWS, INC. All Rights Reserved.

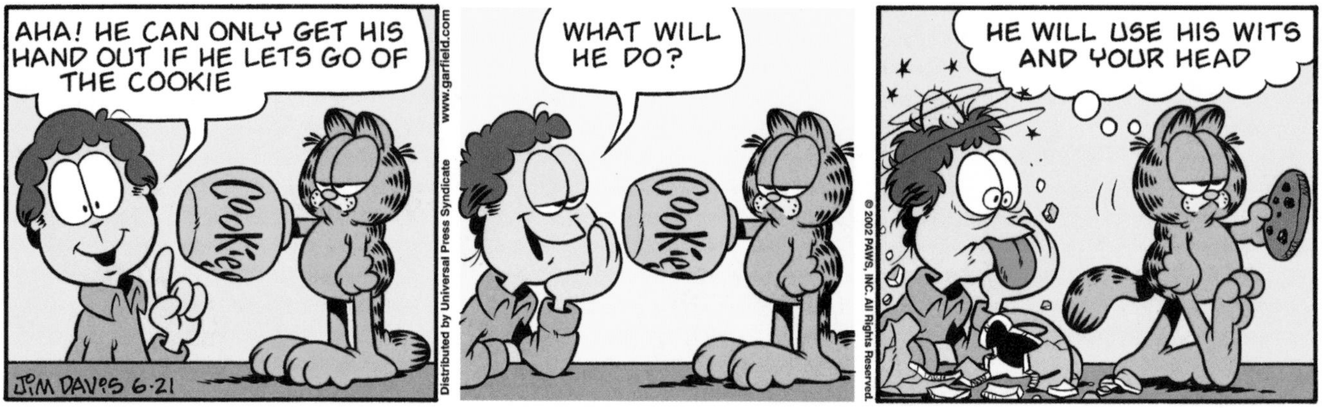
AHA! HE CAN ONLY GET HIS HAND OUT IF HE LETS GO OF THE COOKIE
COOKIES
JIM DAVIS 6-21
WHAT WILL HE DO?
HE WILL USE HIS WITS AND YOUR HEAD
www.garfield.com
Distributed by Universal Press Syndicate
© 2002 PAWS, INC. All Rights Reserved.

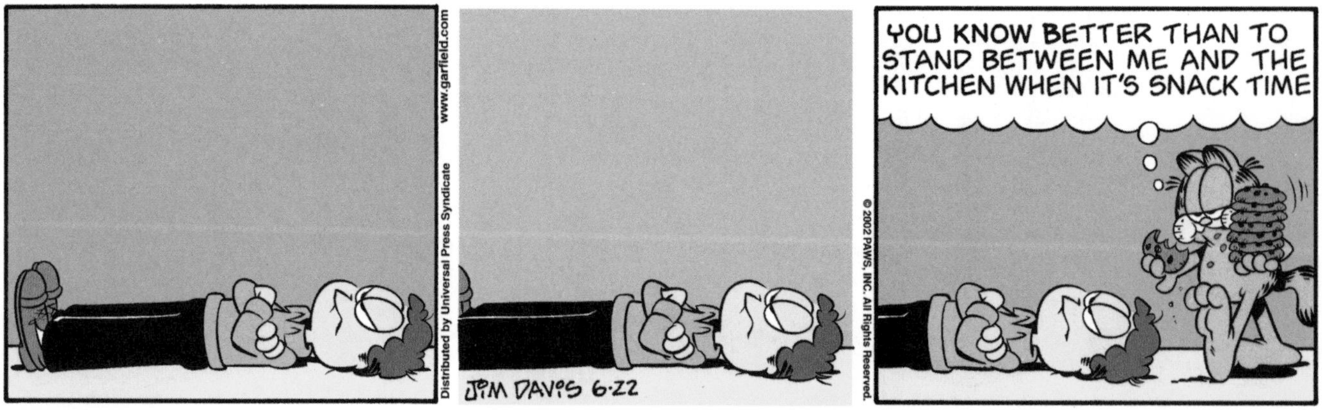
JIM DAVIS 6-22
YOU KNOW BETTER THAN TO STAND BETWEEN ME AND THE KITCHEN WHEN IT'S SNACK TIME
www.garfield.com
Distributed by Universal Press Syndicate
© 2002 PAWS, INC. All Rights Reserved.

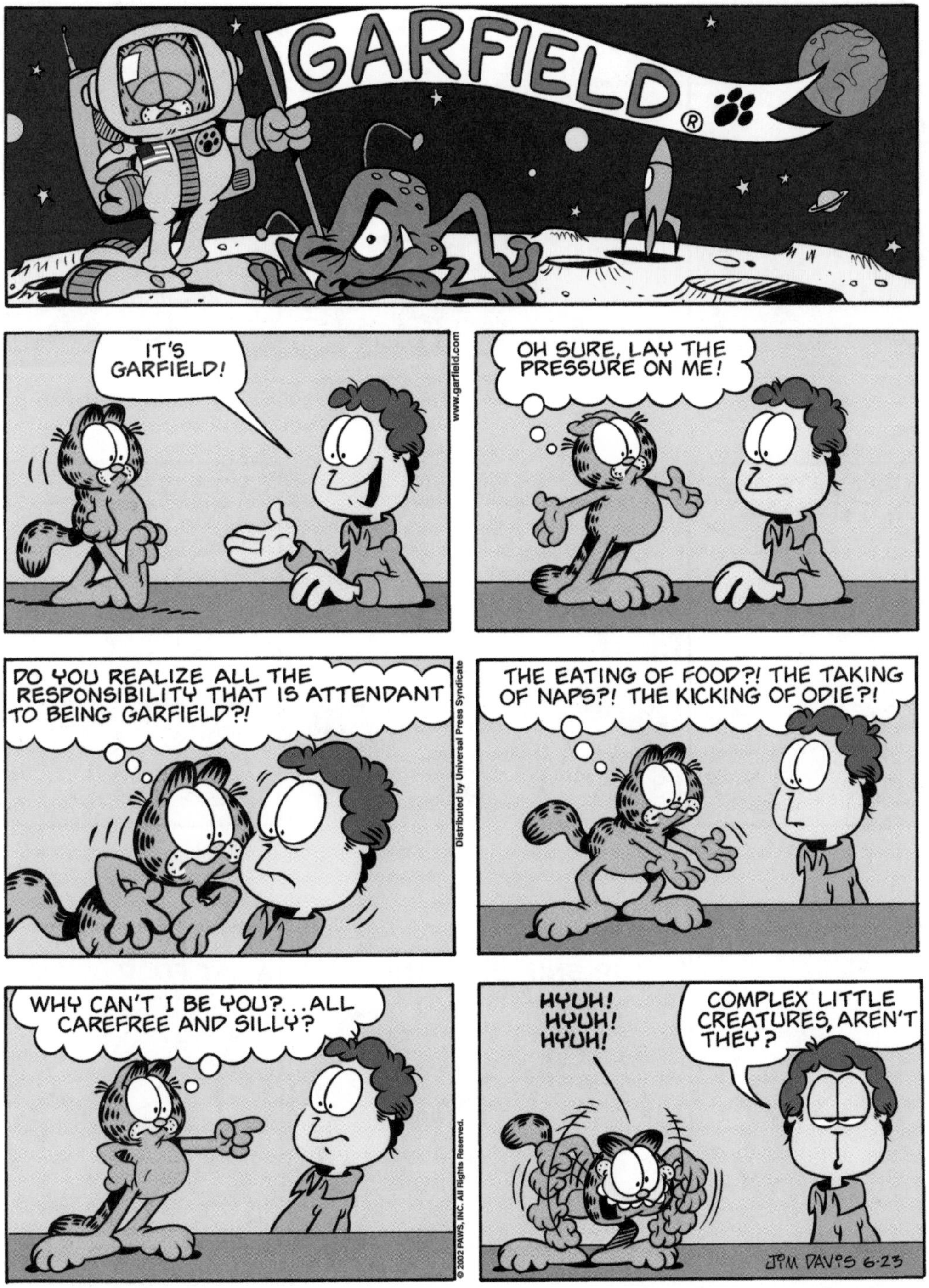
GARFIELD®
IT'S GARFIELD!
www.garfield.com
OH SURE, LAY THE PRESSURE ON ME!
DO YOU REALIZE ALL THE RESPONSIBILITY THAT IS ATTENDANT TO BEING GARFIELD?!
Distributed by Universal Press Syndicate
THE EATING OF FOOD?! THE TAKING OF NAPS?! THE KICKING OF ODIE?!
WHY CAN'T I BE YOU?...ALL CAREFREE AND SILLY?
© 2002 PAWS, INC. All Rights Reserved.
HYUH! HYUH! HYUH!
COMPLEX LITTLE CREATURES, AREN'T THEY?
JIM DAVIS 6-23

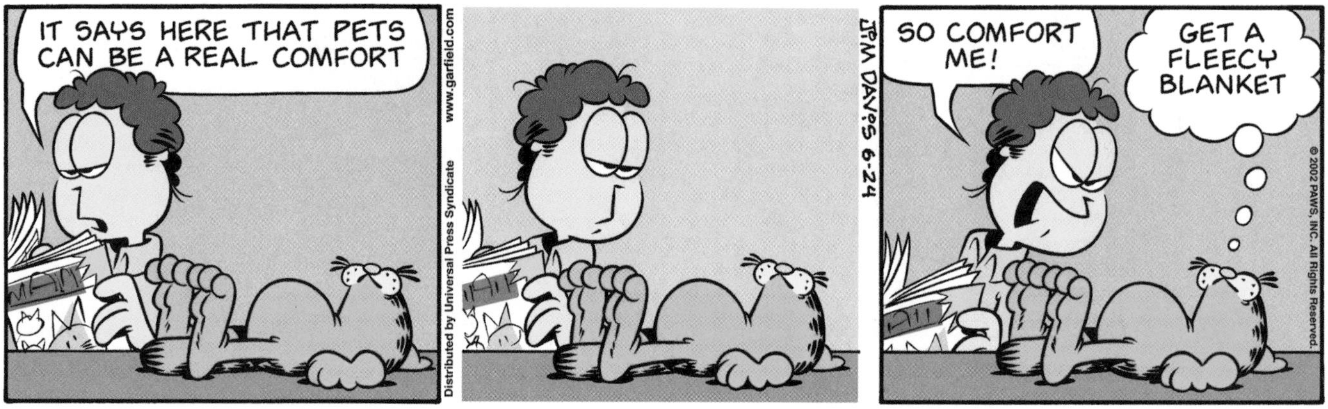
IT SAYS HERE THAT PETS CAN BE A REAL COMFORT
SO COMFORT ME!
GET A FLEECY BLANKET
JIM DAVIS 6-24
Distributed by Universal Press Syndicate www.garfield.com
© 2002 PAWS, INC. All Rights Reserved.

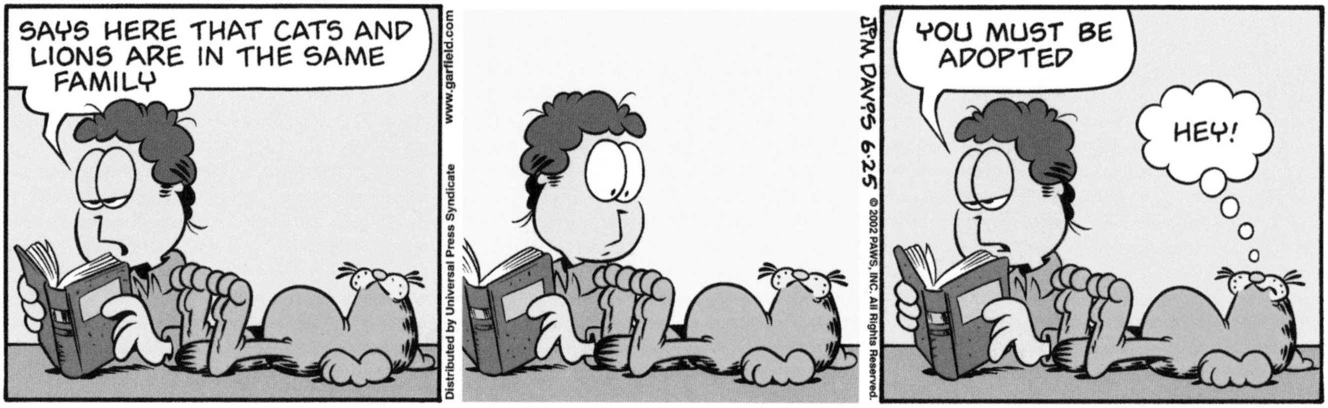
SAYS HERE THAT CATS AND LIONS ARE IN THE SAME FAMILY
YOU MUST BE ADOPTED
HEY!
JIM DAVIS 6-25
Distributed by Universal Press Syndicate www.garfield.com
© 2002 PAWS, INC. All Rights Reserved.

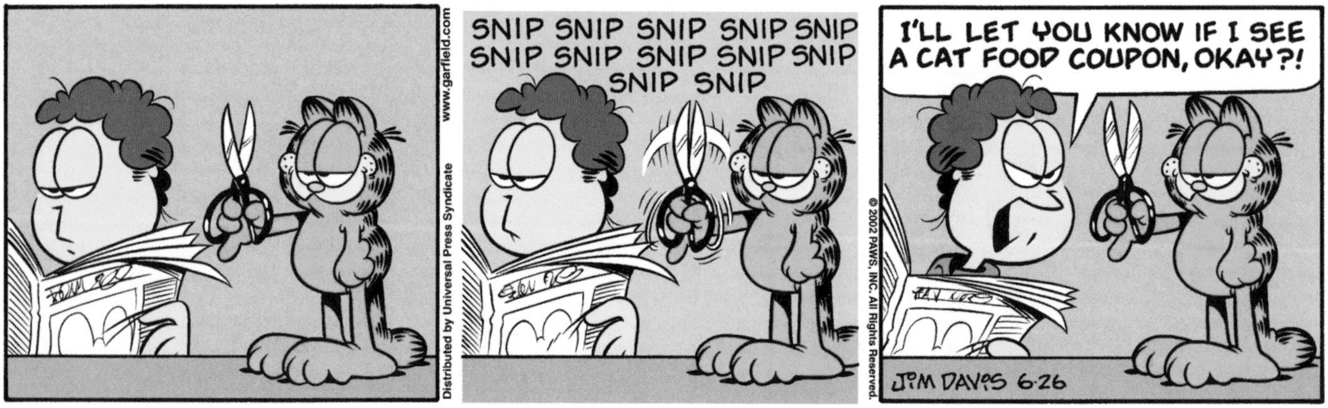
SNIP SNIP SNIP SNIP SNIP SNIP SNIP SNIP SNIP SNIP SNIP SNIP
I'LL LET YOU KNOW IF I SEE A CAT FOOD COUPON, OKAY?!
JIM DAVIS 6-26
Distributed by Universal Press Syndicate www.garfield.com
© 2002 PAWS, INC. All Rights Reserved.

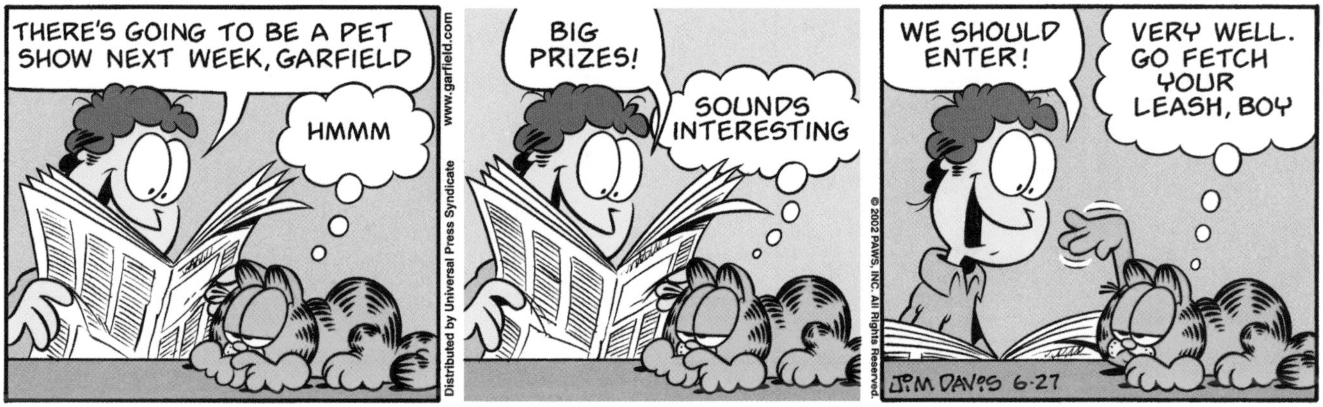
THERE'S GOING TO BE A PET SHOW NEXT WEEK, GARFIELD
HMMM
www.garfield.com
Distributed by Universal Press Syndicate
BIG PRIZES!
SOUNDS INTERESTING
© 2002 PAWS, INC. All Rights Reserved.
WE SHOULD ENTER!
VERY WELL. GO FETCH YOUR LEASH, BOY
JIM DAVIS 6-27

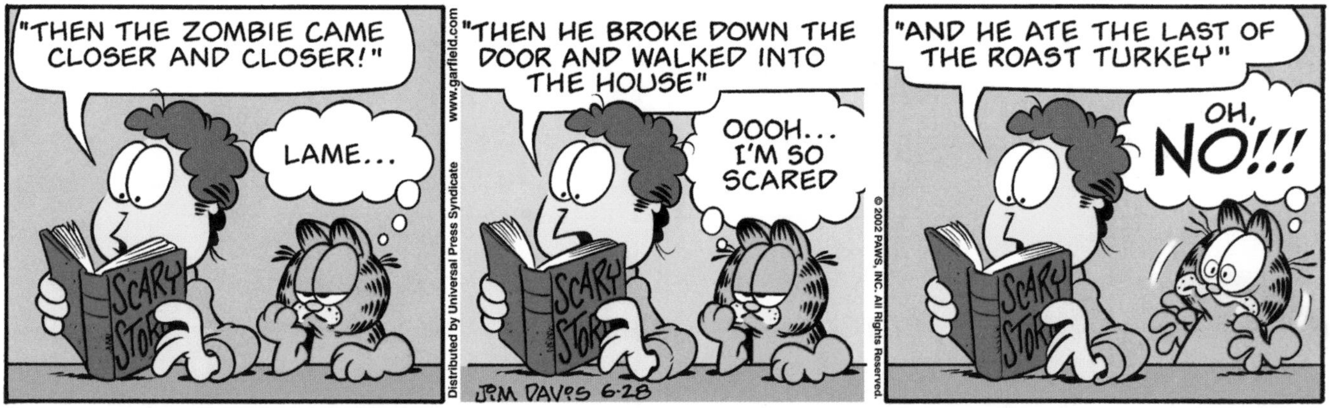
"THEN THE ZOMBIE CAME CLOSER AND CLOSER!"
LAME...
SCARY STORIES
www.garfield.com
Distributed by Universal Press Syndicate
"THEN HE BROKE DOWN THE DOOR AND WALKED INTO THE HOUSE"
OOOH... I'M SO SCARED
JIM DAVIS 6-28
© 2002 PAWS, INC. All Rights Reserved.
"AND HE ATE THE LAST OF THE ROAST TURKEY"
OH, NO!!!

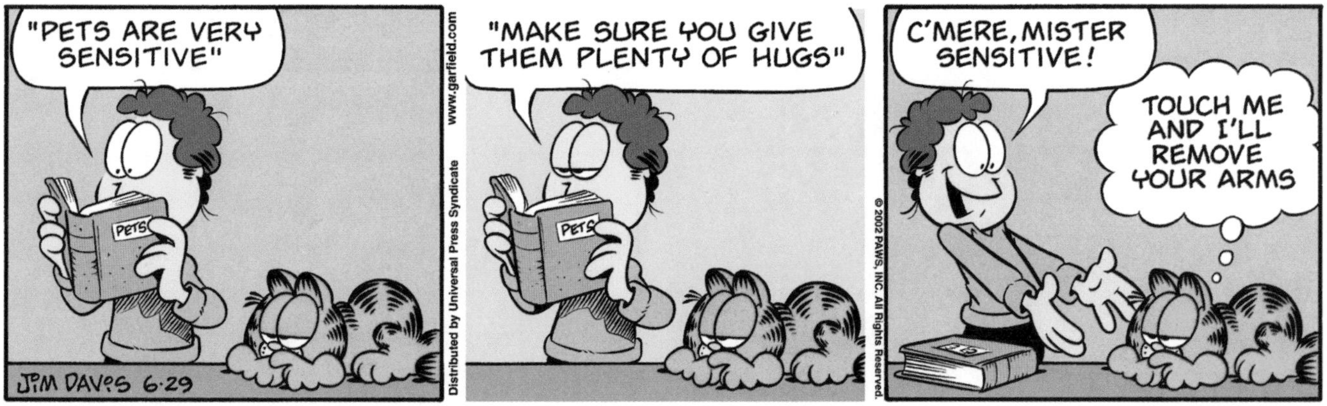
"PETS ARE VERY SENSITIVE"
PETS
JIM DAVIS 6-29
www.garfield.com
Distributed by Universal Press Syndicate
"MAKE SURE YOU GIVE THEM PLENTY OF HUGS"
© 2002 PAWS, INC. All Rights Reserved.
C'MERE, MISTER SENSITIVE!
TOUCH ME AND I'LL REMOVE YOUR ARMS

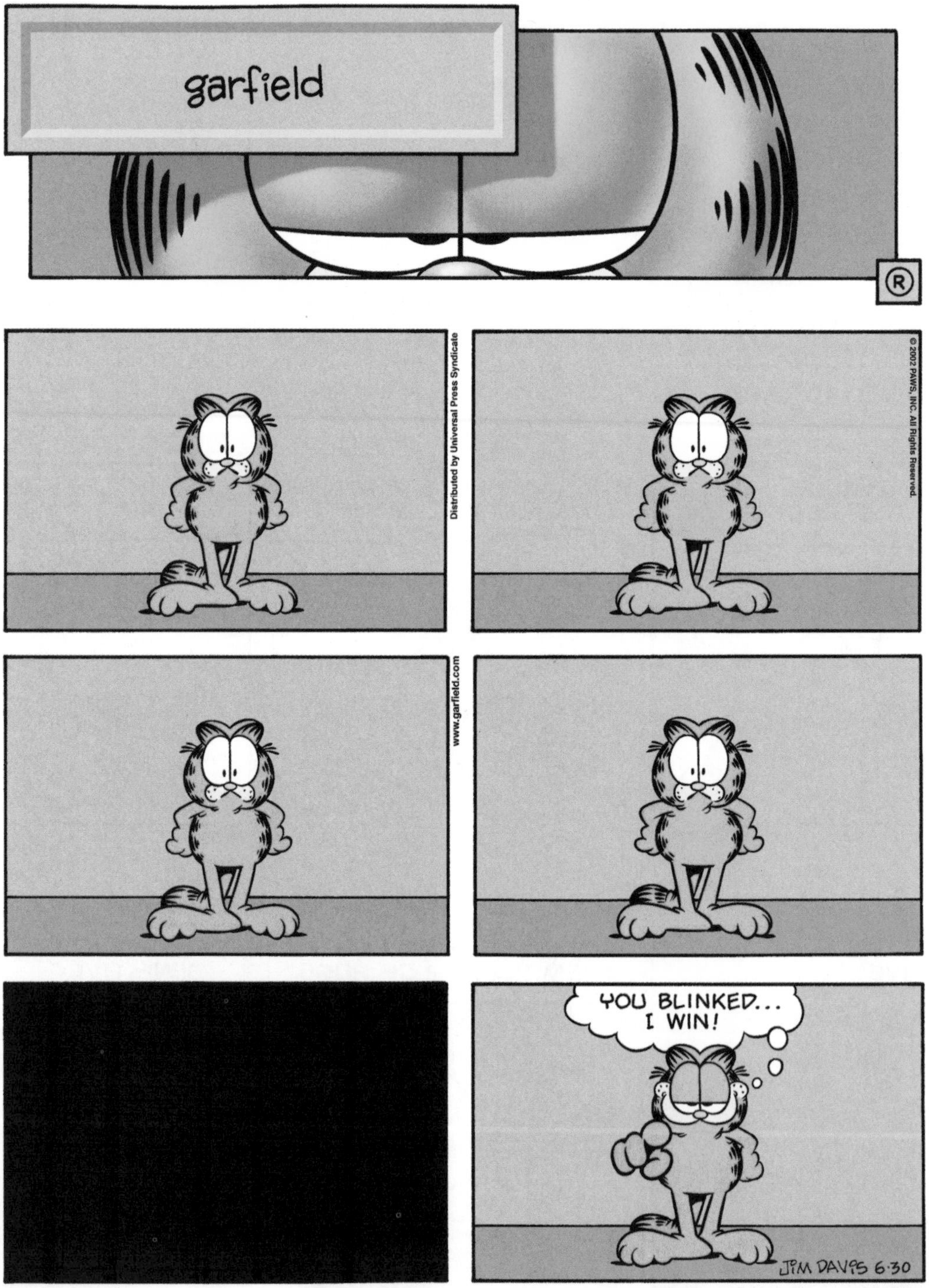
garfield
Distributed by Universal Press Syndicate
© 2002 PAWS, INC. All Rights Reserved.
www.garfield.com
YOU BLINKED... I WIN!
JIM DAVIS 6·30

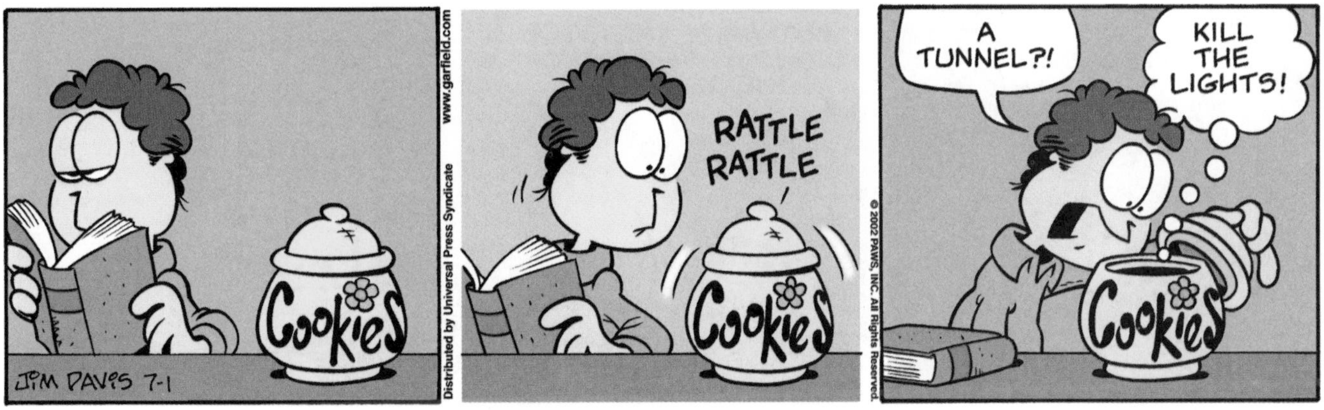
Cookies
JIM DAVIS 7-1
www.garfield.com
Distributed by Universal Press Syndicate
RATTLE RATTLE
Cookies
© 2002 PAWS, INC. All Rights Reserved.
A TUNNEL?!
KILL THE LIGHTS!
Cookies

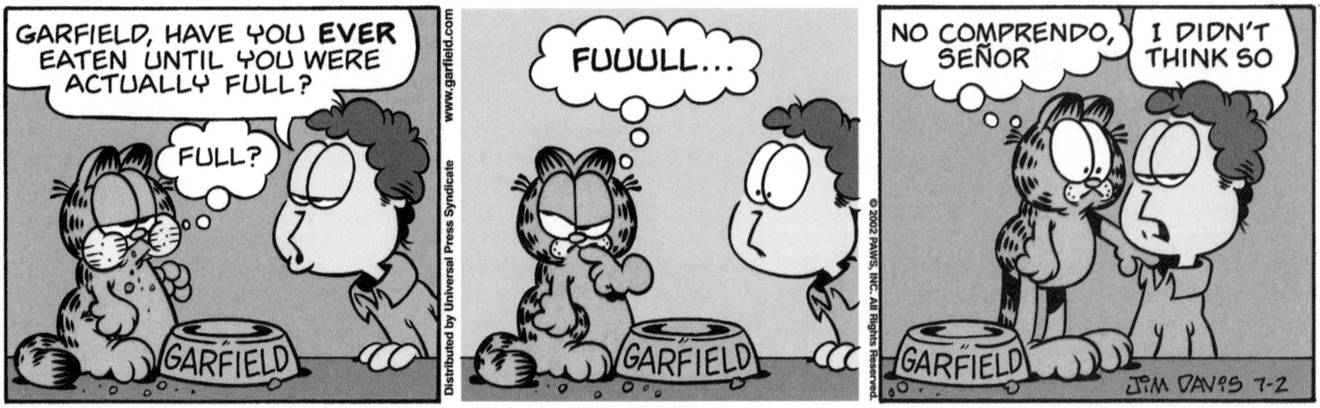
GARFIELD, HAVE YOU **EVER** EATEN UNTIL YOU WERE ACTUALLY FULL?
FULL?
GARFIELD
www.garfield.com
Distributed by Universal Press Syndicate
FUUULL...
GARFIELD
© 2002 PAWS, INC. All Rights Reserved.
NO COMPRENDO, SEÑOR
I DIDN'T THINK SO
GARFIELD
JIM DAVIS 7-2

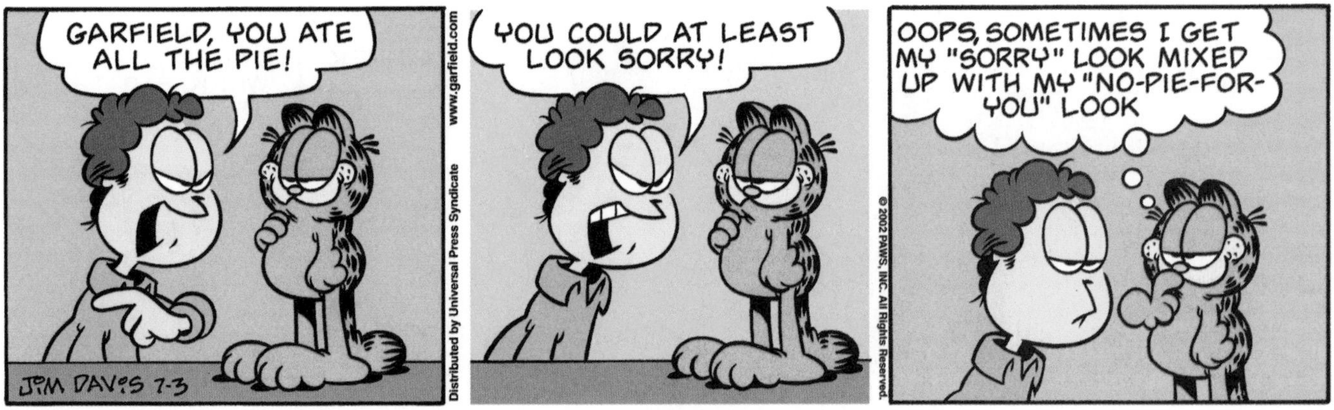
GARFIELD, YOU ATE ALL THE PIE!
JIM DAVIS 7-3
www.garfield.com
Distributed by Universal Press Syndicate
YOU COULD AT LEAST LOOK SORRY!
© 2002 PAWS, INC. All Rights Reserved.
OOPS, SOMETIMES I GET MY "SORRY" LOOK MIXED UP WITH MY "NO-PIE-FOR-YOU" LOOK

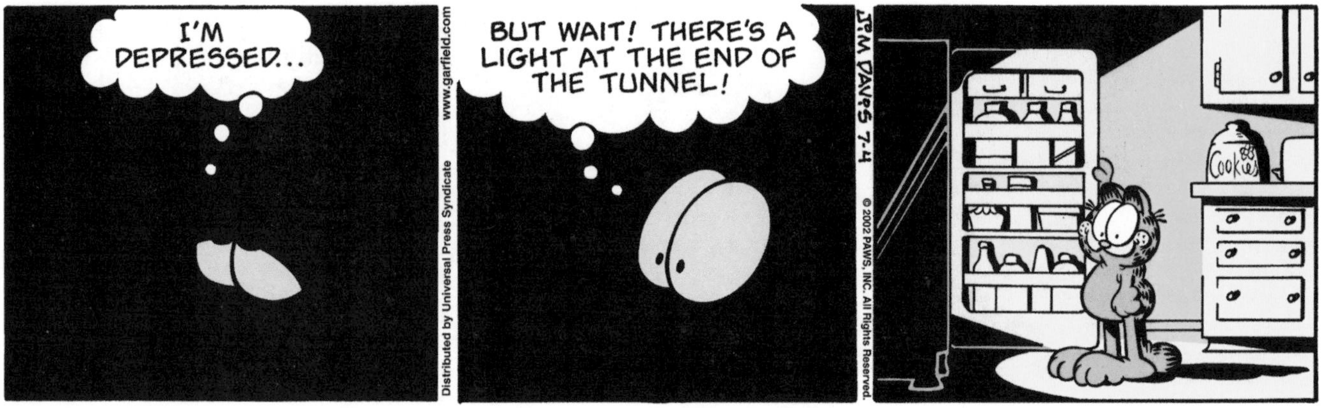
I'M DEPRESSED...
BUT WAIT! THERE'S A LIGHT AT THE END OF THE TUNNEL!
JIM DAVIS 7-4
www.garfield.com
Distributed by Universal Press Syndicate
© 2002 PAWS, INC. All Rights Reserved.
COOKIES

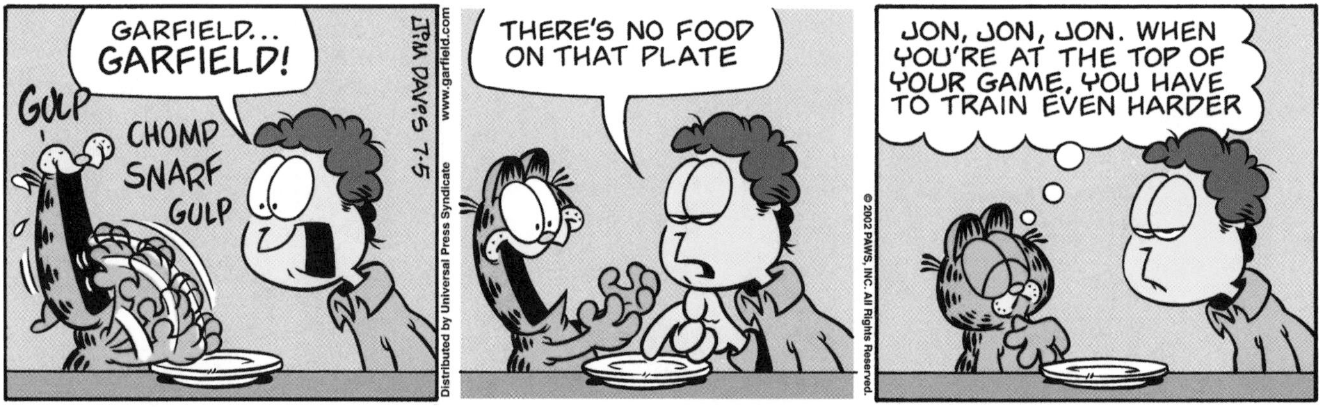
GARFIELD... GARFIELD!
GULP
CHOMP
SNARF
GULP
JIM DAVIS 7-5
www.garfield.com
Distributed by Universal Press Syndicate
THERE'S NO FOOD ON THAT PLATE
© 2002 PAWS, INC. All Rights Reserved.
JON, JON, JON. WHEN YOU'RE AT THE TOP OF YOUR GAME, YOU HAVE TO TRAIN EVEN HARDER

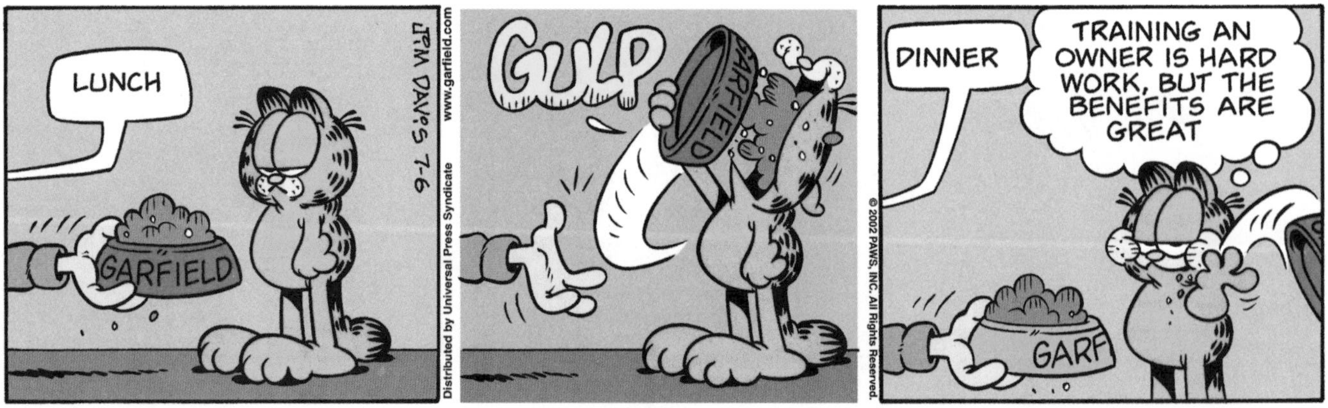
LUNCH
GARFIELD
JIM DAVIS 7-6
www.garfield.com
Distributed by Universal Press Syndicate
GULP
GARFIELD
© 2002 PAWS, INC. All Rights Reserved.
DINNER
TRAINING AN OWNER IS HARD WORK, BUT THE BENEFITS ARE GREAT
GARF

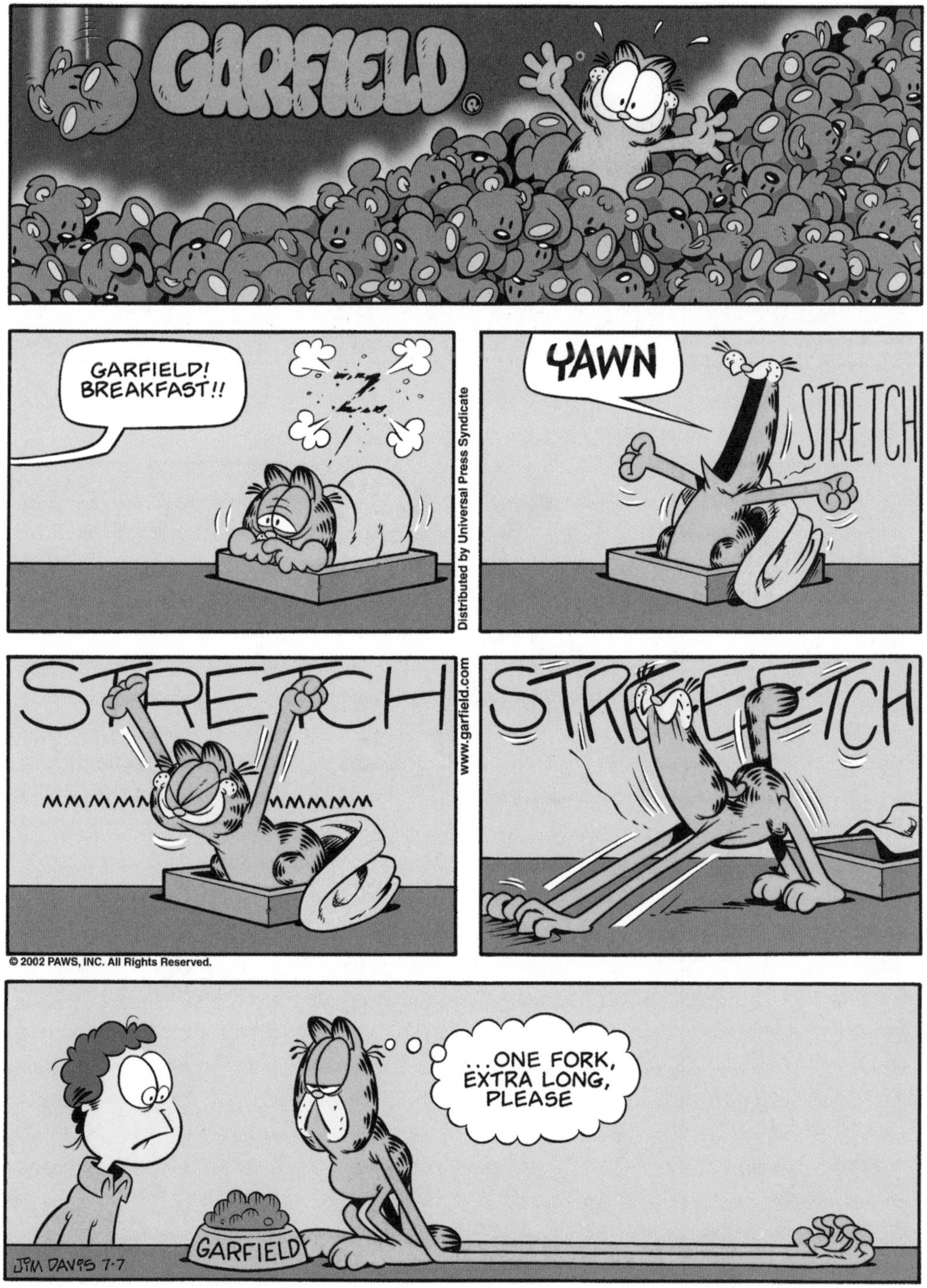
GARFIELD
GARFIELD! BREAKFAST!!
Z
YAWN
STRETCH
STRETCH
MMMMM MMMMM
STREEETCH
...ONE FORK, EXTRA LONG, PLEASE
GARFIELD
JIM DAVIS 7-7

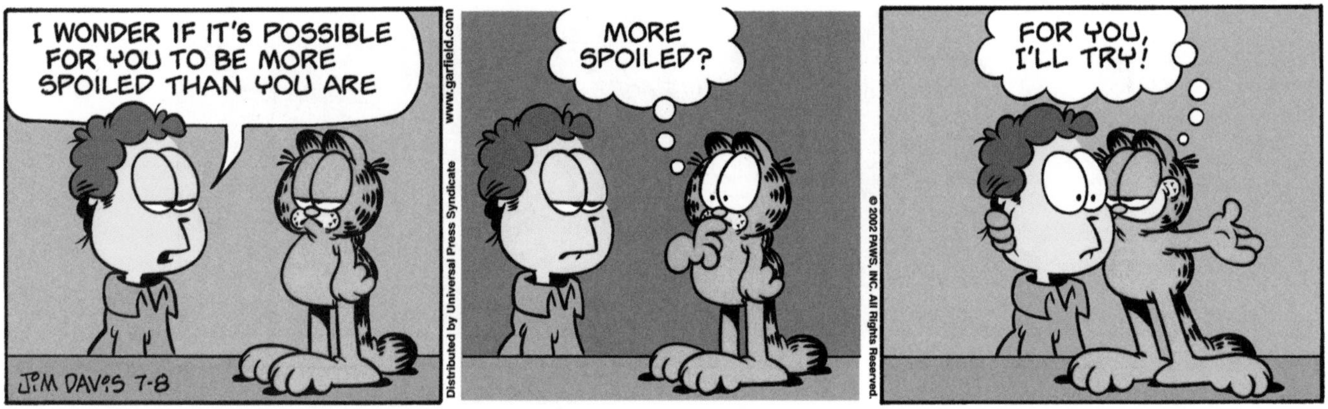
I WONDER IF IT'S POSSIBLE FOR YOU TO BE MORE SPOILED THAN YOU ARE
JIM DAVIS 7-8
www.garfield.com
Distributed by Universal Press Syndicate
MORE SPOILED?
© 2002 PAWS, INC. All Rights Reserved.
FOR YOU, I'LL TRY!

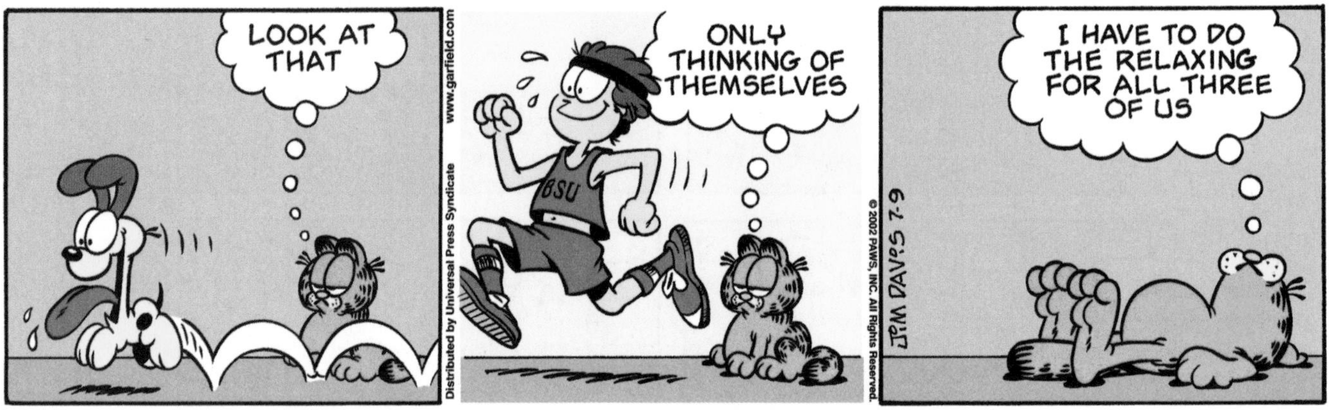
LOOK AT THAT
www.garfield.com
Distributed by Universal Press Syndicate
ONLY THINKING OF THEMSELVES
BSU
© 2002 PAWS, INC. All Rights Reserved.
JIM DAVIS 7-9
I HAVE TO DO THE RELAXING FOR ALL THREE OF US

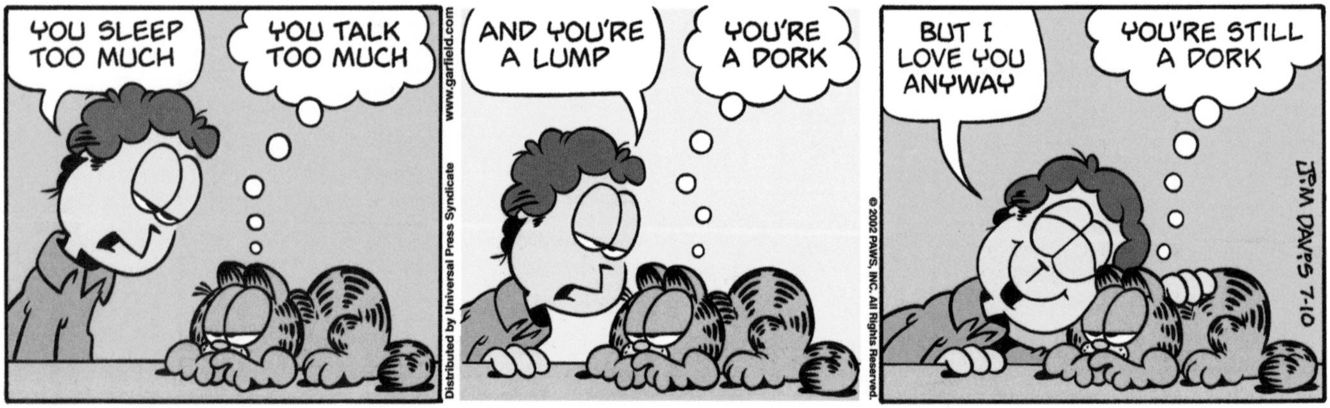
YOU SLEEP TOO MUCH
YOU TALK TOO MUCH
www.garfield.com
Distributed by Universal Press Syndicate
AND YOU'RE A LUMP
YOU'RE A DORK
© 2002 PAWS, INC. All Rights Reserved.
BUT I LOVE YOU ANYWAY
YOU'RE STILL A DORK
JIM DAVIS 7-10

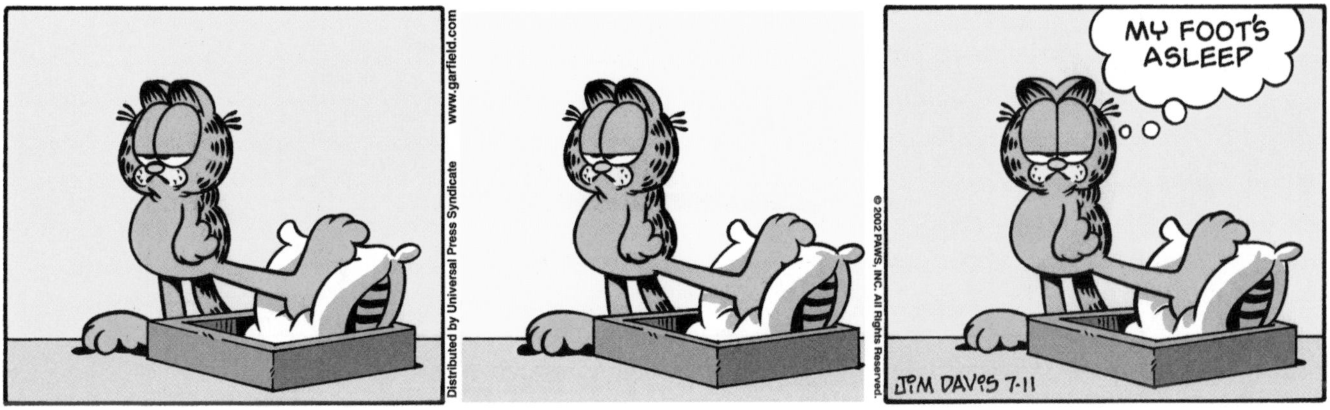
www.garfield.com Distributed by Universal Press Syndicate
MY FOOT'S ASLEEP
© 2002 PAWS, INC. All Rights Reserved.
JIM DAVIS 7-11

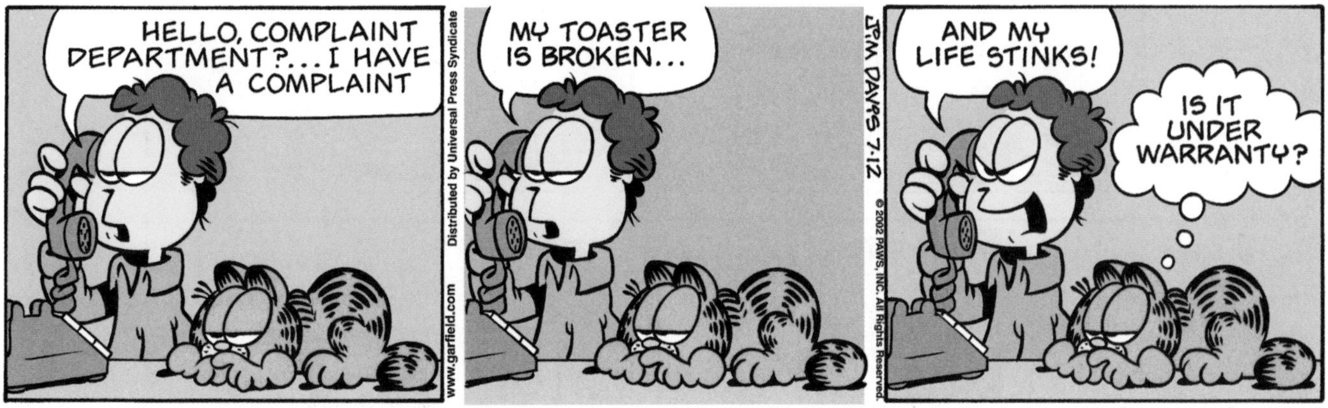
HELLO, COMPLAINT DEPARTMENT?... I HAVE A COMPLAINT
Distributed by Universal Press Syndicate www.garfield.com
MY TOASTER IS BROKEN...
JIM DAVIS 7-12
© 2002 PAWS, INC. All Rights Reserved.
AND MY LIFE STINKS!
IS IT UNDER WARRANTY?

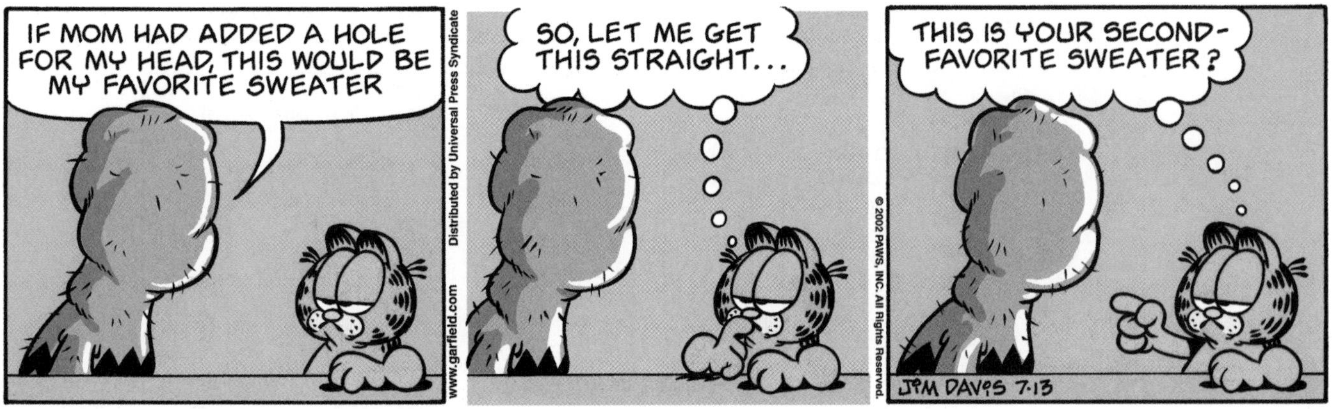
IF MOM HAD ADDED A HOLE FOR MY HEAD, THIS WOULD BE MY FAVORITE SWEATER
www.garfield.com Distributed by Universal Press Syndicate
SO, LET ME GET THIS STRAIGHT...
© 2002 PAWS, INC. All Rights Reserved.
THIS IS YOUR SECOND-FAVORITE SWEATER?
JIM DAVIS 7-13

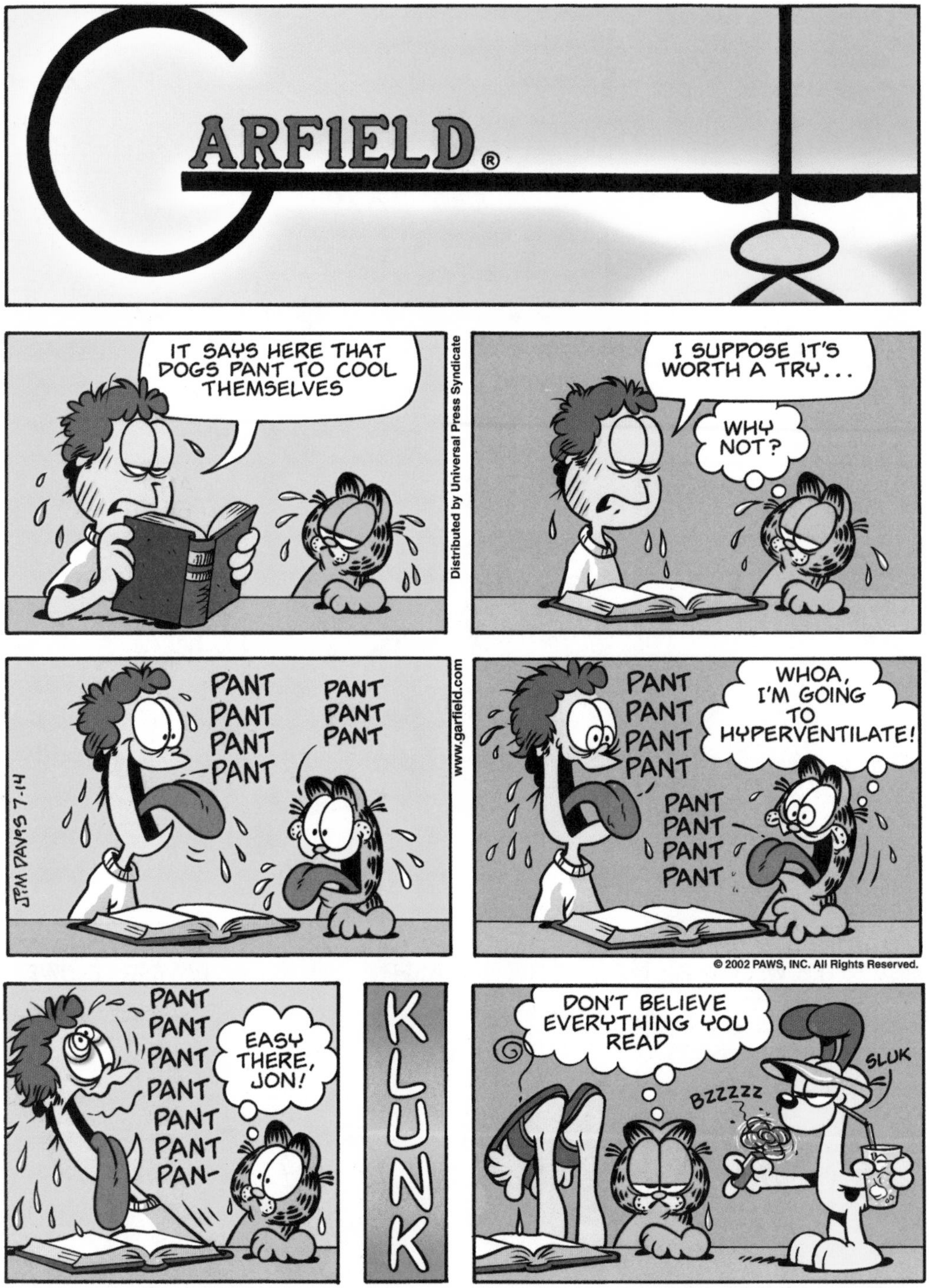
GARFIELD®
IT SAYS HERE THAT DOGS PANT TO COOL THEMSELVES
Distributed by Universal Press Syndicate
I SUPPOSE IT'S WORTH A TRY...
WHY NOT?
JPM DAVIS 7-14
PANT PANT PANT PANT PANT
PANT PANT PANT
www.garfield.com
PANT PANT PANT PANT PANT
WHOA, I'M GOING TO HYPERVENTILATE!
PANT PANT PANT PANT
© 2002 PAWS, INC. All Rights Reserved.
PANT PANT PANT PANT PANT PANT PAN-
EASY THERE, JON!
KLUNK
DON'T BELIEVE EVERYTHING YOU READ
BZZZZZ
SLUK

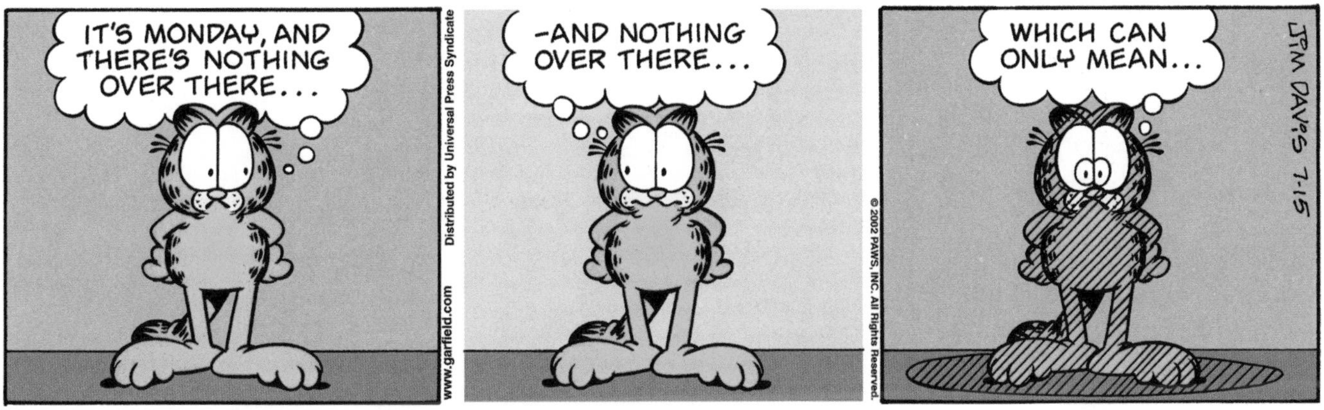
IT'S MONDAY, AND THERE'S NOTHING OVER THERE...
www.garfield.com
Distributed by Universal Press Syndicate
-AND NOTHING OVER THERE...
© 2002 PAWS, INC. All Rights Reserved.
WHICH CAN ONLY MEAN...
JIM DAVIS 7-15

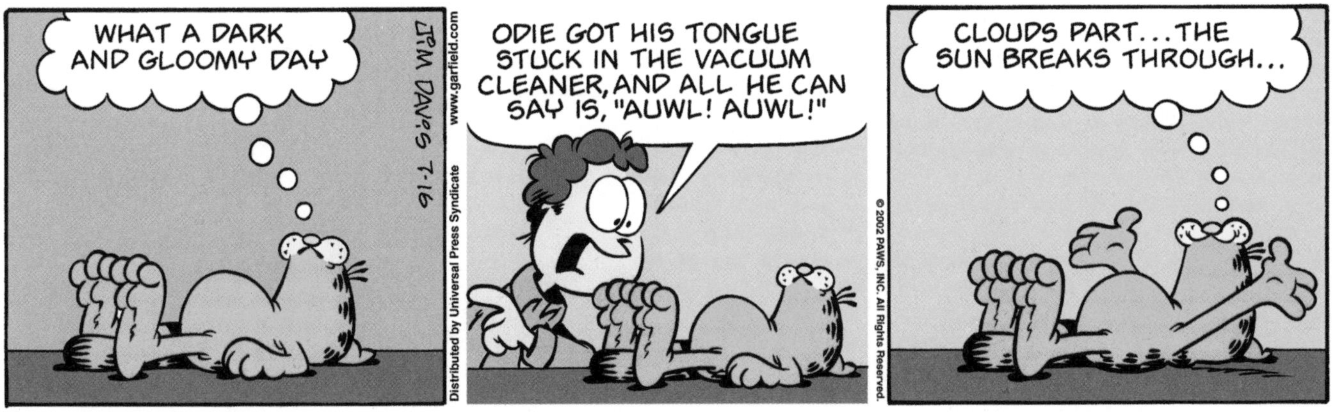
WHAT A DARK AND GLOOMY DAY
JIM DAVIS 7-16
www.garfield.com
Distributed by Universal Press Syndicate
ODIE GOT HIS TONGUE STUCK IN THE VACUUM CLEANER, AND ALL HE CAN SAY IS, "AUWL! AUWL!"
© 2002 PAWS, INC. All Rights Reserved.
CLOUDS PART...THE SUN BREAKS THROUGH...

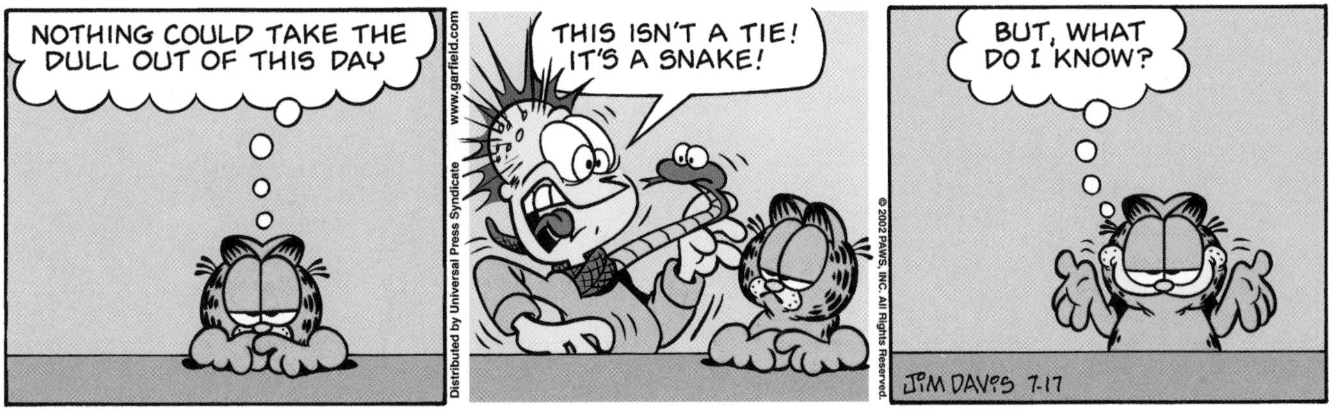
NOTHING COULD TAKE THE DULL OUT OF THIS DAY
www.garfield.com
Distributed by Universal Press Syndicate
THIS ISN'T A TIE! IT'S A SNAKE!
© 2002 PAWS, INC. All Rights Reserved.
BUT, WHAT DO I KNOW?
JIM DAVIS 7-17

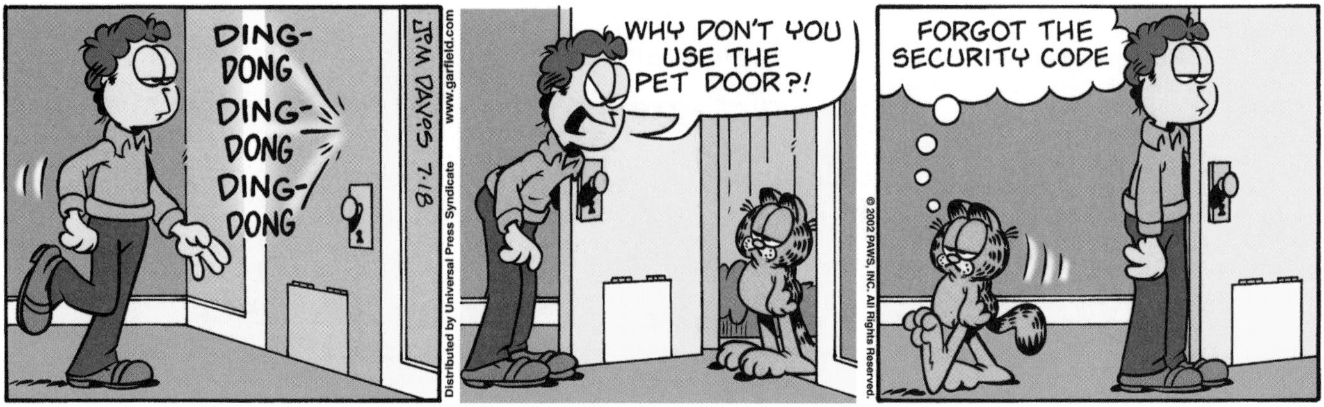
DING-
DONG
DING-
DONG
DING-
DONG
JIM DAVIS 7-18
www.garfield.com
Distributed by Universal Press Syndicate
WHY DON'T YOU USE THE PET DOOR?!
© 2002 PAWS, INC. All Rights Reserved.
FORGOT THE SECURITY CODE

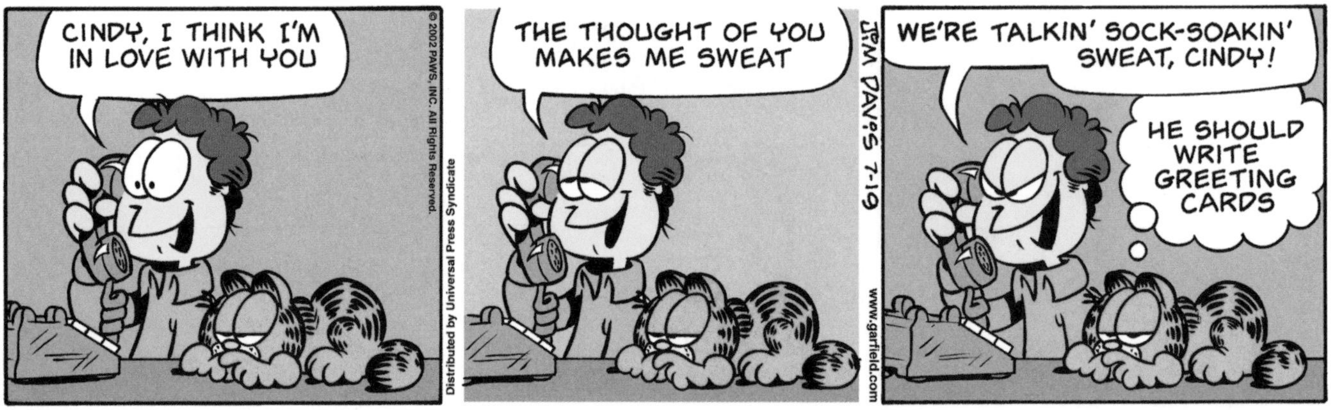
CINDY, I THINK I'M IN LOVE WITH YOU
© 2002 PAWS, INC. All Rights Reserved.
Distributed by Universal Press Syndicate
THE THOUGHT OF YOU MAKES ME SWEAT
JIM DAVIS 7-19
www.garfield.com
WE'RE TALKIN' SOCK-SOAKIN' SWEAT, CINDY!
HE SHOULD WRITE GREETING CARDS

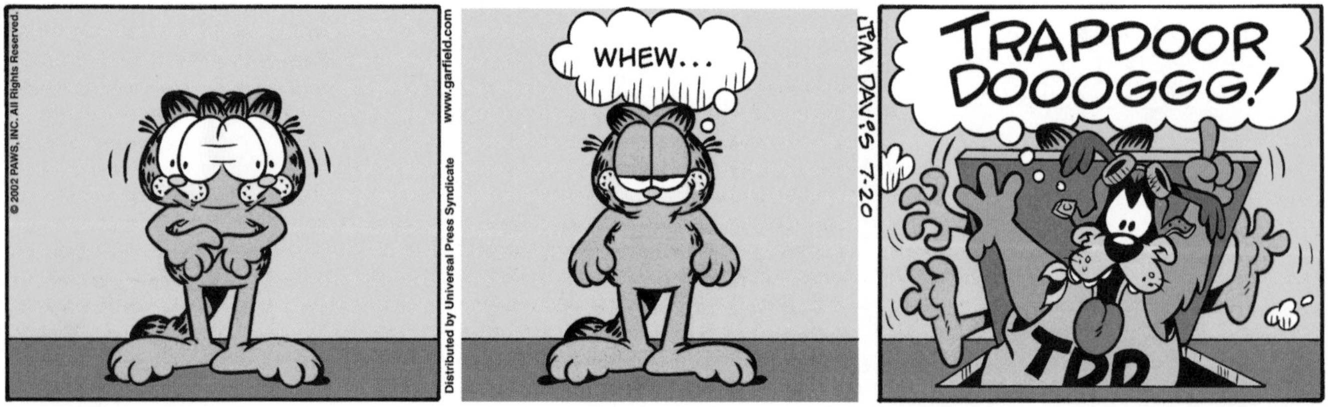
© 2002 PAWS, INC. All Rights Reserved.
www.garfield.com
Distributed by Universal Press Syndicate
WHEW...
JIM DAVIS 7-20
TRAPDOOR DOOOGGG!
TDD

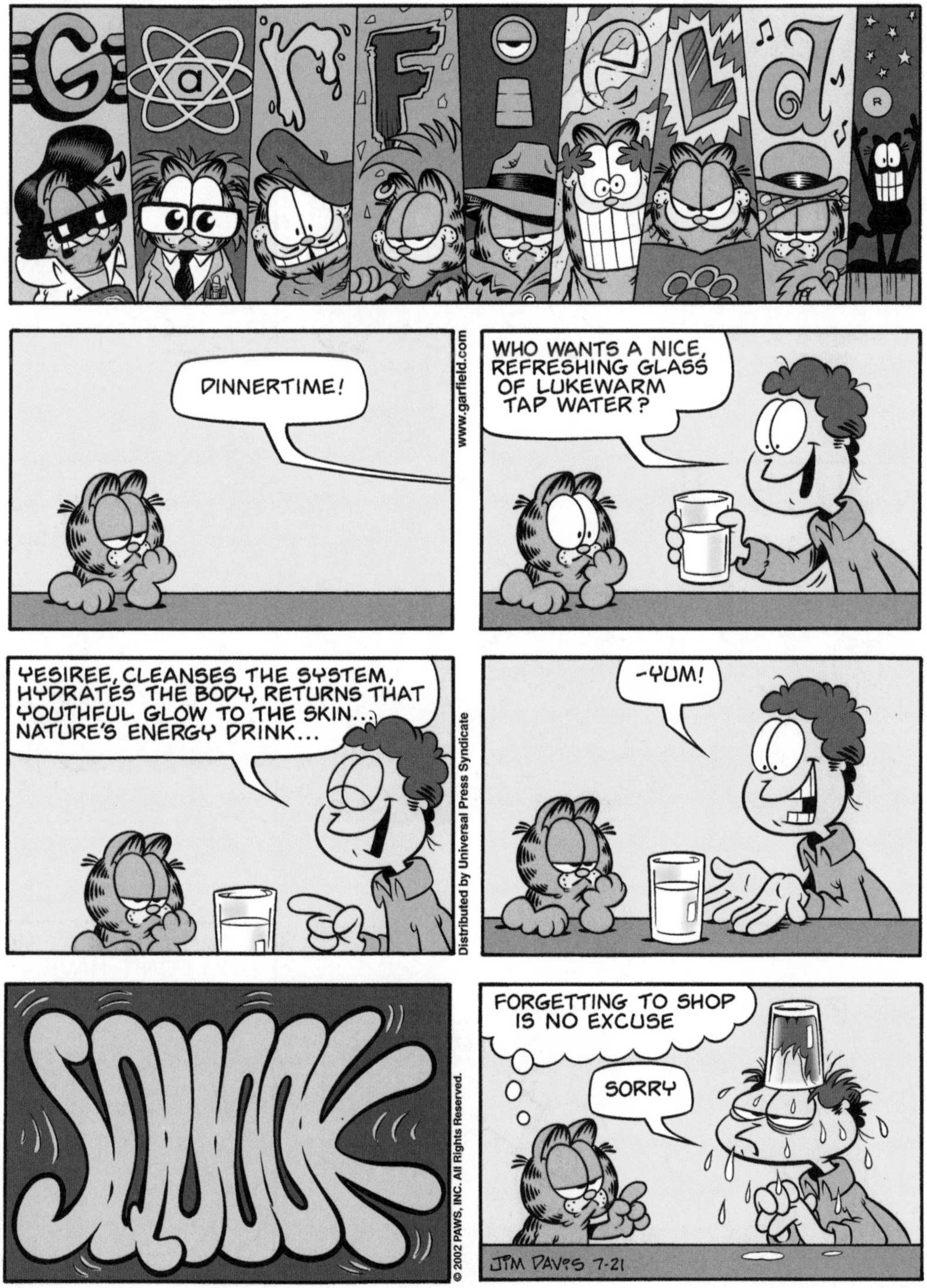
Garfield
DINNERTIME!
WHO WANTS A NICE, REFRESHING GLASS OF LUKEWARM TAP WATER?
YESIREE, CLEANSES THE SYSTEM, HYDRATES THE BODY, RETURNS THAT YOUTHFUL GLOW TO THE SKIN... NATURE'S ENERGY DRINK...
-YUM!
FORGETTING TO SHOP IS NO EXCUSE
SORRY
JIM DAVIS 7-21
www.garfield.com
Distributed by Universal Press Syndicate
© 2002 PAWS, INC. All Rights Reserved.

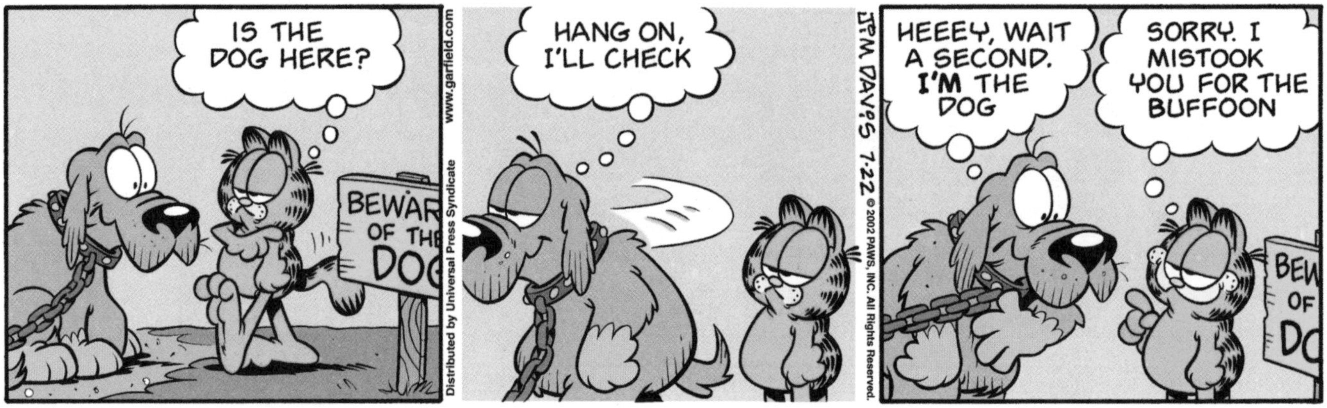
IS THE DOG HERE?
BEWARE OF THE DOG
www.garfield.com
Distributed by Universal Press Syndicate
HANG ON, I'LL CHECK
JIM DAVIS 7-22
© 2002 PAWS, INC. All Rights Reserved.
HEEEY, WAIT A SECOND. I'M THE DOG
SORRY. I MISTOOK YOU FOR THE BUFFOON

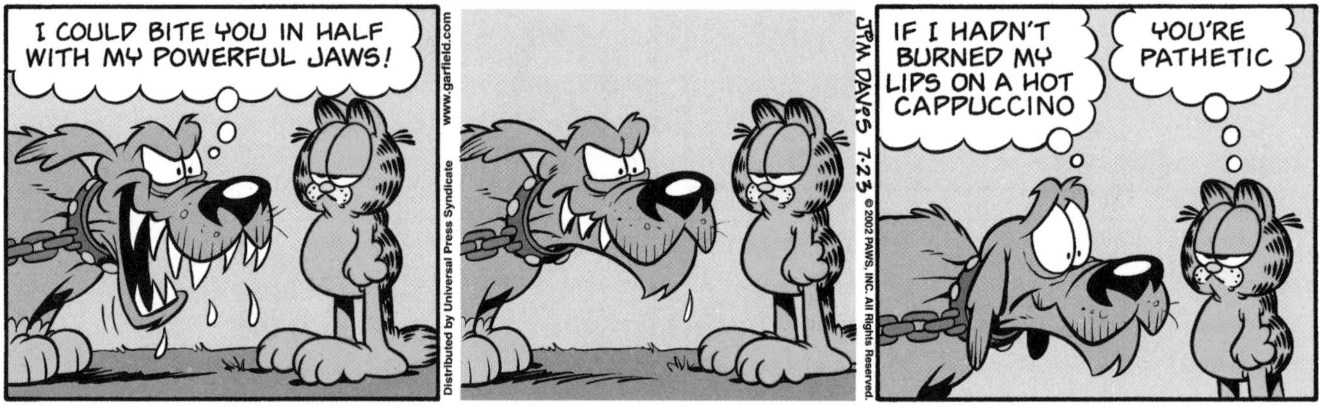
I COULD BITE YOU IN HALF WITH MY POWERFUL JAWS!
www.garfield.com
Distributed by Universal Press Syndicate
JIM DAVIS 7-23
© 2002 PAWS, INC. All Rights Reserved.
IF I HADN'T BURNED MY LIPS ON A HOT CAPPUCCINO
YOU'RE PATHETIC

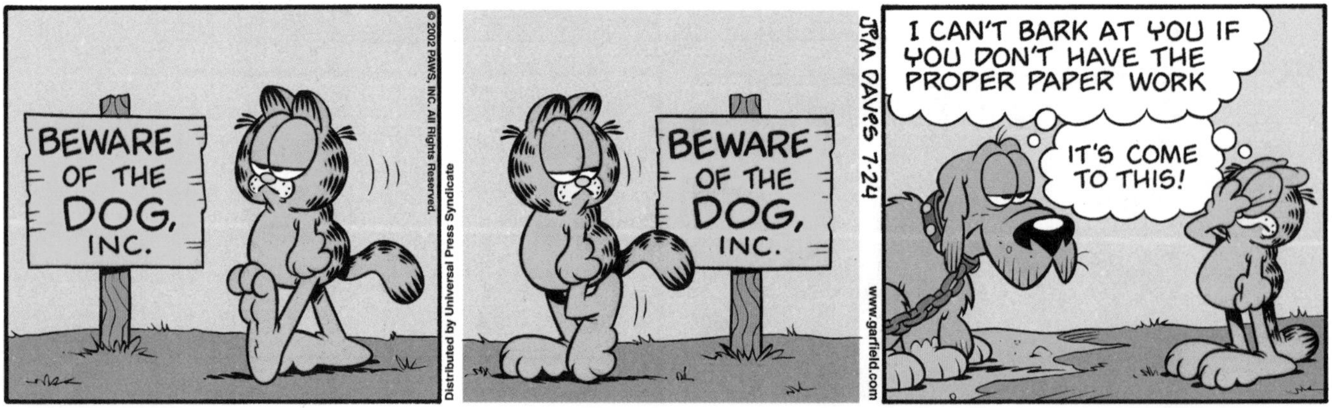
BEWARE OF THE DOG, INC.
© 2002 PAWS, INC. All Rights Reserved.
Distributed by Universal Press Syndicate
BEWARE OF THE DOG, INC.
JIM DAVIS 7-24
www.garfield.com
I CAN'T BARK AT YOU IF YOU DON'T HAVE THE PROPER PAPER WORK
IT'S COME TO THIS!

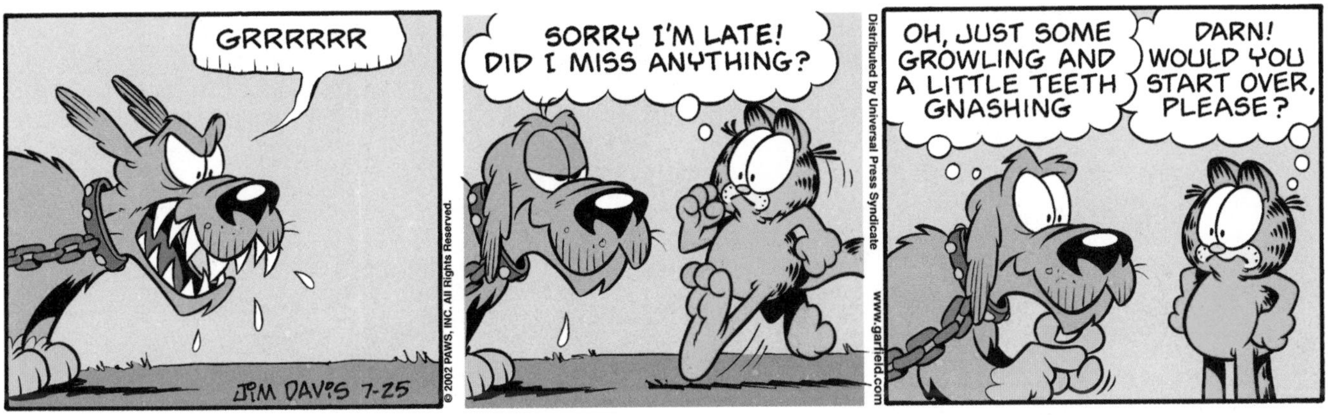
GRRRRRR
JIM DAVIS 7-25
© 2002 PAWS, INC. All Rights Reserved.
SORRY I'M LATE! DID I MISS ANYTHING?
Distributed by Universal Press Syndicate
www.garfield.com
OH, JUST SOME GROWLING AND A LITTLE TEETH GNASHING
DARN! WOULD YOU START OVER, PLEASE?

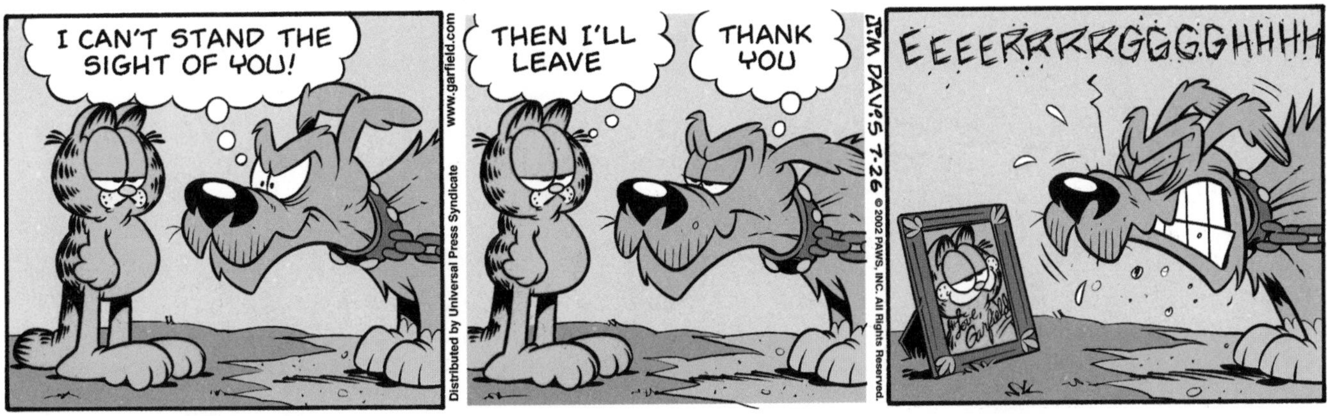
I CAN'T STAND THE SIGHT OF YOU!
www.garfield.com
Distributed by Universal Press Syndicate
THEN I'LL LEAVE
THANK YOU
JIM DAVIS 7-26
© 2002 PAWS, INC. All Rights Reserved.
EEEERRRRGGGGHHHH
Love, Garfield

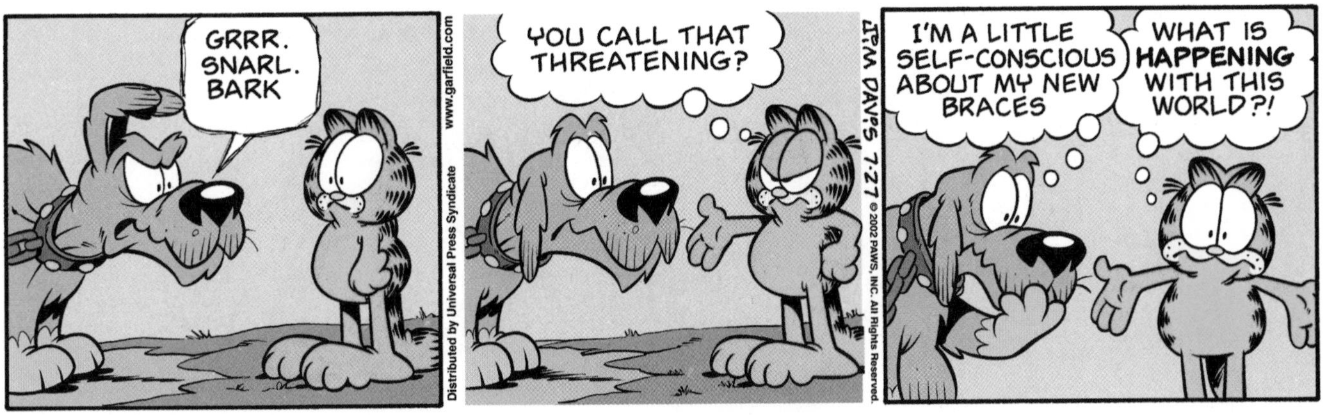
GRRR. SNARL. BARK
www.garfield.com
Distributed by Universal Press Syndicate
YOU CALL THAT THREATENING?
JIM DAVIS 7-27
© 2002 PAWS, INC. All Rights Reserved.
I'M A LITTLE SELF-CONSCIOUS ABOUT MY NEW BRACES
WHAT IS **HAPPENING** WITH THIS WORLD?!

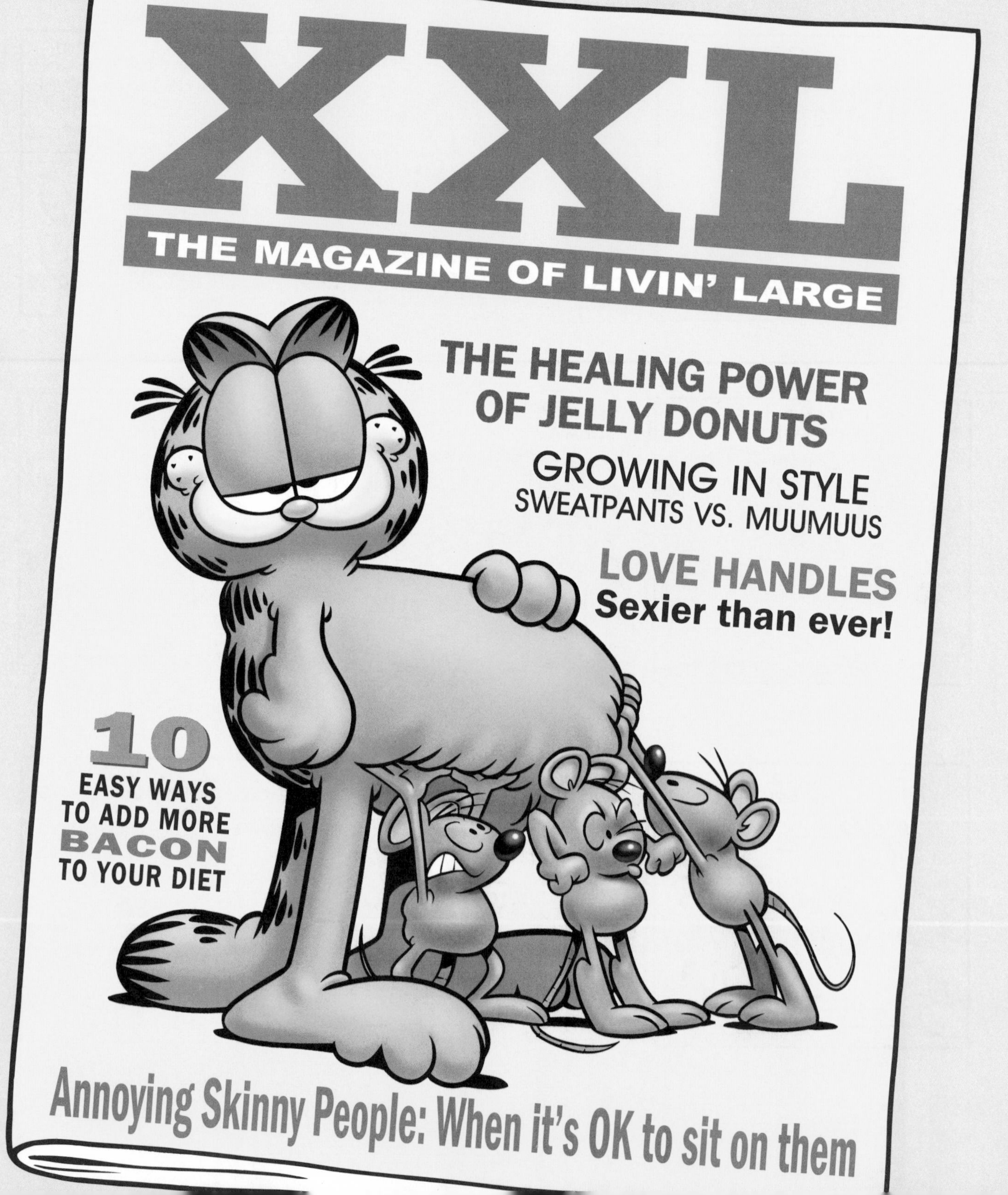
XXL
THE MAGAZINE OF LIVIN' LARGE
THE HEALING POWER OF JELLY DONUTS
GROWING IN STYLE
SWEATPANTS VS. MUUMUUS
LOVE HANDLES
Sexier than ever!
10
EASY WAYS TO ADD MORE BACON TO YOUR DIET
Annoying Skinny People: When it's OK to sit on them

STRIPS, SPECIALS, OR BESTSELLING BOOKS...

GARFIELD'S ON EVERYONE'S MENU

Don't miss even one episode in the Tubby Tabby's hilarious series!